THE EXPLORER RACE and

ISIS

THROUGH
ROBERT SHAPIRO

Isis said, of her request to have a rainbow surrounding a sun enclosing a full moon inside the sun on the cover, "This is a symbol I like to use for myself, because it comes closest to describing the mood I am usually in."

Explorer Race

and Isis

Isis
and Zoosh through
Robert Shapiro

Light Technology Publishing

ISBN 1-891824-11-2

 Published by
Light Technology Publishing
P.O. Box 3540
Flagstaff, AZ 86003
1-800-450-0985

Printed by
SEDONA COLOR GRAPHICS
2020 Contractors Road
Sedona, AZ 86336

Other Books by Robert Shapiro

THE EXPLORER RACE SERIES

THE MATERIAL MASTERY SERIES

SHINING THE LIGHT SERIES (co-channeled with Arthur Fanning)

The Sedona Vortex Guidebook (with other channels)

Contents

Preface

Those of you who have chosen to read this book, and in time perhaps even hear some of this, are invited to let your imaginations
run wild. Do not read this quickly, please. Read a sentence or two, a
paragraph, then stop and imagine what you would do. How would you
live that? What would you create with that? How might it look? What
might it taste like? Use your senses.

This book is intended to stimulate your imagination, not to provide
you with some rigid truth that seems to be beyond your capability to
change. Rather, it will address the Creator in all of you and speak directly to stimulate the benevolence of that energy you are all built upon.

It is my intention to encourage people. People in your time now
need more encouragement than they receive. Sometimes, in the guise
of encouragement, they are told things, and these stories they are told
might have been encouraging when they were first told. But these days
new stories need to be told, so I will invite the new storytellers. Don't
be shy. Tell your stories. Imagine you are telling stories to inspire and
encourage, to support and excite. Remember, you want to help people
to be more, not discourage them and cause them to be less.

We want to encourage the fabric of creation, which runs very deep
amongst the people of Earth. Most people have forgotten how deep
their connections are with each other. Many people have come to believe that so many rips in the fabric of their connections must have
caused a permanent break, but this is not so. In fact, the fabric is so
strong, it can take uncountable tugs and pulls and still remain firmly
connected. It is my intention to speak more of these things and others,
to remind you not only of the fantastic web that you weave of inclusion
in your pre-Creator School, but also to support you on the many little
steps you take to get there.

Let me talk to you briefly about the level up from this one, which is
the Creator School. The next level is the place where the energy that
precedes creators comes from in order that creators might create their
ability, their energy, their capacity to manifest. Their heartfelt vision has
to come from somewhere. On the next level, you have something that,
if you would look at it visually, would seem to be going inside out and
outside in, right side up and other side down. It is constantly pulsing in
and out, and if you went there you would immediately say, "This reminds

me of being inside a huge heart. I can feel it in ways that are not only nurturing and supportive, but I feel as if I could do anything here, and that there are no limits."

This is the energy that must be given to all creators. Because you are all in Creator School, soon you will be made up of this energy, since you are necessarily exposed to this energy on a regular basis. After all, you live within your Creator.

It is, too, that the Creator of this universe is like the legs that hold the table—and yet are the legs separate from the table? No, they are simply a different portion that you do not see all the time. I bring this up because I know you have an interest in such things, and it is my intention to speak not only about the seen and the unseen, but also, from time to time, the unimagined.

Isis
October 21, 1997

An Introduction to Isis
and the Explorer Race

Zoosh
September 27, 1997

(Excerpt from a session for a group from Australia)

Zoosh, I was fortunate enough to hear your brief story of the beginnings of the Earth and how it was seeded. For the people who are here and who have not heard that, would you give us a brief overview?

Earth, the Creator School

This planet, as you know it now, was not born to this solar system, but to a solar system in the galaxy of Sirius. It was transferred here not only because you had a missing planet in your solar system, but also because the planets that existed here were not sufficient for you, the Explorer Race, to be able to achieve what was necessary in this Creator School where you are now situated.

This area in general (several planets around here in this solar system) is a learning zone. It's a place where you come to learn, not a place where you come to live. You can live anywhere, but you come here to learn. You usually discover that sometime before or directly after birth: "What's wrong with these idiots? They don't understand telepathy!" (That's a joke, okay—not a judgment.)

What I'm saying is that regardless of how much you have mastered spiritual studies in other lives, when you come here you will learn. It was believed by various of your teachers and their teachers that you could not learn on a desolate planet, which is essentially what had existed in this place.

If you look at other planets in the solar system, you will not see a great deal of life—living energy. For one thing, you will not see much water—certainly not water in the form you would understand. So you might ask yourself, "What on Earth (pun intended) is a water planet doing in this solar system?" Any uninformed visitor to this solar system might reasonably ask herself or himself such a question. The answer is simply, because it wasn't born here.

Sirius is the galaxy that has lots of water planets. It's also the galaxy that holds the feminine energy in this general part of space, holds it and nurtures it because the feminine energy does not grasp; it contains. Therefore, a feminine-sourced planet was transferred here because it was necessary for all beings who came here, be they feminine or masculine, to be able to achieve the lessons of creatorship in a benevolent space while being challenged almost every moment of their lives.

Now, you could say that sounds a bit harsh to describe this place. Yet you must understand that even though you might easily have a day off, a weekend off, even a vacation, as it were, your body, the elements of life around you, your thoughts, your feelings, your urges, are constantly moving, sometimes together, but often in conflict.

The Challenge of Creator School

This is not because the Creator has played some joke on you, but rather because the Creator wishes you to learn discernment *at all costs*. Did you know that? It is essential in Creator School to be discerning. You must, of course, be allowing and loving and all of these good things, but you must also be discerning. This means essentially that you must know what goes where and why and when, especially if time is a factor (which it is here).

You can learn that here, but you can learn it only if you have challenges, if you come up against something. You can't learn it if there is nothing in your way. If there is nothing in your way, you really don't learn much at all. You will continue to perpetuate a benevolent or even false philosophy indefinitely if there's nothing in your way to cause you to question it.

Creator puts many things in your way here so that throughout your whole life you will question everything you say, do, think, feel and act on. Even after you feel you have absolutely learned something and have been applying it successfully for years and years, you will still have moments when you will question it. This is not, as I say, because Creator is trying to make you suffer or pay your dues, but rather because Creator wants you to experience en masse all the variables that might come up to be faced by a creator.

The Creator Looked for Something It Couldn't Find

Now, why do I keep talking about creators? Well, once upon a time you were all a portion of the Creator of this universe. This Creator was a happy creator, yet there was something nagging, as it were, in the back of Creator's mind, saying, "All of this I have created with the help of my advisors and my inspiration" (because the Creator has this also), "yet I feel like there's something else." So Creator kept creating more and more and more, but no matter how much more Creator kept creating, He still had that feeling. It wouldn't go away. Finally, Creator decided, "No matter what help or what inspiration I get, *more* isn't the answer. There is something somewhere that will be the more that I'm looking for, but I personally am unable to find it."

Creator had to think about that for a few millennia to consider what to do. What do you do if you're a creator and you can't find what you're looking for? Well, as anybody on Earth knows, certainly as any child knows, if you're looking for something, you need to have a dog to find it for you. There's nothing like a dog or even a cat sometimes to find something for you.

This is a new version of the Explorer Race story (comment by publisher).

Yes. I get tired of the old story. So Creator said, "Well, I've made lots of dogs and lots of cats, and a single dog or a single cat isn't going to do it. I need to have a dog or a cat that would have many facets of personality. I need to create something that has the potential of becoming more than I am. How can I do that?" As any reasonable person might, Creator said, "How can I create something that contains more than I have to contribute to it?"

Creator had to consider this for another millennium or so. Finally Creator said, "I will do this. I will birth out a part of myself. Unlike before, I will not pattern it with its destiny. What I will do is allow it to reproduce itself. I will allow it to pass through lessons of this universe to discover its own value. And I will do one more thing that may allow this to become more than I am: I will ask other creators, wherever they might be, to give something to this part of myself that will allow it to become more than I am. In other words, I will pray that that happens."

The Creator's Request for Help

This was, by the way, the beginning of prayer. Creator said, "This I will do." So Creator prayed. In other words, He spoke to creators in other places, other universes, and asked, "Would you contribute something, even inspiration, to this which I prepare to birth out of myself?"

Some of them said, "No, we think it's better you do it on your own." Some of them said no. But three of them said, "Yes, we would be happy to contribute."

One of them was the Creator of All Creators, one of them was the Creator of this Creator, and one of them was a figure you know very well—the eminence, you might say (I don't want to sound too royal), or the focus of feminine energy—who, after all, could not say no—who you know by various names, not the least of which is Isis.

So all of these creators said, "Yes, we will contribute something." The Creator of this universe said, "Don't tell me what it is," and they said, "No, we won't tell you." This Creator knew that if It knew what those creators were going to contribute, then those parts of the contribution would become instantaneously a portion of this Creator and the whole purpose would be useless. If the Creator of this universe wanted Its creation to be more than Itself, It necessarily had to be less than Its own creation!

That part of the deal being struck, Creator chose the most adventurous parts of Itself, the most fun-seeking parts (and perhaps, dare I say, the most reckless parts), and assembled them all together. He said, "You are all going to go on a journey and someday you will replace me." They said, "Oh, we could *never* do that." But Creator said, "Just you watch," and sent them on their way.

Off you went. This was the root of all of you, the root of the Explorer Race. (Yes, there was more to it than that.)

The Explorer Race, a Catalyst for ET Civilizations

"What is the Explorer Race?" you might ask. It is a group of souls sent out by Creator to learn all there is to learn that this Creator had to offer, to learn about creation in its various guises and responsibilities. It was made up of a group of teachers and translators and scholars (I'm talking, of course, about immortal personalities here, not individuals as you know them).

Over the years they would go through countless incarnations, reincarnations and what is called soul-splitting. When a soul has done all it can do in various reincarnations on the theme upon which it is working, it will split, taking on perhaps two different themes. Or it might split in three or five or even seven ways (usually not six) and take on different themes. Over the years all this splitting took place, and the Explorer Race was born.

Now, does the Explorer Race live only on Earth? No. Approximately 90 percent (a little more than that) of the Explorer Race has completed all they need to do, and they're basically parked in an area of space close enough to observe you at a distance, to see what you're doing. The rest of you are not fumbling around in the dark here, but are in fact learning your lessons of, primarily, *discernment*, but also *responsibility* and that old reliable, *consequences*—and now, of course, *application* and *wisdom*, because you're coming down the home stretch.

It is Creator's intent, then, with input from these other creators and with, of course, your cumulative experience, that you'll be able at some point to leave this planet and go out to explore other planets, bringing that survivability with you. Do you know that most of the races on other planets do not have the will to survive that people here have? Yes, part of it is physiological. But you might ask yourself why people who are in a lot of pain and are very sick still have that will to survive. That is not physiological; that is part of your overall personality.

I get ahead of myself. So remember, you all started out as one big mass of gold light of immortal personalities. Now you are still that mass of gold-light immortal personalities, but you are scattered about a bit. Someday you will take that survivability energy, go out into space, and visit lots of ETs out there. Granted, you will unintentionally cause a little mischief (not real problems), but the intention is to stimulate the growth curve of races of beings on other planets who have achieved a rather impressive level of peace, honor, trust, faith, education, spirituality, kinship and so on, but who, with all that beauty and achievement, have unintentionally stopped their growth.

You know that if you as a being, to say nothing of a whole society of people living on a planet, would find something that for you is perfection, you would be loath to change it. That's what most societies have done on other planets, and that's why they are benevolent. They do not have violence, because violence, as *you* all know, aside from its immediate impact, certainly has consequences.

If you have a society that has achieved some level of perfected beauty, you can't have consequences. The only consequences you can have are those that are engaged on purpose when you are teaching your youth the lessons they must learn in order to become good citizens in your society. Thus they have the consequences of learning, but they do not have consequences associated with the growth curve.

You are the Explorer Race. Before you merge together again as a creator to replace this Creator, you will go out into space and search for other life forms, not unlike your science fiction movies. You will encounter some who are less than thrilled to see you, but most of the life forms will be happy to see you. They will be interested in you. After all, most of them whom you encounter over the next few thousands of years have already been here. Maybe they didn't walk on the planet, but they will have visited here and looked around. They will have observed from afar or maybe even have had a base here so they could observe more closely and say, "What on Earth makes these people tick?" You will encounter these people either on their ships or, more likely, where they live. It won't exactly be a chain reaction, but sometimes it will feel like one.

Simply put, that has been designed. That is why so many beings in the universe are keeping an eye on you—not because they are fearful, but because they are anxiously anticipating the reenergizing of their own growth curve. Now, you're not going to bring great discomfort to them, but many of them will require something they do not have: at least 1 percent, maybe as much as 1.5 percent or in some rare cases 2 percent, of what you call negative energy, no more than that. That's all it will take to stimulate their growth curve. They can't take more than that, anyway.

The ETs' Need for Discomfort

That will be pretty traumatic for them. It will be spread out over many years and ease in, because it will give them what for you would be the most minor level of annoyance; that's about it. A minor level of annoyance, for example, would be a draft blowing on the back of your neck, causing you to reach around and close the window. Now, it may be hard to conceive that other civilizations do not have this, but they don't.

If you were to look at their civilizations objectively, you would say, "I understand why, because they've achieved some level of perfection that they are happy with and they don't want to mess with it." The stew tastes perfect as it is, so why add too much salt? As a result, they have achieved a level of perfection, but they maintain that perfection only by being highly controlled—not manipulated, but highly controlled, even down to the birth rate, for example. If the society has reached its level of perfection at, say, 500,000 people, then it tends to maintain that population. Anything and everything that occurred to achieve the status quo associated with that level of perfection is perpetuated. So the population will never exceed or become less than 500,000 (in our example) by more than a couple hundred one way or the other. It is that precise.

Although you could look at these civilizations and ofttimes easily say to yourself, "This is heaven; I'd love to live here." Nevertheless, these civilizations have a great deal more to accomplish. But they cannot do that without having their growth curves stimulated. That's what you will do. You, as the Explorer Race, will go out. Of course some of you will incarnate elsewhere, but a lot of you will go out and explore the planets and bring unenlightenment to various civilizations—at least that's how they will experience it. But they will admire your capacity to survive and also your ability to stay hopeful and even full of humor in the face of things that are threatening.

Most ETs, if put in a position of some threat, would naturally react (which is also *your* spirit's natural reaction) by putting distance between themselves and that threat. This is why a lot of you, if something is threatening, feel less than present, because your personality or your soul takes a hike. Then you have to kind of pull yourself back in and say, "I can deal with this." That is the natural reaction of benevolent beings, and all your souls are benevolent beings.

Explorer Race in Creator School

Since you are here in Creator School and are learning all the things of Creator School, then you have to face the music. As a result, you learn. And since Creator is not vengeful or wrathful in the slightest, Creator says, "Well, you go to Creator School here on Earth for a while, not very long." Creator doesn't allow you to live much over a hundred years; most of you don't live that long, though you hear of the occasional person who lives past that point. Creator says, "Well, this far, no farther, that's enough." After all, you are immortal, and when you leave here after you are done with these bodies and this education, you go on—the personality you know yourself as, not some vague lightbody you're not really aware of, but what you know yourself to be.

Creator doesn't feel that you are being punished. Creator says, "This long in school, and that's enough." Then you go on. Ultimately, you will re-form to replace this Creator. You will do that when the time is right, as they say, but it is not that far into the future. I can't measure it in years; sometimes I say "experiential years," but that can be very vague for you. What I'd rather say is that in terms of the experiential time of this universe—the time left for you to explore the planets, go out and do this stuff that I talked about and then re-form as the Creator—in terms of the percentage of the time this universe has existed: 0.00001 percent.

Most of it is done. But that 0.00001 percent is how much experience is left. Although that might be thousands of years, it's going to change everything, because when you re-form as the Creator, you will be more than this Creator.

Creators

I'll tell you a little secret about creators. Creators can come together and form a council for a short time, but it is not natural for them. They can go to meetings and take a lunch, but they do not easily hang around together. It's not because they're snobbish; it's because they have other things to do. It's also because different creators have different avenues of exploration, and if they spent too much time together they would unintentionally infuse each other with their separate avenues of creation, causing themselves to become diluted in what they are attempting to achieve.

Therefore, when you reestablish yourself as your own Creator, this Creator will be propelled by that and go onward and upward, your Creator knows not where, to the more that this Creator was attempting to find when I began this story. At least that is this Creator's intent. It's not because you're kicking this Creator out. It's simply because two creators cannot comfortably occupy the same space without overinfluencing each other.

So when you graduate and become the Creator of this universe (you will be a Creator of this universe for only a short time in terms of the experience of this universe), you will give the Creator of this universe a boost. He's already motivated to go somewhere where there's more, and you'll give Him a little boost because *you* will be more. He's really looking forward to that. And, you know, Isis keeps whispering in His or Her ear that good things are coming. Of course, she won't say any more than that. That's exciting.

That's the plan. That's the Explorer Race in a nutshell. This might be more than the question prompted, but it is the gist of what I talk about.

I said you wouldn't be here too long. Well, how is that possible? Do you just hang around and manage this Creator's creation for a time and then just bug out?

No. The only way you can bug out is if you create a creator to take your place, or a creator is provided to take your place. Now, that is not absolutely decided yet, but what *is* decided is that you all have creations to do on your own. But graduate school for the Creator, in this case for you, is to take over and manage this creation for a time.

What is the point of going to the fourth dimension?

It's a good question. It really begs another question. If we really exist at these higher dimensions, why bother to make such a big deal about going to the fourth dimension? Well, it's not a big deal at all. It's natural for you to go to these higher dimensions at the end of your natural cycles or even when you are dreaming at the deepest levels of your sleep when you are tethered to your body. Mostly it happens when you pass over. That is the normal way, yes? But what is the big deal about going to the fourth dimension now? The big deal is, you are going to the fourth dimension *while you are alive*, while you are physical. That is why you will have absolutely confusing experiences. When you go through the veils at the end of your natural cycle, you shed a lot of the physical laws of life on Earth. Things immediately become more expansive; more is the case in point and less is left behind. Not to say that any Earth experience is a lowly experience, but it has to be less, more confined, in order for you to learn. So you become more as you pass through the veils and get to the other side.

However, say you are doing this while you are alive. You don't let go of the limits here even though the limits are expanding gradually on their own due to the integration, like swirling chocolate into the white cake mix to make a marble cake. If you stir enough, it gradually becomes a light brown cake. But the swirling and the reintegration take place gradually.

What's the big deal? Why bother? What's all the fuss about going to the fourth dimension? Never before has a whole planetload of people been alive and done this, but it has to be done because *that is your Ph.D. thesis*. It is required of you, and you're all doing it now in part. You're partway, you're between, you're in transit between the third and fourth dimension, and as a result, you're all getting part of that. The young ones especially will go all the way. You will get it in some form. The applied thesis of your graduation here on Earth is that all people will gradually be able to move cumulatively from the third dimension to the fourth dimension by being representatives of all that the Explorer Race has ever accomplished. You have established total karma where the laws are no longer present; you've done all there is to do within the context of your Explorer Race ventures through Earth experiences and Earth school. You can now apply lessons for all circumstances engaged therein. You can then let go of what was and welcome what is of higher-dimensional self or Source, and you are able to do so with grace—grace, the wondrous thing that all beings strive for. Grace simply means the ability to be comfortable in all circumstances.

You cannot do it as an individual *cumulatively* from the third to the fourth dimension, but you can do it. It will require something that you are working on right now—union, which is your natural state of being elsewhere but is challenged here so that you can learn your lessons.

It is possible to gradually re-merge into union. For one thing, union is never completely broken here on Earth—the absolute bond between you and all other beings.

Why don't I say "all other people"? Because it's more than that. It's all other beings—animals, plants, rock, lightning, rain, earthquakes, all that—which in their own way live and have their life cycles. But let's just isolate it to human beings for a moment for the sake of simplicity. You have more union now than you have differences, and you always have. You all function basically the same physiologically with some variances from individual to individual, however minor. You all breathe, you all eat, you all drink water and so on. This is intentional so that no matter how challenged they may be under the most extreme of circumstances (war, for example), the bonds of union will never be broken. They might be challenged, but they won't be broken.

As time goes on, more and more union is coming to you. Gradually and naturally more and more you become aware of people suffering on the other side of the globe, which you may or may not be able personally to do something about. If you're able to do something personal, perhaps you do. If you're not able, then what do you do? Maybe you include these people in your prayers or you ask the universe or spirit. In some way you ask if these people can be relieved of their burden and be comforted.

More Union Is the Goal

All of these things are associated with union. Even the news—perhaps they tell you more than you need to know about things that are going on. They will also let you know about things that need to be changed and that you personally may not be able to stop. But you can say, "May these people be relieved of their burdens, be nurtured and comforted," in whatever way is meaningful to you. And by saying so, many of you or even a single person, you again include more union amongst all of you.

I might add that it is not an accident that there is a massive amount of population on Earth now. It is tough on Mother Earth, but the more people there are, the more likely you are to bump into each other and the more likely you are to discover what you have in common. As I've always said, your common ground is what's building now. It will continue to build even though for some of you it will be difficult because some of you will have to give up things associated with nationalistic pride and even joy. But you'll have to give them up for the greater joy of all beings on Earth. Just give them up for a while; maybe Mother Earth has the capacity to feed all peoples on the Earth. But in order to do that, more people will have to start farming and more people will have to start loving the plants they are raising and harvesting them in a loving way, so that the food actually feeds you, heart and soul as well as body and mind. That's a big one for you, but you can do it.

You have capacities that are beyond what you are now. As you re-form into greater and greater union, you will be able to pass from the third to the fourth dimension when the time of the real lock-in takes place. Right around 3.47 to 3.75 dimension is the real testing ground before you get to 4.0. Once you pass 3.75, it's downhill from that point on. The testing ground is taking place and you're in that testing ground now. Granted, you'll occasionally backslide to 3.43, but you won't slide any further than that. You're mostly in the testing ground now. That is the reason union is coming to you more so that by the time it comes to the real push, you'll be able to have complete union—not only unconsciously as you do now, not only subconsciously at times as you do now, but *consciously.* Granted, it will be for only moments, but in order to make great accomplishments, sometimes moments are all that are needed.

All right, Zoosh speaking. Greetings. What shall we talk about?

We never talked about this "more" that Isis and the 2 creators put into the Explorer Race.

I know, that's true.

I didn't ask the question in the earlier material: Did anybody else put something into the Explore Race?

We talked to some degree about the mechanics of how Creator was going to actually be able to evacuate the premises. As a matter of fact, I think the one true consistency in my work—and you know it perhaps better than most—is that all of my answers without exception are designed to stimulate questions, so sometimes they come from unexpected quarters.

About the input from those beings, obviously what they put in could not, as I've mentioned before, be identified or known by this Creator of this universe. Otherwise He would know it, and this would defeat the purpose. It had to be something, however, that would create a tension so that Creator would in fact be pulled up. You understand, if Creator could have pushed Himself up and essentially bilocated, He would have done that a long time ago. We know Creator's going to be propelled by you, because when you take over it's going to create a little oomph to allow Him to move up. But it's not enough oomph, so there has to be something that also pulls Him up, thus combining the masculine and feminine, since He has been responsible for creating a circumstance that is polarized. This means that polarization can work *for* Creator. You can tell I'm being circumspect.

Ah! I understood that he couldn't know then, but I didn't realize he couldn't know now.

No. If I say it now, it will really throw a wrench in the works, so the only thing I can actually say here is to describe the mechanics more. But certainly I have to bend over backward to avoid saying what it was they put in.

Who just told you something?

Isis makes little jokes sometimes. She's humorous.

I understand that we can't discuss what was added to the Explorer Race.

Well, we really can't do that; otherwise we'll . . .

Spoil the party.

Spoil the party—well said.

Then we'll do a little bit with what you can say.

What they were able to do was include things that would be compatible with this creation but were not a portion of it—essentially, threads. They would add something to the Explorer Race that would be threads to the more that Creator is heading toward. And since you will probably follow in Creator's footsteps to some extent (maybe not all the way), having those threads come down to this universe was acceptable.

Like from the next level above.

Yes, that is just for illustrative purposes, not that it is factually so. What has been added, then, is of this creation, meaning it can come into this creation. It does not, however, directly add to this creation. It's interesting the way it works: They're kind of like drinking straws, in the sense that they sample this universe, pass that sampling up (and of course, the Explorer Race) without actually removing anything from this universe. It samples it as you might stick a finger in the soup and then into your mouth to taste it to see how it is coming along. However, it doesn't actually take up any of the soup of this universe. It just samples it, like sticking your tongue to the ice cream, as it were.

It brings enough of the awareness of this universe to that next level so that there is sufficient familiarity. If this Creator were to be propelled to the next level without any shred of familiarity, the first thing that would happen is that when He got there He would be fragmented, not broken or damaged. But there is so much more.

Creator is actually a being who is so much in the now that it would be very much like dropping a drop of water onto the concrete below: It would go in many different directions. Creator would instantly go in many different directions at once and become fragmented for quite a while, exploring as much as possible. It is so much larger than Creator can ever explore strictly from curiosity, you understand—the urgency of curiosity to explore as one being—that it would be quite awhile before Creator managed to reassemble Itself.

So it was believed necessary to bring enough of the familiar so that Creator would have a means to find Its way. Being pushed is fine, but if you're not pulled, you could get pushed in the wrong direction. So He's going to be pushed and pulled and also have that thread, as it were, to follow.

When Creator gets there, It will be met by Isis. Isis will spend a significant amount of time guiding Creator around. Creator will be like a kid with a new toy. It's going to want to go in all directions at once, but in fact He'll be guided slowly. This is a circumstance not unlike a meal, where each flavor is to be enjoyed and treasured step by step rather than have all the flavors at once. Mixing the ice cream with the turkey may not necessarily be so wonderful.

I thought He was going to go with the other hundred parts of All That Is who are waiting for Him, and that they were all going up together.

Yes, but regardless of who He goes with, He still has to be welcomed (I'm stepping carefully here. There's very little I can say.)

Because He can hear you. I understand.

Absolutely. He can hear me thinking. I can't even think about it.

Can we talk to Isis? Can she say things other than this at some time?

I don't know. Let's see what she can say now, eh?

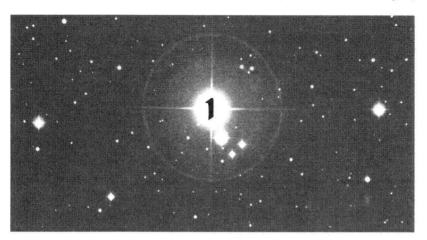

Isis and Your Creator

September 30, 1997

T his is Isis. Your Creator is young, as creators go. This is why your Creator would even consider taking on such a project as the Explorer Race. Older, more experienced creators did not take up the idea, much less even consider becoming responsible for it, because it is such a commitment. But because this Creator is young, like the young everywhere, youthful enthusiasm allowed him to become excited about the project. To do something new and exciting is always the venue of the young.

Your Creator

So when the choice was made, it was necessary for this Creator to have a great deal of advice and advisors, for He could have easily become distracted with the many variables associated with creating a replacement during the time and place of your creation. Replacements for Creators are not rare, but one does not usually create one's own replacement in the same area as one's creation. If you do, most likely it will be a duplicate of yourself. The only way to avoid that is to ask for assistance and to have very little control or personal involvement with your replacement-to-be.

Your Creator is very hands-on, so to give up involvement was not a real option. The only way to keep your Creator from accidentally meddling too much here in this universe was to give Him assistance from creators beyond this realm. I was perhaps the most active participant. The other two mentioned [Creator's father and the Creator of Creators] also participated because there had been some familiarity, some contact with these beings and your Creator before, so that was comforting. There had been only distant contact between this Creator and myself, so my involvement allowed me to be the unknown to this Creator, which is very advantageous if you wish to be influential, as I did. Being a mystery somewhat myself, it caused this Creator here to be sufficiently intrigued so as to accept an unnatural state of condition for Itself. You must remember that this Creator is above all curious. And being young amplifies the curiosity.

So it was necessary for me to be enigmatic. This served or fed this Creator's curiosity while not necessarily giving Him too many answers. In this way I was able to support and sustain this Creator's goals, yet not become directly involved with the project. I felt it was necessary for me to have some distance. So when this Creator requested outside input to the Explorer Race, I was able to provide direct input to the beings of the Explorer Race.

Instead of bringing a cord only, as described by Zoosh, I brought the cord and also myself. Because this Creator was interested in the way I conducted myself then, I was welcomed in this creation. So I sent a portion of myself here while retaining the larger portion of me beyond this level, as you say.

As a portion of myself here, I was able to provide a bias to each and every immortal personality that arrived in this creation (not before your arrival, but when you arrived here). This means that all of your immortal personalities, in any of their incarnations in this universe, would be biased toward functioning in the most benevolent way, yet be dedicated to the Explorer Race project. This was necessary, because being involved in the Explorer Race project as a fleeting experience—coming and then going, perhaps to another universe—could possibly despoil the other universe, because you are all of what you are when you go elsewhere and it was essential to limit the impact of such Explorer Race lessons to this universe alone.

So I added that bias. Although it did not sequester immortal personalities to only this universe, if it was in their favor or providential to go to other universes for other lives, they would leave. As one would go through a veil, they would leave all their Explorer Race experience here, making certain lives unavailable to them in incarnations beyond this universe.

These immortal personalities accepted this essentially blank spot (not a real limit) in their access to their lives as a commitment to this worthy experiment here. As a result, even if they were beyond this universe [chuckles], since they could not access the lives here involved in the Explorer Race, it would create a curiosity—a tension, as it were.

Imagine yourself in another universe in a life there. You would examine your lives, as is typical in other places, and there would be blank spots. You could tell that a life had existed but it was otherwise unavailable to you. You would consult with your teachers, your guides, all those who helped you, and everyone without exception would say, "Yes, there was a life, but it is there unavailable to you where you are now, though it may be available to you to examine some other time." That's all they really could say ("some other time" meaning, of course, should they return to this universe for some other incarnation). I don't have to tell you what attention that would create, especially for the very curious.

This was also intentional, so that the investors (for that is what they truly are, those who would participate in the Explorer Race grand experiment) who would do so would be inclined to invest more and not less.

Some individuals, as you know, have had only one Explorer Race life, but this is rare. It is usually at least three and sometimes many more—and that is because of this tension. It is not true tension as in a mechanical tension. But for any curious being, to be unable to examine in detail a life in the way you examined so many others would create a definite longing or urge to know.

This is what I added to the Explorer Race. I have always believed that in order to accomplish anything, the first and foremost necessity is commitment. If anything worthwhile is to be accomplished, you must be absolutely committed to the goals of that accomplishment. If you are not committed, the chances of that goal or effort achieving its desired success are sufficiently reduced. You know this.

The Rise of the Feminine Energy

Can you tell us about your involvement within the Explorer Race as the goddess in all of our legends and our myths and our religions? Can you talk about your activities here?

There is a whole book here at least, maybe three. I will touch on it lightly. Sometime in the future we can begin projects. I can talk at length about many things. Perhaps a series of two or three books might be acceptable?

Oh yes, please.

A nutshell, yes? My involvement here with the Explorer Race to support and establish and nurture the divine feminine was initially a direct desire within myself to support and nurture the value of the feminine anywhere. But secondarily, it is in homage to those who have chosen to have physical lives on the star system Sirius.

Sirius is the most important location in this universe of the feminine energy. It is committed absolutely to spreading the value of the feminine energy to all points that desire it in this universe. It is the source in this universe of such energy. And because of the request by the elders there, I was invited to participate fully. Moving with you through your locations as the Explorer Race, I have very gradually infused the feminine energy.

There was a time when the feminine energy was less welcome. This is when you were beginning to experiment with and pursue the ideals of polarity. Yes, polarity has ideals as well as challenges. The ideals are simply that polarity can offer an absolute understanding in a sequential manner of the value and differentiation of the masculine, of the feminine and a polarity (which you are not experiencing now) of the combined masculine-feminine.

This experience of the combined masculine-feminine is in fact a polarity, because when the masculine-feminine are combined, they are each distinctly themselves. It is not a polarity when the masculine and feminine are blended, but when they are distinctly each and only themselves but combined, this is in fact a polarity. You are not experiencing that at this time, for it would be too confusing. But you will; it is a step on the way.

Is it what Zoosh has called the third sex?

Yes. I was then for a time a little more distant from you, as you were exploring the polarization of the masculine regardless of what sex you were. But considering the fact that all of you without exception started as primarily feminine energies—yes, every single being who has ever manifested as the Explorer Race started out as a primarily feminine being—most of you had only this energy. Some of you had some slight degree of masculine energy, but it would not be possible for you to answer the call to become part of the Explorer Race if your energy was more masculine than feminine, because the masculine energy is predominantly involved in self-destiny. With self-destiny one tends to create one's destiny directly, hands-on. It does not necessarily mean control, but self-intent. With the feminine energy, destiny is associated almost exclusively with allowance, and allowance has attraction as an absolute ability. One can attract or be attracted. The reason that you were all attracted to the Explorer Race and were able to come here (mechanically speaking) is because you were primarily feminine.

Now, while you worked your way through the experience of the Explorer Race, there were times when you gradually became more masculine and less feminine. It was during one of these times, especially when many of you were manifesting on Orion, that I pulled back a bit and was not as involved. That is not to say that there was anything wrong with Orion in these times, but it was a time of the exploration of destiny on the level of adventure, something which is at this time on your Earth again somewhat in existence.

I remained a little bit at a distance for most of you. Then as you began to move from Orion through various brief stops and ultimately to Earth, who is a fine teacher for you all, I was able to infuse more of the feminine energy. I will be very active with you, and I have been since about the late 1800s. I will continue to step up my activity with you, because as your time goes on, in 25 years or so the willful destiny of the masculine energy will begin to fall away and the acceptance of destiny from attraction will become more appealing to the masculine energy.

This will also be seen by most beings in spiritual circles as a leap of faith. During this time of the leap of faith a great deal will be accomplished, because when there is a leap of faith like this, there is no resistance. And when there is no resistance, a great deal can be accomplished in such a brief moment as to be less than one measurable second. This is likely to happen in 25 years. It may take as long as 35 years, but I don't think so.

The feminine energy, then, for many beings is rising. This is perhaps most significantly available to those who are feminine (women), but it is surprisingly available to men as well. You will find that men who utilize and know how to utilize the energy of attraction will become much more common amongst you. They will often be spiritual men, but sometimes just average citizens, and they will be able to use this energy in the most benevolent way.

Isis and Mother Mary

Is what we call Mother Mary's energy connected to you?

What you call Mother Mary is directly connected to me. Mother Mary is not so much a person, in the story that you have come to know in the Christian religion, as what I would prefer to call, in the Russian terminology, an icon—meaning someone who is beyond that by which she is normally identified. Mother Mary is a cousin, a direct connection to me. Her true participation in those times was as a teacher, as a student, as one who performs the benediction.

I don't know if you're familiar so much with this term. It is usually associated with religion, but a benediction is not just a prayer one says over one's followers or one's family. It is truly associated with initiation. The term *benediction* has come to be used instead of initiation but *initiation* is perhaps a better term. Mother Mary, then, is involved directly with initiation, to the point of focus associated with the true divine feminine.

You have an all-encompassing knowledge of much beyond what we have reached so far. Correct?

I have some secrets. I might not be able to reveal them all to you, but I will reveal what I can.

Wonderful. Robert is perfectly comfortable channeling you, right?

Yes, at the moment. But in the future it will require more of my energy coming through, so we will have to step him up a bit.

Thank you so much.

Goodnight.

And see you again.

Yes—and benevolence.

The Biography of Isis

October 23, 1997

All right, this is Isis. What shall we speak on tonight?

Welcome. You said that we'd do your biography.

Oh, yes. I will follow the format as much as possible, but I will have to make one exception: I cannot state when I became aware of myself, because that would suggest that there was a time prior when I was not aware of myself, and this I cannot say.

Beyond all time and experience, I have always been aware of myself, so I will go back as far as I can go and speak of things that would be relevant to you and our readers. That is the best I can do.

That's wonderful, but you don't have to follow a format, just whatever feels right to you.

Isis Maps Her Journey

All right. I will start out speaking about, not the level just above this one [see *Council of Creators** for description of levels], but the level

---

* See Book Market in back of book.

above that. Above that there is a state of being where consciousness or self-awareness (if we can define consciousness that way) is in a constant state of flux, meaning that in a moment of experience, one is aware of oneself, and in the very next moment one is aware of all selves everywhere, not only at that level, but levels above and levels beyond (I'd rather not say levels below).

In this way one learns, at that level, the experience of individuality *and* inclusion during a visit there. Again, I cannot really say during a life there—you experience yourself there, but there is really no birth and death and all this. So that level, then, is involved almost entirely in that activity. It was when I was in that level that I discovered all of these places, cultures and beings that I would like to visit, so when I journeyed onward to the level just above this one, where one experiences creator energy, as I discussed last time, it was during my time there that I was able to define more clearly not only what personalities I was attracted to and their cultures, but also where those cultures had been, where those personalities had been and all of the potentials for future growth.

It was when I was studying their potentials for future growth that I realized it would be possible for me to influence some of these individuals and cultures in a benevolent way. Most of the cultures I was most interested in were crying out for guidance that would help them to achieve some goal or worthwhile expression of life for which they had no fundamental wisdom. So they were asking spirit and praying for someone to come and show them not only the ideal they might emulate, but also some guidance in doing so. One learns on the creator level a great deal about the emulation of ideals and how and when it is valuable and, conversely, when it is inappropriate.

You are discussing the level above us, but are you working with these cultures on that level or on our level?

I'm looking at cultures on this level where you are, but I'm on the level above at this moment in the course of speaking about my life.

So those were the cultures I was most attracted to, and when I had mapped the individuals and the cultures I was most interested in, then is when I journeyed to this level.

On my journey I decided not only who I'd see and where I would go and to what cultures, but also what individuals and at what stage of their development as individuals I would journey to see them, for sometimes individuals, even in their reincarnations, can become their best possible selves and produce the greatest value for themselves and others with surprisingly little encouragement. So I will speak of individuals I visited first, if that is all right. Most you will not have heard of, but some you will.

Isis In Sirius, Where She Appears As a Lion

The individual I went to see first is, in a manner of speaking, in residence at a fairly high dimension now in your time: the seventh dimension of Sirius. When I went to see this individual, he was living what amounted to a life as you would experience in physical life on a benevolent planet in Sirius. This particular individual chose to have consistently reincarnating lives in that galaxy because this individual was working toward becoming a guide or teacher of the theme that would develop for that galaxy. And of course individuals such as this need to be encouraged as much as possible.

So when I went to see this individual, he was at the stage of his incarnation when the most broad-minded view he could have about individuality and expressions of individuality was what was seen by him—what was actually seen and sensed, what he could see and touch and so on as you have here—was all he acknowledged. He did not feel that possibilities, that potentials or even wishes or desires had enough tangibility to be strived toward.

So when I appeared to this individual who always—all these individuals in all these cultures had asked for someone—so when I appeared to this individual in that life in his incarnational cycle, the individual needed inspiration to find a means to be able to touch that which had no form, because this individual, in that life, had poor-quality eyesight. He could see somewhat, but by your standards had about half of your vision capability.

But he had the ability to hear, and his sense of touch was very strong—so strong that if he was within 70 or 80 feet of something, he could already begin to feel it, become aware of it. His instincts were very sharp, so what I did was appear to that person in the form of a lion—a friendly lion, if you would. By communicating with him as a lion, giving him the lion as the symbol and supporting and sustaining that instinctual ability, I was able to show him how to use animal instincts to perceive potentials.

Sirius in your time is known not only as the place of the feminine energy, but also as the place that supports and sustains and generally creates variety.

This person would some day become a sustaining teacher for cultures on Sirius to encourage such things. So, by giving him this greater sense of animal instinct—not to *be* the animal but to have the instincts of the animal—this individual was able to use his imagination.

Lions have a tremendous capacity for vision; they can *see*. On your planet you will see these lions with their big manes; sometimes they seem to be just sitting there, but what they are doing is not only seeing the future, but helping create it, not only for lions, but for all beings. They have this capacity. The regal countenance ascribed to them is not simply a casual description. Their regality lies in the responsibility they have taken to help create the best possible world for all beings within the context of expressed variety.

The lion, you can see, was the perfect animal to befriend this being and pass on to him such skills as are possessed by the average lion. Therefore, that being was able to assimilate those qualities over his lifetime and build on those qualities in succeeding lives on Sirius. Rather than have a reincarnational cycle all over the universe, this person was having a reincarnational cycle only on Sirius and would remember the cumulative knowledge and wisdom from one life to another.

Isis First Uses the Sphere

So that's the form I took. It was during this first visit that I began to use the sphere in what you call the third eye or the crown chakra. In that case I used the sphere. Here's the nose of the lion. The head slants back and the eyes are here. If you would see this sphere of light, perhaps an inch and a half around, it would be there only when the person was present, to give him the idea that the sphere of light was attainable.

It was also necessary for that person to identify, outside his own being, the capacity the lion had to see the future and help create it by giving him an icon or model. You understand? Something tangible he could touch—because this person's primary talent was touch. As a vision, putting that inside the lion's head would be no good. It had to be something the person could reach over and touch; it had to be something that was not normally "worn," for lack of a better word, by other lions.

That was when I began to do that. This person, now in higher-dimensional form, is involved in the guiding and directing of inspiration on Sirius.

Isis in the Pleiades—the Sphere as a Tool

Now, the next individual I went to (I will speak of another one along the same lines) was on the Pleiades, and I visited her when she was a child. This was her last life in her reincarnational cycle in what amounts to physical life. If you were to see her, she would appear physical. It was many years ago, naturally, and she was going to live several hundred years in that life. I went to see her in the form of—the closest to it would be what you call a fairy—again as a ball of light. This time it was floating a little bit in front of my forehead. Of course, the child asked, "What is that?" I said, "That is the sphere of wisdom." A child wants to know, "Where can I get one?" or "Where is mine?"

Do you see the advantage of using something like this, the sphere? It gives people and beings in general something they can understand. They look at it, they see it. It seems to be like a tool—as a carpenter has a hammer and nails. You might not know how to use it, but it looks like something you could use, and it also takes away from idealizing me alone. That is really essential. If they idealized me and I did not have this floating sphere, then they see only me. I would become like a religious figure to them, which I wanted to avoid. A sphere, even though it wasn't something they possessed, was something they could understand. It was something that was a part of their lives in other ways, because there would be other spheres in their lives.

I felt it was important. I worked with that individual throughout her whole lifetime in order to help her understand the value of play as it is integrated into learning experiences or, as you say, education. But education on the Pleiades is much different than on this planet.

On this planet at this time, most education is about things that have little to do with life and a great deal to do with studies of one sort or another. On the Pleiades, all the education has to do with life and is based on things you need to know, not only to survive, but to understand. While you might never have to plant crops and grow them on the Pleiades, you need to understand how it works so that you will appreciate the food you eat and appreciate the beings who are that food. That's just an example.

I worked with that individual who is now right around the seventh or eighth dimension helping to guide Pleiadians. You can see that when I work with individuals, at least some of the time it has to do with helping them help others.

The Nine-Life Sequence with One Spokesman

Now I will mention one other individual, someone you don't know, because it is something you can understand, living on a polarized planet as you do. There was a planet, not in your galaxy, quite a ways from here (it's hard to give it in terms of distance) but in this creation. This one individual planet was involved in primary experiences when your Creator was beginning to experiment with polarity.

Now, it wasn't the kind of polarity you experience here on a daily basis, but it was the beginning of polarity as associated with passion or strong feelings. It was the beginning experiences of what you would call seduction—not referring to this in a sexual fashion, but rather as someone taken off his own path because of persuasion or interest in the path of another. In this one place, this person represented several others. It was what I call a nine-life "sequence," meaning that one person speaks for eight others. It is like twins. Here you have twins and triplets and so on. It is a similar thing there, only in groups of nine, where one person speaks, interacts and so on, and the other "twins" of that series will process it, think about it, consider it and choose what to do. So one person speaks and the others essentially act, but they are all part of the same being. It is an interesting way of life, and it allowed Creator, I think, to experiment more quickly with polarity and passion in such a place.

The results or the consequences, as Zoosh likes to say, were very swift. I went to that place because a person there had gotten to the point where he was beginning to be seduced by power and didn't have enough wisdom yet to appreciate the impact of power and control on others. So I was involved in assisting this person, giving him a positive role model (a good term) so that he would find a different and more benevolent polarity. The reason I'm bringing it up is that this was sustained for that individual's reincarnational cycle all throughout that chain of lives.

It is a nine-life sequence, but the nine lives exist in the same moment. It's not one after the other, but at the same time. At some point the lifetime is over, and on that planet the nine lives would be over all at once, then there would be some reincarnational cycle. A chain of lives means one life after another.

It's like a group being, one being.

A group being, yes, but in the case of the reincarnation cycle of that being, they did not stay on that planet anymore. They reincarnated on different planets, and that chain of lives ended after about seventeen lives. Then they split off into two other chains of lives, one of which passed through this time in your planet. That person was known as Hitler. I mention this to you, not to suggest that I am a bad influence but rather that when I went to see them, they were already heading down that road. That was their first incarnation in this universe.

I was able to give them (I can't say him or her because it was many individuals) a positive role model, but when they split off into two chains of lives, one cycled through Earth and the other didn't, but explored lives in the etheric.

The first chain were lives in the physical with the greatest amount of physical experience possible. The lives themselves wouldn't be involved so much in thought or feeling, but the primary experience of each life in that incarnational cycle would be primarily physical. I am not casting any aspersions on physicality, but it is important to note that no matter how much you might inspire an individual, if they *must* become something, they will.

I'm bringing this point out because that was a learning experience for me. When I worked with that individual I attempted to inspire them onto a more benevolent path. If I had to do it over again, I would not, because perhaps they would have learned in a way less impactful on others. I cannot say.

They might have learned without having to experience the Hitler identity. However, I believe somebody would have been; it wouldn't have been Hitler, perhaps, but it probably would have been Bormann. That was an event that was destined to happen for your planet, unfortunately.

I want to make this clear so that you understand that we all—myself and other beings of consciousness—are learning as well.

When that first group split off, what percentage of that nine-being group came here? Were others in that group incarnated at the same time as Hitler?

No, the nine were one. I know what you are saying, because twins are two people, but on that planet the nine were one.

And here that nine was . . . ?

. . . Hitler.

One. But you said it split into two.

Yes, there were the incarnational lives, and there were two chains of lives, one of which isn't going through here and the other one is. But I don't see it like that.

But Zoosh uncreated Hitler.

Yes, it is a moot point at this moment. I bring it to your attention because it's important not to put us on a pedestal. I do not take any blame in this case. This is something that had to happen, and if it hadn't been the man known as Hitler, it would have been Bormann, with some slight chance for another person not particularly well-known at that time. I feel disinclined to give that name; it's not someone known in that movement of the time.

What you're saying is, there was a drama that had to be played out, and somebody had to play that role.

Yes.

Zoosh once said you were from the sixth level above.

Yes, that's true. But remember, I said at the beginning that I really would begin to speak of things that would have some relevance here. I do not think there are even words to describe the sixth level. I would have to struggle to find words to describe even the fourth level above. So I started.

But you had other experiences. You were functional and conscious long before this Creator created this creation?

Yes.

So you're editing that out and talking about things that are more relevant to us?

Yes, because it would take so long and be so esoteric, I don't know if it would even apply here. If there is interest in the future, then we can go into it, but now I prefer to give things that relate in some way to your field of interest here.

The Feminine Culture on Sirius

Now, there were societies that also interested me. The society or culture, as I called them before, that I started out with was also on Sirius. It is a feminine society and at that time had to do with the acculturation of different types of beings, and in some rare cases, the reculturation. If this culture of feminine beings on Sirius felt that a culture was not working benevolently and was somehow working destructively, then they would make themselves available to guide that culture if that culture desired it, though they wouldn't impose themselves.

I liked the idea that they would help others who needed help. I also liked the idea that they wanted someone who could act for them as a sort of advocate or go-between to help them see beyond their personal capacities so they would have as much inspiration as they needed to work with different groups of beings to support cultures. By supporting cultures, for instance, they would help by inspiring people within a culture to dance or sing or have some form of ceremony or rite, for example, or inspire beings to establish worthy forms of education and so on, things they could understand.

They were beings of a high calling within this Sirian society. I presented myself to them during one of their ceremonies when they asked for someone who could help them with inspiration. Up to that point in time, they'd had three experiences with cultures so foreign to their own that they had not known how to inspire them. One of the cultures was the Warrior League on Orion.

This Sirian culture for a long time did not have any positive ideals, nothing beyond their own personal culture, and they wanted some. They were asking for ideals, but these had to be representative of something godlike, you understand, that would benevolently help them find a greater balance. This was ultimately accomplished through creating a form of women's warrior league, which was how these individuals initially represented themselves. They then trained Orion women to achieve warrior mastery—in this case this does not mean actual battle, but the capacity to resolve all disagreements that could lead to war and resolve them equitably—which, I might add, was the original root of being a judge in a court. Originally a judge was intended to resolve disputes, not to simply conduct the court and be the voice of the law. So that was a worthy task. I give you that example because it directly reflects on your culture. That was perhaps the first time I was seen with the sphere on the top of my head. This is the way I am more commonly seen or remembered in your now culture, because these pictures of more recent cultures in your time have demonstrated me that way. You understand?

That is not simply symbolism. Remember, I chose the sphere, which I feel is a very useful choice in this universe. This universe is largely based upon very specific shapes, and the sphere is perhaps the most foundational shape of this universe. All universes are not like that, but this universe definitely is. I had to utilize some shape that all people in all societies in this universe would be familiar with. In that way, the shape would be familiar as a symbol, and that was critical. No matter how a culture perceived me as a being, they would ultimately be drawn to the idea that somehow the sphere had something to do with what I said to them and how I guided them.

I wanted them to perceive that wisdom comes from the sphere rather than from me. In this way I have been able to avoid being deified in most societies, though it was a struggle in some. I must admit I have been deified by some, yet when I saw that coming, with no way to avoid it, I made myself less available in those societies.

Some societies require someone as a deity so that they do not have responsibility for the way their culture exists. In my perception that is how it is; when there are deities in charge or who are responsible, they can be thanked and/or blamed.

And that's not what we're here to learn.

That is not why you're here. So I have made myself more available generally to cultures you are familiar with because those cultures, even if they struggled with the idea of a deity, were still motivated to take responsibility on a personal level or were striving toward that. So in some cases I gritted my teeth and went forward.

Atlantis and Lemuria

When you came to this planet, what was your first interaction here? What was the time or the civilization?

Perhaps the most well-known interaction in terms of your now-conscious awareness of a world was Lemuria. In that place the beings had a very evolved culture and did not actually need me. It was right around the time that Atlantis was coming into its own, choosing to be competitive with Lemuria and trying to emulate or set an example that would project the image that Lemuria was living past its time. So competition as you know it today was really being invented on Atlantis. The people of Lemuria needed to have someone who could act as a go-between (to guide the people of Atlantis if they requested it—they did not—but that was the Lemurians' motivation) or show Lemuria as being more powerful than it really was.

If Lemuria had waited around at the same dimension as Atlantis, then Atlantis would have probably destroyed Lemuria, because it felt largely intimidated by Lemuria at that point. Lemuria basically wanted someone to be a temporary . . . not statesman but someone who could create an image that lasted long enough to represent Lemuria to Atlantis, and be pervasive enough so that Lemuria could, from the point of view of Atlantis, seemingly dissipate. However, what they were really doing was moving their entire society to a higher dimension. Since Atlantis had the capacity to interfere with dimensional shifting, Lemuria basically needed to get away.

And not be interfered with in the process?

That's right, not be interfered with. Atlantis had the capacity and the competitiveness from its own point of view to want to prevail, no matter what the cost to Lemuria. So I was called in to distract Atlantis, which I did. That was an unusual circumstance, but I certainly felt that Lemuria needed to be preserved.

How did you do this distraction?

Well, for starters, they could see Lemuria from where they were, so I created an unblockable, impenetrable mist they couldn't see through. They could not see from any direction. While doing that, I spoke to the unconscious minds of all sleeping Atlanteans and the conscious minds of all waking Atlanteans so that they would have programmed (some mentally and some spiritually) the value of all life. This was done for a very short time, while the Lemurians got away. I might add that Atlantis was then, certainly thereafter, becoming highly involved in controversy within its own ranks about the experiments they were doing with life.

Toward the end, when Atlantis was largely uncreated and somewhat destroyed, they were just about at the point of resolving to stop all the genetic experiments they were doing. Had they not accidentally uncreated themselves, I think they would have resolved that.

And because they didn't, we're back here doing it again?

Yes, and yet it is a worthy thing to do. Science and technology in your time has gone past its own capacity to see what it's doing. People are so thrilled and excited about technology that they might easily do something that happened on Mars. The Martian society years ago used to have fluid on the surface, not exactly water, but something very similar to it. Their technology evolved to a point where they discovered they could utilize that fluid as a fuel to drive their ships. Because there was such a desire to take these ships as far and as fast as they could go, they used up the surface fluid.

Right now your society is rather frighteningly close to something similar. (I'm bringing this up as an aside because it is contemporary.) Your oil companies are largely considered the bad guys by many individuals. But in one case the oil companies' suppression of something that is supposed to be a cheap fuel is very good indeed. It is possible to run an automobile engine, as you know, on water. If this were done, it would not be too long before there wouldn't be enough water for plants and animals and people. So I totally support this suppression.

Really? Could we use up that much?

It seems like there is more water than you need, but if you think about all the plants and animals and people that continue to come to be, you need all the water on the surface. The water below the surface is only slightly available, because if Mother Earth felt that you were pulling too much water from under the surface up to the surface, she would simply pull it deeper, and that would be the end.

But I just read that we have access only to 10 percent of the fresh water on the planet. The rest of it is at the two poles and glaciers.

I don't know if that is true in its complete volume, but I would say that technology's capacity to say, "Let's use water for fuel," would prompt everyone to use it: "Let's use it to heat the house, let's use it for everything." It's very easy to look at a large volume of something and say that there will always be enough, but by breaking it down into its natural elements, you literally *eliminate* it. It's not a renewable resource for you, only up to a point. So here I make the oil companies the hero.

For once. Eventually, though, we won't be using oil, either.

No, but that is a ways off. Between you and me, I'm going to encourage you to do a little bit of homework, not too much. Look into societies for which there has been some representation of me, traditional societies, and ask me about my interaction with them, what I meant to do, not necessarily how I was portrayed.

Yes, I will do that.

That will be a really short list. Now we will continue.

The Fate of Atlantis

I didn't realize that Atlantis was uncreated. I thought they moved up another level. Are we those beings who were in Atlantis?

Uncreation in this case does not mean their souls, but the land. You have to remember that we are talking about an actual continent. People like to say, "Oh, Atlantis blew up." Think about it. If it did, it would have displaced a lot of physical mass. If you had the capacity to shove a continent under water, that water would have to go someplace. This continent was essentially uncreated, whereas the souls, the living beings, experienced what amounted to death.

Some of it exploded and fell in, but most of it, you're saying, was uncreated?

Not exploded. There wasn't much in the way of explosion. I do not see any explosion. The uncreation happened accidentally, though there is no such thing. I say accidentally because it was not the intention of the people. The benevolent people on Atlantis wanted to change the role of government and create a society that would be more benevolent. They had ringed the entire continent with crystals they were working with. It was a small society but a good one. It's just that they had been controlled, so early on in their experiments with crystals, they were attempting to reconstruct or reformulate the process by which the

Atlantean government thought. They were trying to change a thinking process, but they accidentally changed a materialization process. That's why I say uncreated. If something is uncreated . . . imagine you're standing on a ship at sea out of range, and you're looking at it. It essentially dissolves in front of your eyes. It doesn't splash into the sea, but it dissolves.

Now, I'm going to say something interesting about that. What happens if you remove a continent? Doesn't the ocean go down? It did. For several thousand years after that Mother Earth had to bring up a lot of subsurface water so that the ocean wasn't a puddle. You know what I mean—If you remove a massive continent, and we're talking *massive*.

Lemuria was slightly different in dimension. It didn't have to be very big because it was interdimensional. Atlantis never realized this during the time of its existence—Atlantis, you have to remember, started out at about the same vibrational intensity as Lemuria.

The culture of Atlantis began around the same vibrations as Lemuria. It gradually densified as it got more into the experience of the separation of an individual from what that individual created.

That's how it gradually densified and why that happened. It happened over time, and regardless of what you write about and how you try to preserve knowledge, it is difficult to preserve knowledge of higher dimensions when a society is densifying.

If the society is going the other way, then the future memories and the past memories of higher frequencies come to you. But as you are densifying, they go away from you. Lemuria was somewhat protected, but not at all of its vibrations, so it was necessary to create a screening so it could get all of itself out of there.

What dimension is it right now?

Right now Lemuria ranges, as always, in dimension. It ranges from the sixth dimension to the twenty-first. At the twenty-first dimension there are small parts of itself, but the bulk of the society is in existence around the eleventh dimension.

Many of the beings who were on Atlantis have reincarnated now on Earth, but the beings on Lemuria have not?

Beings on Lemuria, as far as I know, are still there. There is no reason for them to incarnate. Their incarnation there is permanent unless they choose to stop it. They do not have the birth and death cycle there.

They have nothing to do with the experiment we're involved with [the Explorer Race]?

No.

But the Atlanteans did even at that time?

I think the Atlanteans backed into it, because they were experiencing a lot of the fundamental densification that you came here to resolve. You might say that they contributed and became involved in the reincarnational cycle of the Explorer Race because they were moving backward in research, in a sense. They were experiencing consequences, and with consequences there is always something to be done to resolve it. They contributed. So I think that's how they slid into the Explorer Race cycle, but not of their own conscious choosing.

Zoosh has said that there were eighteen civilizations on this planet after it got here from Sirius, before our civilization. Is Atlantis one of those eighteen?

He's probably counting Atlantis and Lemuria. Atlantis was one, and of course Lemuria, although it is still in existence, was at one point closer to here.

Are these two civilizations just before ours, or are they far back in the sequence?

You have to remember that Atlantis slid through time a lot, because every time they slipped down to a denser vibration, they changed their time sequence. So it's very difficult to put an exact time on when Atlantis existed. In the beginning they existed at one time cycle—more of a constant time, not sequential time as you experience it. At the point of their uncreation, they were about at 3.48.

Which is right where we are right now.

I think that's probably why Zoosh is very concerned about you, because you are right about that same place. There is a difference, though, you see.

They were going down and we're going up.

That's right. Zoosh has indicated to me that he feels that is the safety mechanism. We hope so.

Well, we're going to make it this time. What percentage of souls on Earth right now have had incarnations in Atlantis?

A moment. I'm going to say, in the past fifteen years from this point back, then up ten years—I'm going to make a twenty-five-year opening there—the percentage in that twenty-five-year doorway is 7 percent. In your now, it's 2.5 to 3 percent, depending on who you count. Some of them have passed away in the past fifteen years, some are being born and some will still be born in the next ten years. But that will be about it for births associated with lives actually lived on Atlantis.

Isis' Commitment to this Creation

Would you go back to what got your attention when our Creator saw the ribbon of inspiration? What was your connection there? Where were you and how did you get involved?

I was at that level where I was conscious of the individual and all beings with that interplay. In moments when I was conscious of all beings, I became aware of the Creator of this universe's journey. At the time I became aware, I think it was right around the time that Zoosh had gone to the place to wait for your Creator to become an individual. It was interesting, but I didn't note anything.

I would still check. I would become aware of their journey all the way to the point where your Creator of this universe here attached Itself to the thread of the Explorer Race experience. Right around that time, I could see the value of coming to this universe at some point because I felt that your Creator here would make a very valuable contribution with this experiment—which is really drawing to a close now, in terms of the time factor.

It was right around the point when your Creator caught the thread of what would come to be the Explorer Race that I made a personal commitment to myself that I would participate in some way.

Before, you said you saw that the Creator was very young and He needed some babysitting—or something to that effect.

I don't like to call it that, but the Creator was (and this is critical) sufficiently inexperienced that It would not be reticent to take on such a task. Anybody in a business, a corporation or even a family knows that the older or more experienced individuals might not wish to take on a task, but the young, when they come in, take one look at it and say, "Well, let's do it!" That youthful enthusiasm is what allowed your Creator to take this on. I think it has been discussed before that other creators said no.

Yes, the ribbon went by everybody.

It went right past everyone, but this Creator, being young and having not done that much in creation, said, "This is something I would like to try."

And you felt that you could help Him?

I felt that He would want the help, which is something that is not always the case with creators, and that He would appreciate it. Appreciation is necessary in this case, because when you appreciate something, you very often welcome its repetition. This means that I could come and go from this universe and be welcome when I returned for some reason. I felt that this Creator would appreciate my contribution, and that was important.

The Master of Discomfort

What were your interactions? The Explorer Race on this planet is one tiny little period of time at the end of the experiment, right? You had many interactions with the Creator and this creation before the actual Explorer Race on this planet? Can you talk about some of those?

Yes, briefly. One of them that might be of interest to you is when your Creator was attempting to create a usable dialogue between Itself and that negative energy.

The Master of Discomfort.

Yes, that's a good term, the Master of Discomfort. In order for your Creator to communicate well with this being, there needed to be a common means of communication. Your Creator is primarily benevolent and the Master of Discomfort is primarily, in its outer expression, malevolent, though on the inner expression is also benevolent.

It was necessary to hook up your Creator with the inner being of the Master of Discomfort, because at that level of that being, it can speak to any and all beings about anything. That is the high mastery level of that being.

I was able to assist there because of my exposure to the many and the few (as we can label that level), where one experiences one's own consciousness and in the next moment experiences the consciousness of all beings. One can be aware as if you were all of those beings, sometimes all at once and at other times, individual beings within the whole.

When I became aware of all the uncountable beings (because the number was too high to count), I became aware of the Master of Discomfort. I had the capacity to understand the personal motivation and the personality at its most intimate level of the Master of Discomfort. I was able to create for your Creator a sense of common ground by showing that the ultimate desire of the Master of Discomfort was to achieve absolute and complete balance between discomfort and comfort, to create what would be a perfect balance—just enough discomfort to stimulate all of the beneficial effects it has, such as growth, but not so much discomfort that it would actually cause pain.

This is the Master of Discomfort's intent, and this is why, as the Explorer Race goes on and experiences other societies, the Pleiades at some point will experience from 1.5 to 2 percent discomfort. At that time the Master of Discomfort will be able to be its perfect balance and give that perfect balance to the Pleiades.

I was able to help Creator with that. Essentially, I showed Creator what would happen in the future with the Master of Discomfort; then Creator could interact best in communication with the Master of Discomfort in the future. That was what I was able to do.

The Sixth Level

Are you totally separate from what we call the Friends of the Creator? Is any one of them an aspect of you?

None of them are aspects of me from my personality, as you call it. Yet having experienced all beings, I cannot say that I am totally separate, because once you've experienced the level where you are aware of yourself and you are in the next moment aware of all beings, after that it is never possible to differentiate yourself only. I've not only experienced all beings, I've experienced all beings intimately. I have an awareness of all beings as a general experience, yes, but to have experienced all beings intimately means that I've got an intimate understanding of the heart and soul, as you say, of all beings. That's why I can't say that I'm *not* something, though I can say I *am* something.

You were saying they were separate?

They are themselves, and I know well who they are.

This is jumping a little, but you're leading into it. How many peers do you have? How many other beings have experienced everyone at the level you do?

There are others; I have met some. As far as I know at this time, they are not in this universe. I am here because of my personal interest in this project.

What I mean is that there are many beings at that sixth level above and beings at levels in between. I have not seen any of them in this universe, but there are others like me. I don't think that most of you on Earth at this time have had contact with any of them, but surely, looking around quickly at those incarnated on Earth now, there are at least 17 individuals living on Earth now who have had contact with one or more of those beings in some form.

Do you create something? What is your focus?

I don't know if I can explain it. It is a good question. Let me take a moment.

I'm sorry, it is not verbal. I do not think it is possible to describe it in words. The closest I could come to describing it would be in high-speed motion that you would have to experience.

Picture this: Be here now in your body and at the same moment accelerate in all directions. By the time you get to the outer boundaries of this universe in all directions, some portion of you would be touching everything in this universe and its outer boundaries and have the capacity to go beyond there to everything else. At that point you would understand about one-half of one percent of the sixth level. This is the closest I can come. It is not a thought as much as an imagined acceleration you've experienced before.

But with you it's a living experience.

Yes. I'll tell you something, as wonderful as that sounds—and I did like it while I was there—I have discovered that the value of individuality as you experience it here on Earth comes not so much from the growth curve, but from the innocence of it. When you are able to experience so much, you experience innocence as a group experience. But when you are beyond the veil, when you are in that veil of ignorance, you can experience innocence at a much more personal level.

I think that is an experience to cherish, because it allows you to really have childhood twice in your life—the experience of being the physical child and the experience of what is called senility, which is really intended to be a second childhood wherein one redevelops one's innocence. It does not always work that way, but it is intended that way, so that one comes into the world innocently and exits the same way.

Beautiful, and leaves all the baggage behind.

Yes.

Well, this is fun. Have you ever talked through channels before? You must have many times.

I have spoken through many channels and continue to do so to support the objectives of those channels and/or the groups that surround them, yes.

Do you use many names, or always your own name?

Usually I will use names you know on this planet that are associated with me. Isis is my most frequently used name.

What are some others?

I don't know if you know of them because they are not in your time, but a name I used once was Nebon (nee-bon´), the "n" being almost silent. This was in times ancient from your now perspective, about eight to ten thousand years ago in the area now known as Bali.

But it doesn't survive now in Bali?

No, it has not survived in their mythology. It was just for those times. That's why I haven't brought these things up. We'll focus on what you know, then later, for other volumes, we can get more into the unknown. I feel we need to stay somewhat in context.

So people will understand.

Yes.

Interacting with the Creator

Let's get back to your interactions with the Creator—were there other things you did for or with Him or for us?

We had some common ground in terms of the experience at the sixth level. Part of this Creator is at higher levels, and I have seen this Creator in Its other portion at the sixth level.

Can He hear you while you're telling us?

He can hear, but it won't affect His wisdom. In this case it won't. For Him to know that He's at a higher level—the sixth level is just a term. What does it tell you? The sixth level is a feeling, an experience, not so much a thought. So it does not really interfere with Him. We had a common language anyway, because this other part of Him is there. Even though He's not in touch with that part, it was easy for Him to understand it. It's as if you have some knowledge, but you've been hypnotized to forget it. You can still access your abilities and talents toward that knowledge without necessarily having the specific knowledge you don't recall.

When Creator individualized, He individualized on what I thought was this level, from the Creator of the Inverse Reality.

Yes, he did. That is true.

He separated before that, then?

I am not sure when the separation took place, but it took place at some point. I'm not sure that this separation was before His personal experience of His own being. Part of Him would have been seeded at this other place, but at some point He didn't allow that piece to go onward and upward and wait for Him. I think maybe before He created this universe, He may have sent that part up so that He could follow that pathway more easily.

What we had heard was that it was a deliberate thing. We would have to separate ourselves, so He wasn't going to ask us to do something He hadn't done.

Yes, that sounds like Him, all right.

So you two had this resonance?

A common language.

What other things? Did you influence anything in the creation or interact?

I tried not to, because one thing that is essential to understand when interacting with any creator is that it is so easy (you understand this on an individual basis as a person) to deflect someone from his personal vision even with the most benign intentions. It's as if somebody is making soup on the stove and wishes the soup to have a flavor of tarragon that is like an aftertaste, so that after you swallow every spoonful of soup, that tarragon flavor is there. But if you come along and add some other spice, the flavor of the soup is changed. So I decided I would (I like this term) butt out. (I heard that one from Zoosh once, and I thought it was *very*, very funny.)

So you just sort of kept an eye on everything.

I watched and waited. It was beyond time, but for the sake of simplicity, for the last few million years in this creation it was okay to say things to Creator, but when Creator was just beginning this creation, it *wasn't* okay. It would have been very easy to have unintentionally influenced Him.

The last few million years is the end of it? The cake is baked?

Yes, the cake is baked, and if He wants to change the flavor of the frosting a little bit, that's okay.

This is going to be really neat. You're fun to talk to. I was a little intimidated because I don't know very much about you.

Well, as the channel learns to allow me, it gets more comfortable.

The Planetary Influence of Isis

October 28, 1997

All right, Isis.

Welcome. You asked me to get references in societies where there have been some representations of you.

And you were going to prompt me with things more associated with what is understood on Earth, yes.

Almost all the references I have found seem to relate to the Isis/Osiris/Horus Egyptian story. No matter what book of mythology you look in, that's what it says. I have some pictures and some articles.

I would like to look at them. Do they all have this appearance? If so, one is enough, yes?

They mostly focus on what's been excavated in Egypt. I even bought Isis Unveiled *by Blavatsky, but there's nothing in it about Isis.*

Ancient Egypt and the Feminine Energy

The relationship to the ancient Egyptians was that of creating a reverence for and appreciation of the feminine energy. In societies of those times, the feminine energy was not always fully appreciated because of the apparent difference between the sexes on Earth. A man had more physical strength, if not more mental strength—at least the ability to be ready at all times should defense become necessary. A woman was not always able, even if she was a warrior. Women warriors were certainly known even in those times.

So the term "Isis" was applied at the time to educate those who would receive education about the value and especially about the strength of the feminine being. Given the times, it was as close as you could get to introducing the idea of equality of the sexes, in terms of the educated person's perception in those times. Granted, such education was meant for a select few in their society, but it was intended that they educate others who would not receive such education. To some extent this was done.

My part in this was to work with various beings in their dream states. Dreams were very significant to the ancient Egyptians. A man might dream something one night and mention it to his teachers or advisors and discuss it, but if no one else had dreamt that, it would simply be considered and set aside. Yet because dreams were considered visions and were considered as relevant as conscious communication (if not more so), when others started having the dream (in which I appeared the same way to all of them), they began to take notice. It was during these dream classes that I was able to instruct the priests of the time, as well as some of the royalty, that the feminine of the beings had the capacity to empower strength. Because of who and what they were, they would necessarily test such things, stimulated by consultants or advisors to the wise or powerful.

Feminine Energy and the Warrior's Strength

This is one test that was done: A warrior was pitted in battle against another warrior—not to the death, because they were both good warriors and no one wanted to waste a good warrior. One warrior fought entirely on his own; the other warrior had his wife and all his female relatives standing near him, not in the direct field of battle, not entreating or praying for his winning, but filling their hearts with the Sun and the Moon energy, with their arms out like this—straight out with their hands. Palms toward the center, but tilted slightly upward.

They would give that strength to the warrior. This test was done exactly that way, sometimes with one warrior, sometimes with another, all over the land of those people, and it always turned out the same way. The warrior who received strength from his women would always succeed, or he would have the strength to go on when the other warrior became exhausted.

With such profound proof that the mind of no man could deny, there was a recognition that a female goddess was essential so that there would not only be a model of behavior for women based not upon male ideals, but feminine ideals—meaning the goddess ideal—but also that the masculine beings—the priests or wealthy class—would also have a model of feminine behavior to idealize, and more importantly, to respect.

This was truly a turning point for that civilization. Before that time, women were appreciated and loved as in any society, but were not admired as equals. That is an important point, "admired as equals." Here was a circumstance in which the people understood that their women giving strength to the warriors was vital. This is understood even today in that part of the world.

I might add that, surprisingly, it isn't understood in the rest of the world even though other parts of the world consider themselves to have powerful militaries. You might ask how the not-very-powerful militaries of those areas have managed to survive. The reason is that to this day they understand that the woman amplifies the male warrior's strength. I am not saying that is necessarily what I was teaching the people, but it is what they proved to their own satisfaction.

So once the test or the hurdle was passed, it was then possible to begin teaching the priest class to recruit for the priestess class. I was then able, through dreams and visions, to begin to establish a river of wisdom that would be held in trust for all beings in the priestess class. Even in these times, when women study in such groups and practice ceremonies, rites and loving rituals, such wisdom is held in trust not only for themselves and other women, but for all people—men as well. It is not for women to go out and seek men and give them this knowledge, but for men to come to the priestess and ask her for such knowledge. I might add that the origin of the ceremony in early England of the queen knighting someone is rooted in the idea of the worthy warrior seeking out the priestess (in this case the high priestess) to give him the wisdom that will give him greater strength and, of course, power.

I'm trying to relate some of these things to more contemporary historical facts so that you can see the influence even today.

Atlantis and Greenland

Can we back up and get an overview here? Atlantis was uncreated and Lemuria went into another dimension. Is what followed considered the civilization we're in now?

No.

No? There was another one before or there were several?

Atlantis was essentially unfinished, not completing things. Other civilizations that were more native peoples over the Earth had to play out what was left. They were not necessarily working on anything that might be considered Explorer Race foundations. I'm not saying that Atlanteans were necessarily Explorer Race, but they were establishing foundations for Explorer Race. For example, there was a civilization that used to be much more populous in what is now Greenland. Shortly after Atlantis, there were about five times more people there compared to its present population. It was not always so cold; it had more warm weather than it has now. And it did not have the icecaps very much, just a little. Comparatively, the icecaps in the north were 7 percent of what they are today; in the south they were about 10.5 percent. The world was warmer and more hospitable; this is why Greenland was more hospitable to so many people.

The people of Greenland, then, took on most of the unresolved issues left over from the uncreation of Atlantis. For example, they took on the resolution of equality of all life. At that time that society was benevolent, but the people fished for food. Not every people who lived near the sea did that, yet what seems normal and even rational today was not necessarily the norm then. This seems innocent enough; the people lived off what they gathered and to some extent what they planted. Most of these peoples were not in contact with world travelers, so whatever they planted had to be locally available.

They didn't trade.

That's correct. The way they played it out was as follows: Most members of their tribe (if I can call it that, though it was evolved people) consumed food from the sea. I'm going to call them a tribe because most of those people are not there anymore; they migrated. It began slowly at first, again through dreams and visions. In their case, almost immediately twelve- to thirteen-year-old boys and girls started having the same dream. Whales would come out of the ocean, walk upon the land as if they had legs and come up to the fires of the people. They would sit down and tell stories of the sea and of other whales as if they were stories of family life and ancestors. When this dream was told in one family, then another, it was considered enlightening and interesting and stimulating and funny. But after a few weeks, when the people begin to compare notes, as you say, they found, much to their shock, that something like 32 or 33 young people had had the same dream the same night.

The Knowledge of the Sea Creatures
and the Appearance of the Traveler

Then the elders put their heads together (that's another good phrase you say) and said, "What does it mean?" They began to ask their nature spirits, "Was it a message to begin treating sea creatures as equals?" They were told by the nature spirits through their shamans that sea creatures had a great deal of knowledge and wisdom to pass on to them. If they would begin to treat sea creatures with much greater reverence and appreciation—and in time, love and respect—then the sea creatures would give them all this wisdom.

The elders considered that for a while, then they asked their spirits, "What will we live on if we begin to be taught by sea creatures? We cannot eat our teachers; how will we survive?" The spirits told them that there would be a man who comes from far away. He would have things in his boat. "He will give you these things and you will plant them. They will be seeds that will give your people the food you need until you go with the man or his ancestors to where he came from." That was the message almost word for word.

So the people developed a more reverential and appreciative attitude toward sea creatures, and they waited. After about twelve years a man came, though not in the kind of boat you have today. It was what you would call a vehicle, but it came from under the water, not unlike a submarine of your times, though it was shaped like an oval. It was a vehicle from another star system, but it was based on Earth. There were other people inside, but only one man got out. Before he got out, he bade those inside farewell, for he was going to live with the people as an anthropologist might do. They said good-bye and gave him two big sacks of corn; one was blue and one was red. He took the sacks and went to be with the people.

It took time, but they raised the corn. It grew very well because it was warm and wet there, even though it was in the northern latitude. (Remember, there wasn't much of an icecap.) He taught them ways that are not unlike the ways of being now practiced by several North and South American native peoples. He himself had learned these ways from those people, not the other way around. You assume that he had taught them, but no, he learned from them. He was a person who in those days was referred to as the Traveler. Even today, stories, myths and legends exist with native peoples all over the world about the Traveler who came from far away and brought gifts to make the lives of the people better. Then he told stories and said, "In a few years you will have enough corn to live well, and then you will be able to have all the wisdom of all the sea creatures. When you have all of their wisdom, then if you wish, you may come with me."

So the people worked on the land. The corn grew quickly, and within three and a half years they were beginning to assimilate the wisdom of the people of the sea: dolphins, whales and other fish, sometimes small fish. Sometimes fish would come that did not ordinarily live in those waters. They would come if there was a warm current—eels, hm? The beings you know as mermaids would come and discuss with the people the abilities to use benevolent magic to transform all discomforts. This was the final education from what you now call mermaids—or mermen, for that matter, though they received their education from the mermaid.

Then came the time of choosing. The people were told that there would be an ice age coming, that all of their land would be covered and they would have to move. They had a choice to go with the Traveler, who would bring them to other places. It would be up to them. The people asked, "How will you move us if we go?"

The Traveler said, "I will call for my people, and they will come and bring sky boats to move you."

The people said, "We cannot stay here if the ice is going to destroy our land." So the Traveler called his people and the sky boats came. Some of the people asked to stay on Earth; the others said, "We will go with you to your land," which in this case was Pleiades. Of those who wished to stay on Earth, some went to what is now North America in the area of Canada, joining tribes there that would have them. Others came to what is now the northern United States and joined tribes there.

There was celebrating and greetings, for the people who came to these places had the wisdom of the sea, and these places were inland. There were rivers and lakes and thus fish, so knowledge from the fish was greatly appreciated. That is why even to this day some of the most secret and holy relics and shrines of the peoples in that part of the world are based on aquatic themes, though not everyone knows this. But it is not so secret that I cannot tell.

What they resolved, as you can gather, was the most critical lesson that did not play out on Atlantis, which was the separation of classes. This played out on what is now Greenland, by people as one class and aquatic creatures as another. It worked out well. I mention that civilization because it has been so influential in many ways. Even to this day you will find sacred relics all over the world that have aquatic themes. That is because some of the people asked to go to other parts of the world and were dropped off there, where they educated others. Some small degree of influence was exerted because of their interaction with what became the Polynesian race. There was a lot of influence and wisdom that integrated itself into different groups of native peoples through stories and through the application of the wisdom of those stories. As it was in ancient Egypt, advisors and consultants want to test knowledge to see if it works, and if it does, then it is not only revered, but perhaps more importantly, practiced.

I was able, with the people of Greenland, to advise them through one of my students, who at that time were in the form of mermaids. Mermaids are real.

Are there any now?

Only inside the Earth, but not many. Most of them have been evacuated, as you say, taken to places where they will be safe from certain radiations that mankind is utilizing too much.

Because they were partly human, they were able to teach the Greenland people?

Yes. The people of Greenland could see that these beings were like them in some way, but also aquatic. Because they were partly human, they could communicate in ways humans would understand and still act as interpreters. Even though aquatic creatures had been able to give visions and tell stories through the sensitives of these people, the true feelings of aquatic creatures had been difficult to impart, and mermaid people were able to do this.

Other Native Peoples

That's beautiful. So when Atlantis and Lemuria left, there were groups of native peoples all over the planet?

Yes. Groups of native peoples have been here for a very long time.

But it wasn't the time of any civilizations yet—China or India?

Not yet, no. But there were native peoples there.

Are they our ancestors, then? Does that bridge us to the present time?

It's not measured by years so much as by the evolution and acceptance of the heart of the human being to living a challenging life on Earth. Many beings who came from elsewhere did not survive on Earth because life can be hard here. But those who did survive needed a great deal of encouragement to embrace Earth. So I would rather measure time through the resistance to, or the embracement of, Earth. Lemuria went up in dimensions because they were not able to tolerate the energy and competitiveness of Atlantis, and Atlantis uncreated itself. In both cases there was a degree of resistance to the way Earth is.

Yet if you looked to native peoples all over, those who survived and thrived had embraced Earth the way it was. They learned how to live with Earth as it existed and they appreciated Earth. These peoples, some of them, are in existence today in their descendants.

But genetically these tribes were our ancestors? There's not some other jump in the genetic programming?

Correct. In the sense of being ancient Earth peoples, they are that. I am not prepared to say they are wholly representative of your genetics. Certainly some genetics continue to be contributed by extraterrestrials, but as I say, the extraterrestrials who came here to settle, unless they were accepted by tribal peoples, usually did not last because Earth life was too challenging for them. They thought that if they were born someplace else and brought their culture with them, settling as colonists might, their lives would be perpetuated. But not so. Immediately they would have experiences associated with lessons on Earth, and this was very difficult for them. If they were adopted or nurtured by native peoples who understood what to do in that area—the geography, you understand, where they were—then they might survive, but many of them did not. In some cases they were able to request rescue, but in most cases they simply didn't survive because their emigration to Earth was a one-way trip. They had been dropped off and were not expected to return.

Can we say that from these people rose the civilizations that we know of as our recorded history over thousands of years?

Yes, you can say that.

Mysterious Origins of Egypt

No one knows how Egypt became a civilization; it was suddenly just there. Can you talk about that? From a tribal culture, how did it become this great . . . there was extraterrestrial influence, wasn't there?

This was, to some extent, an experiment. There were very advanced beings living underground in this area. Those beings, in consultation with other beings, asked whether it would be possible to encourage the surface dwellers to establish a sacred, benevolent wisdom school. That school would be used for the perpetuation of useful wisdom, not only on the practical level but also on the intergalactic level. It would provide an acceleration in cultural sophistication and make it possible to create an earlier contact between the peoples of Earth and the peoples of the stars.

The underground civilization worked for many years to establish a means by which they could train surface peoples and have those surface peoples go back and still be appreciated. There was a lot of concern that a separate class would survive or be maintained because of the magic that would be given to these trainees—magic necessary to propel any wisdom school into a more rapid foundation than might otherwise have developed in the area.

Now, at that time Egypt was not a desert—it has become a desert in recent times, but it wasn't then—so the peoples were fairly abundant and could live easily off the land. It wasn't a struggle as it is today. Yet the biggest challenge for the underground dwellers was how to do this without adding to the complication of separate classes. At first they tried with dreams and visions, but it didn't work because the people on the surface already had a pretty good life and they didn't need a different one. So those underground beings realized that they would have to wait for someone who would respond to the dreams and visions.

They waited for about eighty years, and then they were able to give dreams and visions to a young woman who was intrigued by them. She spoke to her mother about them, and her mother said, "If you go to find out more of these things" (since one of the visions was to go to a rock wall not far from her encampment, a place people usually did not go because of wild animals), "you must bring your brother, who will guard you." The young woman agreed. In the vision she had to go alone, but her brother went with her.

The underground people did not know what to do, since the brother had been given similar dreams and visions but had not responded— he'd thought of them as only dreams and had forgotten them. They said, "How can we do this?" They let her go to that wall week after week after week. They were waiting for the time when her brother would do something else because she had always been safe. It finally happened after about three and a half weeks. Her brother said, "I will keep you in sight, but I won't come all the way. If I see any danger, I will run and protect you." She agreed.

Well, as is typical for anyone, you cannot stare at someone constantly. She got up to the rock wall and the underground people waited until her brother looked away in the distance. When her brother looked back again, she was gone. He ran over, but she was gone. The underground civilization had opened up the wall and brought her underground. Utilizing time, they were able to give her about thirty years' training and experience and knowledge and wisdom in about ten minutes of surface time. She was told that she would return with all this knowledge and wisdom and practical experience, but would have been away only ten minutes Earth time, so she would not miss her mother and father and family.

It was very hard for her nevertheless, since she was clearly educated and told that what would be taught to her would help her people to not only become entirely self-sustaining, but to establish great wisdom schools for now and the future. She felt this was important, so she received the education, which was essentially the fundamental priest- and priestess-class education that would follow in times to come. This included not only wisdom that you now consider spiritual, but also practical wisdom such as agriculture and animal husbandry (as you call it), science, religion, mathematics and, to some extent, geometry. All of these things and more she was given.

Sure enough, after the brother had been rushing around looking for her for ten minutes (though not rushing home to say he had lost her, which would have been pretty serious), they opened the rock face and let her out when the brother was on the other side. He ran around and said, "Where were you? Were you hiding and playing a trick on me?" as any young man might think. She told him, in a condensed form, what had happened. Since he loved and appreciated her, he believed her.

She said she had been entrusted with knowledge and wisdom that would help her people, that she had been given knowledge and wisdom meant only for women and had been entrusted with knowledge and wisdom meant only for men. She asked if he would like to have the knowledge and wisdom that was meant only for men. He replied, "I will have to ask my elder." (In those days every young man and every young woman had an elder—not always grandparents, but usually other older individuals.) So they consulted his elder. She spoke a bit to the elder about the wisdom, and the elder said yes. But the elder added, "May I be with my student, the person I counsel" (her brother) "while this education is given?" She looked inside herself and said, "Yes, so you can help him." Well, it is a long story, but this is how it got started.

That young woman was the model for what came to be known as the image of Isis that you now have. The circle was a little something extra. But in other ways she was the model.

And was her brother the model for Osiris?

Yes, because by the time they became much older, the first wisdom school had already been built. So they had a place where people would come to learn, then go back home, bringing the knowledge. They would be able to raise much more abundant crops and build permanent structures that would shelter them from the rain and the elements, just as any society is created.

Now, the education that took place for the young woman was given by very advanced beings. Most of those beings, who existed at a quicker frequency (also known as a higher dimension), are still there under what is now loosely referred to as the Middle East. Their attempts to influence people with dreams and visions (like the ones they

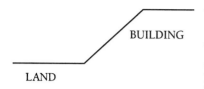

BUILDING

LAND

broadcast to the young people of those early times) still continue. They are waiting for some young person to go alone to one or two different rock walls they still have. They will someday reestablish their wisdom schools there.

So the great Egyptian culture that rose was not an accident. It was very successful because the wisdom taught there spread all over the world. Even though there has been much turmoil, strife and struggle, they shaved about 2100 years off the time when modern civilization would meet and interact with extraterrestrials. So it was a success.

It was always intended that the wisdom, not the civilization, would last. Remember that the wisdom schools were not intended only for the people that this young woman and her brother were a portion of, but for any people who came there, whether by sea or land. All were given the education freely and all were shown the result—abundant crops, happy animals, all of these things—and went home to their lands. Not all of them survived, because times were challenging, but many did.

That is why even today certain similar myths and legends that cannot be logically explained away are associated with ancient peoples all over the world. You could say that the reason some stories are similar is because people are similar, and that is certainly true. You could also say that certain world events affected everyone, and that is also true. Yet there are other things that are clearly associated with the recognition of the sacredness of all life. For instance, people in those times were told at the first wisdom school that the best way to honor all life was to treat all life, be it plant or animal or stone, as something sacred and equal, and make pictures that would last beyond the time of their civilization. This is something almost universal among sacred peoples: "Make pictures," their guidance told them. Of course, the people thought initially that the pictures were meant for themselves. But wiser ones eventually realized they were not. That is why all over the world there are consistent themes in weaving, painting, sculpture, cave art— everything associated with plants. Look at the designs; they are often associated with plants, and one consistent design that you find all over is this [draws]. If you look at the overall design, you might say, "Well, that's a normal design." But was it always a normal design? It

FRONT→

SIDE VIEW
WISDOM SCHOOL

was not, and I'll tell you why that design is so pervasive, especially with ancient peoples. That was the side view of the first wisdom school!

Here was the land [draws], and here was the building.

Isis and Her Student

Since they were influencing this young lady from underground, how did she become known by women? Did you continue to work with her?

I encouraged her. She insisted throughout her life that she was not Isis. She said, "I am the student of Isis." Think about it; if someone says, "I am the student of . . ." Think about *your* culture: Swan Son—the son of swan, yes? How much of a leap is it to say "the student of swan"?

And pretty soon the student is swan.

Yes, it is really that she said, "I am the student of Isis," for I was one of her guides—always in the vision state, never physically. If I were to have come to her physically, she would have treated me like a god, being a simple girl of the time. It was important that I be more like a grandmother—nurturing, supporting, guiding, teaching, loving—but not someone so magnificent that she would immediately separate herself from me. That is why even to this day teachers who have the best effect on students have such qualities.

Had you been guiding her long before she got this vision from underground?

No. It was after she went underground that I began guiding her. Thirty years of experience for one so young, even though it was only ten minutes of Earth time. Yes, thirty years of experience—would she not desperately miss her family, her brothers and sisters, her mother and father? She needed someone to love her and cherish her. I did this on the spirit level with her every night when she slept. I would be there to hold her in my arms. When she slept, which she looked forward to, she would, as she said, sleep in the arms of Isis. So I became a beloved friend, which is a much better teacher, and I would help her in her sleep time with her lessons.

Then how did your sphere get transposed to her?

In time, as she got older, she would tell stories she could remember about me. She would draw pictures as she saw me, and sometimes she saw me with the light, the circle at the top, and the horns, as you see them. Horns have to do with authority, but I did not wear horns; that is strictly an Earth adaptation.

She would tell of this, and the people needed what you call icons—not idols, but pictures. Remember, the people were encouraged to create pictures for themselves and for the future (but they didn't know that until later). They would use the authority symbol of the time, which was horns. The horns were intended to show wisdom, strength and (perhaps most important for any peoples associated with those who lived close to the land) continuity, or perpetuity.

Their more ancient gods and goddesses had horns, so it was perfectly natural for them to create a picture of her as she looked then, with the circle of light on top, then add the horns. She knew that if she dressed up like that, she would become so separate from the other young women that when she died her wisdom would die with her. She was trained to make certain that she was a loving teacher, but never a queen or goddess. When you are a queen or a goddess, usually your wisdom dies with you because people feel separate from you—you are the exalted one. But if you are the loved and benevolent teacher, that is quite different. Although she said nothing when the people wished to make such pictures and idols, if you would—let's call them ideals—she would not dress like this, though many wanted her to.

In later years others did dress like this, but not on all occasions. Usually it would be to bring in pharaoh, wife of the pharaoh or someone like that for the purpose of modeling herself after the idol—the ideal. In the beginning it was not intended to create a separation, but rather to be an ideal to live up to. So that's how that got started, as it does with many other ideals. When you think about the cross and how it has become the symbol for modern Christianity, yet think what the cross was in those days—a tool of execution and punishment—it is ironic, is it not? Certainly in the future the Christian symbol will evolve into the equal-armed cross, which is a more benevolent rendition of the symbol. In some cases it has already done so; I have seen it in your time.

Horus, Osiris and Isis

What about some of the other melodramas, where they had a child named Horus, where Osiris was killed, and where they had a wicked brother—all that was handed down to us.

You must remember that a lot of history and the molding of the children of any society is done through stories. If you want to create a pattern of knowledge or wisdom in your culture, in your children, you will create stories. And you can gauge a society very much by the stories it holds sacred. As your friend Zoosh says, never forget that. That is an absolute rule that I have seen no exceptions to in all my travels.

So these were added later by people bringing in good and evil and something to control them?

Not just bringing in good and evil, because that is too academic an appraisal, but more the idea of creating a separation between one group of people and another—the good guy/bad guy idea. It wasn't for the concept of creating good and evil; that concept was not even considered. Look at your own culture; the good guy/bad guy theme is very strong.

Oh, absolutely.

As a result, your culture is even more polarized. In time the glorification of such stories will pass, and the future stories of adventure will have more to do with exploration and discovery than good guy/bad guy.

Wonderful! Now, at the beginning of the mystery school, you told the girl your name was Isis.

I said, "Grandmother Isis."

There must be other interactions with you around the world that are not in our stories where you used your name.

Isis in Africa

Yes, sometimes I did, and sometimes I would use other names, because the term *Isis* is acceptable in some places. But in other places, other names might be more appropriate. In an ancient civilization in Africa, I once presented myself to the woman chief of a tribe. In those days that was much more frequent. I would show her, through visions and dreams, as I like to do, the means by which she could learn how to heal injuries. I also showed her how to make it much more comfortable for women to give birth by using the right herbs and berries so that the mother-to-be would feel less pain. Then I also taught methods by which she could learn to nurture the baby properly.

She was the chief of the tribe, so she had many responsibilities. When she was being supported and became the elder, the grandmother, I would give her this wisdom and she could pass it on as she saw fit. These were very independent people; you didn't tell them what to do, you didn't give them complete instructions. There was some autonomy needed, faith in their judgment.

So I gave her this wisdom, told her about the plants and the barks and the roots. This took some time, and I noticed that during the time of the instruction she would experiment, as was proper. She began teaching a group of young girls this knowledge. So I was able to support that wisdom in that ancient tribe. It was very satisfying. Unfortunately, that tribe is no longer in existence; too bad.

I think they were able to perpetuate some of that wisdom, because after that chief died, she talked to me and said, "This is a good thing, this way of teaching with visions." She requested to be taught in that manner, and I took her as an apprentice and taught her how to teach with visions in the dream state.

For the next 10 to 15 thousand years she went all over the Earth in the form of spirit messages and worked with young women in all kinds of native tribes to teach about the plants that were near them. She became very good at this and still does this to this day. Right now she's on another planet doing the same thing. She said that probably she will come back here soon to begin again.

Before the Great Pyramid

In Egypt, did you influence the beings underground to send those visions, or was that their gift?

I was able to influence them. They wished to be more aggressive or assertive in their education plan, but I was able to be the cooler head and encourage them just to invite someone who would wish to be involved.

They wanted to go up to the surface and start the school themselves. I told them that was certainly guaranteed to create a separate class of individuals, that it was essential that a reasonably well-liked and accepted member who was open to such things be allowed to do it, and that the process would take much longer than they wanted to invest in it. But they decided, since patience was their group lesson, that they would try it my way.

A lot of our understanding of wisdom teaching and priestess' and priesthood has to do with the pyramid in Egypt. Was there a pyramid there from a previous civilization? Was this before the Great Pyramid?

There was no pyramid at that time; as a matter of fact, there were really no structures. The building of the wisdom school was the first permanent structure—and when I say permanent, I mean something that would last for more than a hundred years. That's why the shape of the wisdom school was so defined, and one sees these shapes in today's architecture. For example, here's the land and this is the side view of the wisdom school [points to earlier drawing].

And houses still have sloping roofs, imagine that.

It is kind of pyramidal. See? It had this sloped back, so this would be the front.

FRONT→

SIDE VIEW
WISDOM SCHOOL

So this is before the Great Pyramid, then.

This was before the pyramid, yes. Remember, she was taught mathematics and some geometry, so she had an understanding of how to build structures without suffering or struggling. We're not talking about rolling rocks across the plain using timbers, because the whole idea was to create a structure that would live long after the civilization that was using it (though not to this day) and would be buildable without distracting the people from their own culture. She was taught enough benevolent magic so she could ask certain stone slabs to volunteer; then she could move the slabs, utilizing energies that would allow the slabs to float. Even to this day some structures (not in Egypt) continue to stand that were moved in this way. Perhaps the most frequently photographed of these structures would be Stonehenge, which was built by floating rocks to that place.

By students of this wisdom school?

Teachings from a Visiting Civilization

No, I don't think so. The teaching in that case came from an extraterrestrial civilization that stopped off and taught a few people. It did not last, though, you see. There it is: When you have education coming from beings who appear so exalted and different from you, such education tends to not be maintained because it is not coming from one of your own kind. There is immediately great reverence, but also distrust, and ultimately that will lead to strife.

So the wisdom that once existed at Stonehenge was lost. But in the wisdom school in Egypt, this branch of wisdom is still in society even though it is not widely appreciated or practiced. There are people in your societies all over the world who have the capacity to move objects without touching them. This is not only in your genetics, but is usually associated with these people in some ancestral way, back to someone in their line who at one time attended the wisdom school. A line can be not only a bloodline, but a reincarnational line.

There was a man in Miami who did that. They call it Coral Castle, on the South Dixie Highway. He moved the stones around. Can you see that?

Yes. He was not from another planet. People said so, but other people said, "We can prove he was born here!"

Were the beings who taught people to build Stonehenge called the Druids? Or were the Druids their students?

No, the Druids did not build Stonehenge; it was something they inherited. But the extraterrestrial influence was short-lived. By that time those who were receiving their education were so highly distrusted by prevailing societies that the wisdom of the Druids, though it was for the most part benevolent . . . well, the Stonehenge builders' descendants were the subject of dangerous gossip. So they had to go underground to preserve their wisdom as much as they could, though much of it does not exist in your time today.

And they were taught by the extraterrestrials.

No, they inherited it. They were not taught by the extraterrestrials. The beings who were taught by the extraterrestrials built Stonehenge, but those were not the Druids.

Did those beings, then, teach the Druids?

Their ancestors taught one person, who went on to establish what came to be known as the Druids.

What star system did the beings come from who taught the beings who built Stonehenge?

Archimedes.

Archimedes. We had a Greek scientist of that name.

Nice name, isn't it?

More on Isis' Student

Yes. Back to the girl who was the student of Isis. She did such incredible work. Has she reappeared in our history? Do we know her by other names, or is she living with you now?

She was disappointed a little after her life. She felt initially that she was being deified, not quite realizing that the people needed something to inspire them. So for a long time she didn't incarnate again on Earth. But she did have a couple of lives in the past few thousand years, and perhaps [chuckles] because of having such a prominent life, she decided to live quietly. She is not amongst you now.

Well, she did something awesome as far as the Earth is concerned.

She was a wonderful student, totally dedicated to improving the quality of life for her own people and all peoples who would apply. Applying even today is so important. The appreciation of the questioner is still not strong in your society. Any question is truly an application, meaning you are applying for the answer. In this sense the questioner is still not fully appreciated. In some Eastern traditional societies, yes, the questioner is appreciated, because it is understood in some of these more ancient societies (anciently rooted societies, perhaps) that the questioner might bring out just as much wisdom for the teacher as for the student by making the teacher stretch and attempt to deduce or ask for guidance. So appreciate whoever asks the question, for very often the answer will stimulate growth in all.

Beings from the Underground

I like that. All right, back to what we know of Isis. She also was known as the protector of the underworld. How did that get started?

Well, think about their wisdom school. Where did those beings . . .

Oh, underground.

Underground, that's how that got started. The underworld in your time means something entirely different. In those days the underworld simply meant civilizations underground, whereas in your time the underworld is significantly more frightening. Remember that the underworld in literary references does not refer to the criminal society, but refers to beings of the worlds beneath—meaning innerworldly beings, or perhaps magical beings or slightly twisted magical beings.

We won't go on with this, but that puts a new light on Hades and the Persephone legend, some of those things. That was your interaction, then—the eventual growth of an Egyptian society that had pharaohs and kings was really an outgrowth of this original wisdom?

Yes. When you have a wisdom school and people come from all different areas, eventually that area grows, gets bigger. Where are these people going to stay, especially if they are there for years at a time? That created a city where no city existed before. It is always the case, in my experience; a wisdom school attracts [laughs]—unlike, I might add jokingly, many schools of today where a student often runs from school. But when it is a wisdom school, that is quite different. If the child was going to discover how to float a ball above his or her hand, the child would run to a school like that with a smile. But if they are going to learn facts upon which they will be tested, then they run away from school.

Maybe schools will change.

They will definitely change.

Is there anything else you want to say about your interaction with Egypt?

That is enough for now.

So your name isn't known in other civilizations, then. Did you interact with India, China?

Not by this name, no.

So you have had other names.

I used other names if it was helpful; I did not use the name Isis in the African society.

We wouldn't recognize the names you used?

Equal, Not Superior

No, I would use the name, in any event, names and words I am going to interpret. If a society has people that are named after events, then I would be a grandmother of some event—Grandmother Dreamer or Grandmother Who Sees, you understand, something like that. In this way the people do not see me as something foreign. If creators or gods or goddesses or priests or priestesses, what-have-you, intend to do the best for a society they work with, it is always best to be perceived as an equal, not as a superior. If you present yourself or allow yourself to be presented as a superior, the chances of your good works living beyond the lives of those people are greatly diminished.

In all the other cases in which you interacted with humans, you attempted to work with them through their dreams and visions?

Yes; even in the Egyptian time I recognized that the people needed to have ideals, so I did not worry about being deified. I knew that much of the meaning would be lost in your modern times and that ultimately people of the modern times would not look upon me as a deity—which they really don't. Even today I am looked upon in that Egyptian model, as it were, as more of an ideal than a god.

Well, there are goddess groups now where your name is invoked pretty regularly.

Yes, I work with these people, but I also advise them that it is always my intention to improve the quality of their lives so that they might improve the quality of the lives of others as those others apply to them. In this way I present myself to them on very practical levels so that they can see I am looking at them eye to eye rather than examining the tops of their heads.

Is there another civilization or group of beings that you had an impact on under another name that we would recognize?

I'm not sure if you would recognize them. Remember, I have been almost like a zealot in my attempt to go unnoticed if at all possible. In some Eastern societies I have worked with beings who trust and value benevolent visions. I have attempted to do that in the past, and where it has been successful I have been thankful; where it has been unsuccessful, I have learned. Ultimately it is necessary for all beings to learn, and I am no exception.

Can you tell us about a successful one and maybe an unsuccessful one? You're a wonderful storyteller.

Isis in India

Thank you. In one case in India—there were many fewer people in those days many years ago—there was a man who had time. It was toward the end of his life and he was fortunate in that he was appreciated by his sons and daughters, and they would bring him food and give him shelter. Because he was a wise man, he was accepted and welcomed wherever he went. Yet with all of this richness of life, he was often a little lonely because he said to himself, and occasionally to other men of his age, that he missed the inspiration to succeed and live life that he'd felt when he was a young man. He wondered if there was some story or vision he could receive to inspire him at this time of his life.

Hearing his desire and visiting him in his rest time at night, I spoke to him and gave him a job. Very often older people need a reason to live beyond being loved by their children and grandchildren. They need something to do, for which they can see the valuable results. I told him that his job, if he wished to practice it, would be to think up stories he could tell to children that would dramatize, in an exciting, fun and benevolent way, the most important lessons he had learned in his life.

He was to invite other old men, if they wished to come, to sit in on the groups and listen as he told these stories to the children. Then he was to ask them (talking to them first, saying these things) to tell *their* stories in the same way. In this way he would not only cause them to be more welcome guests when they arrived to tell stories, but it would also be a good way to pass on hard-fought lessons of wisdom that could best be passed on in a fun way to children.

They would not attempt in any way to make it sound educational, not lecture the children afterward, but just tell their stories and let them go. They would trust that the children might remember the stories and as they grew up, understand their importance, but not be burdened with such lessons as children. The man did this. He was able to pass on such storytelling methods to other older men of the time, and this became very successful.

Of course, there were other people at that time in that society who were telling stories; this was not new. But it was new to this man and his people, because in his society at that time, when a man got older and he had been a good man (good to his children and so on), it would be a time for which he would receive back from them their love and appreciation and would not be burdened with any of the work of life, including raising children. This was another way to honor him, not only to listen to what he had to say, but more important, to give him a reason for living beyond being honored. So that was pretty successful.

This is separate from the story line, but the imagination of human beings spreads spherically out in all directions, and when stimulation is needed or even if it is prompted, it will be available from whomever can provide it. Imagination is the one true connection that allows your conscious mind to unite with your unconscious and thus to the One. I believe this is why your friend Zoosh says that the imagination is the divine part of the mind.

Once somebody said that imagination is the memory bank of the soul.

It is an acceptable way to say it.

So you stimulated the imagination of the soul of this man and that gave him a purpose for life.

I gave him a vision, a dream. Have you not ever had dreams such that when you woke up, you said, "That was real!" Those are the kind of dreams I give people. It is not just a casual dream, but a dream that causes you to leap out of bed inspired.

Yes. Do you want to tell about another one?

Horns of a Dilemma

I will tell you one story, since you have requested, of a circumstance that didn't work so well.

Alas, live and learn. There was a time when I was working with animals, not unusual for me. There was a species of animal that was gradually evolving toward what you now know as the longhorn. This type of being had very sharp horns to protect itself, because such animals were originally wild and needed a means of protection. Yet sometimes they would unintentionally damage younger members of their species, because the young ones are more delicate. So I suggested in a vision that these animals manage a horn that was not quite so sharp. The ones I was speaking to, in this case more than one individual, were those that were the dreamers, receptive on the dream level, ones that would sing the song of the old ways to the young ones. All animals come from someplace, usually not here, and there must be someone that sings the song of the old ways to them. Thus they will know when they come here, not unlike some humans, where they are from and where they will return to, so that no matter what happens they will have some sense of purpose.

So I was communicating with these beings and they said, "Well, we will include that in our songs, saying that some of us have more dull or rounded horn tips and some sharp ones." In this way they would give permission for such to occur, since future generations are affected by these songs. Even your own peoples, human beings, are affected by songs. In your time many young people are troubled because the lyrics of songs have been troubled for a time. Change the lyrics to something more benevolent, and in time the children are less disturbed. It is not *only* that which disturbs children, but it is partly so.

So these animals that would become cattle someday tried that, and sure enough, there came to be some born in the future that did not have horns so much, but little rounded stubs. As it turned out, however, they didn't have as good a balance. I didn't fully realize at that time that the hollow space inside the horns functions as an extension of their sinus cavities. And I went back essentially with an "oops!" story, in which I said, "Excuse me." I might add that most of them did not survive, but one did, who was very old at that time. He kind of smiled at me and said in the nicest possible way, "We do appreciate your efforts, however."

[Laughs.] How very sweet. They were also at the mercy of the sharp-horned ones who'd want to fight with them?

Yes, it was a failure. I learned after that to pay more attention to the functional aspects of all beings.

The Adventurer

October 30, 1997

Isis here: You know what I'd like to talk about? I want to talk about my interactions with the Explorer Race before you got here.

The Adventurer and the Explorer Race

When the call went out for the beings who would come from far away and participate in these adventures here (in this universe as a member of the Explorer Race), I remember noting especially how far the distances were, not only in terms of time and dimension, but the level of commitment it required for some beings to come and participate. One in particular, who participated in the early days of the Explorer Race but who is now waiting for everybody else with the larger group, took so long to get here that the Creator of this universe was literally releasing personalized souls to become the Explorer Race when the being arrived. This was very impressive when you consider that, of the souls who came, this being was the only true explorer amongst the bunch!

Can you say anything about his origin?

It's impossible to describe it in contemporary terminology in any language on this planet at this time. This being was so enthusiastic about the Explorer Race that had this being been of a creator status, it would have picked up the Explorer Race thread before your Creator did. It so happened that when the thread that became the Explorer Race idea was being created in its bits and pieces, this being was there for that creation. Although it was only a portion of something else, it was personally involved as a portion of the substance that became the thread. It was on what you would call . . . we'll do a picture here [draws]. The thread was going that way [to the right on drawing]. This being was already committed to going the *other* way!

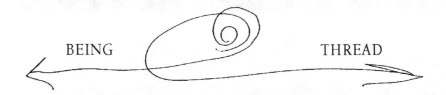

So he had to turn around and go back?

No, you don't do that when you make commitments there.

Oh, he had to fulfill his commitment and then come back?

He did his entire commitment, completed it, resolved it, everything, all the while looking to return, not listening (in order to do a commitment, you must be present), patiently waiting so he could return. After he completed his commitment, the thread was so far away by that time that he had to travel at the speed of elliptical time. That requires another illustration—elliptical time. This is time [draws].

TIME

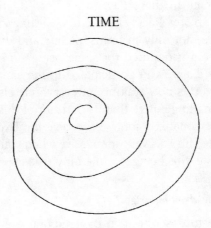

ELLIPTICAL TIME

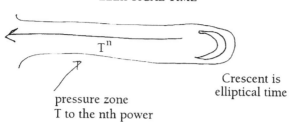

T^n

pressure zone
T to the nth power

Crescent is
elliptical time

And this is elliptical time [draws]. There's more to it than that; how can I illustrate it? This is what you would call a pressure zone [draws line around arrow and crescent]. That crescent is elliptical time. In the pressure zone, time has the capacity to speed up to the nth power [writes "T to the nth power"]. It took such a means of physical motivation (not mental or emotional motivation) to get our Adventurer there.

Understand that if you take time to the nth power, first you go through all the colors of light; then the passage beyond that becomes a cacophony of all thought everywhere. You cannot move through it on a straight line. If you do, you will inevitably strike or come into contact with a thought or a concept around which thoughts tend to cluster and become. If our being did that, he would have had to become involved with it and work his way out gradually.

So not unlike flying through comet fragments or asteroids in an asteroid belt, he had to move at this furious rate of speed, yet not hit anything. He obviously took a circuitous course. Continuing to accelerate, the next level is what I would call *depth*. (Air has a certain quantity of depth; you don't realize you're touching it until you touch something else that has a different density.) In order to go through that . . . barrier, let's call it, you have to be prepared for sudden increases and decreases in acceleration. This means that you cannot maintain any thought or feeling; you have to be entirely without them to get through this. That's how time to the nth goes; if you're going to travel through it, you cannot propel yourself through on your own. Occasionally you will have your own capacity to navigate, but for the most part you will be pulled. So your mind and your feelings have to be completely blank, and just doing that for a length of time takes considerable effort.

The next level you go through as you're heading to the nth (but you're not even halfway there yet) is extremes of feeling all the way to complete lack of feeling, a null zone. Since you have already been practicing no-feeling—not merely the calm feeling, but no feeling whatsoever—it is not such a big step in terms of the null zone of feeling, but it *is* a tremendous impact of extreme feelings. You would not know from one moment to the next what's coming.

So to be able to pass through there requires not only a level of spiritual and material mastery, but you really need to have been exposed for some length of time to lessons of quantum mastery, which is about consequences, or you need to have been working on it. Otherwise you can't get through, because all of these things you're going through affect the outcome of other things. They are not simply personal barriers, but actual places of existence that provide what you experience, as you're traveling through it, to all beings everywhere. If you are accelerating through that, obviously you must not make any impact on it. The challenge is to be able to pass through this without stimulating or causing *any* consequences. As I say, you'd have to have been exposed at length to at least material mastery and quantum mastery.

Meeting the Nucleus of Its Own Being

Once you've managed that, if you have (and this being did—that's why I call him the Adventurer), you then have to face perhaps the most difficult task of all: You must go through the zone of applied and practiced individuality. This is the area where all concepts of individuality are born, created, worked out and even applied. Since this being was an individual, it could not help but at some point meet the nucleus of its own being passing through there (because it would naturally be attracted to it); conversely, the nucleus of its own being, feeling its applied personality passing through, would rush toward *it*. As much as you would wish to embrace it, you could not even acknowledge its existence, because doing so would mean that you would stop and remain there. This being had to go right through, remember, without causing any consequences.

That was very difficult because in the occasional moments when an individual personality is allowed to return to this place, it is the homecoming of all homecomings. It is the time not only of completely understanding every single facet of your personality—why you've done everything you have ever done in any incarnation or will ever do—but completely understanding how the bits of you came together, what those all mean and why. It is the complete capacity to understand every single aspect of yourself as it relates to everything else.

It's a fantastic experience, and it is usually not experienced until you have achieved at least absolute quantum mastery—and not many beings have. So our being, our Adventurer, had to sail through that as if he were passing through a piece of paper: "Whoop! Oh, okay," then gone—nothing, no reaction.

Passing through the Mother of All Love

Then the next and really last hurdle on the way is that our Adventurer had to pass through what I would call the barrier, or the sense of compassion that underlies all creation, all uncreation (for that exists) and all nurturance. It is the component that makes up what is felt by all beings as love, and it is also what holds all matter together. If you could go back to the source of all love, then go to Love's mother—what created all the stuff from which Love was created—that's what we're talking about. Passing through that without causing consequences means that you must be able to pass through without having the slightest need for anything. If you had even the slightest need, compassion serves all needs. So our Adventurer passed through it, and after having done that, he was able to breathe a sigh of relief and put it on his wish list to return someday.

Imagine passing up all this for the desire to come and participate as an active member of the Explorer Race.

Who was pulling him?

He wanted to go, but in order to get through all this he could be pulled only by a being with whom he had a personal acquaintance. He had a personal acquaintance with Earth as she existed before she became a planet. Earth, as you know, is working on quantum mastery, but at her higher levels of being right around the ninth dimension of herself, she has achieved this. This particular being on his way knew Earth. At that time Earth was not in your solar system, but it wasn't far away. She acted as a locating navigator; she pulled him and he, with his acquiescence, pushed a little bit.

This being, then, came with the desire to live one life on Earth. He lived on Earth when Earth was in Sirius, in the form of the origin species of the dolphin. (The dolphin beings look different on this planet than in their original form, though in their origin species they are, in fact, water beings.) So this being passed quickly through the Creator, and within a short time (compared to everybody else dispersing and going out and creating chains of lives), he went straight to Sirius and lived a life on Earth. He brought with him the spirit of adventure, especially in passing through Creator and mingling and cocreating, as it were, being a portion of all the other beings.

Explorer Race Personalities

The reason I want to talk a little bit about the Explorer Race before it got here is to reveal some of the actual personalities that make you up and how they have played out their lives. The Adventurer wanted to experience the creation of the Explorer Race, since he had been there—

actually, a portion of his substance was part of the original thread. In that sense, he was following a piece of himself.

After this being completed his life on Sirius, about 525 years Earth time, he was very happy. He could feel the trends in the future, could feel the success of the Explorer Race. This being is primarily a feeling being, which is probably the reason he needed to go to Sirius, a feeling place. He was the first being to take up the rendezvous position where most of the beings (souls, if you would) of the Explorer Race are now waiting for the rest of the Explorer Race to complete its experience.

What Zoosh called the 93 percent?

Yes. This being has been waiting all that time, though it does not feel bored.

How does his energy of adventure get into the rest of the Explorer Race beings? He went through just at the time they were coming out?

All the beings, as they were coming out, were melded with each other—they were a portion, after all, of the Creator. This being had to pass through the Creator and become a portion of the Creator to do it. So I would use the analogy of their being like twins or triplets who have individual personalities, yet there is a great alliance between them. There is what you would call a blending, and it was the blending that perhaps allowed the Explorer Race to evolve quicker than otherwise. The individual souls who came out of Creator to form the foundational soul beings of the Explorer Race were excited and happy and interested, but they would have been more cautious if they had not been infused by the Adventurer. As a result, the length of the entire experience was collapsed by two and a half times. This being speeded up the whole thing.

How does that work? We were told that there were only three seed beings that would come back together to be the Explorer Race, who would be fused into a new Creator.

You have to remember that within those seed beings are other parts; there is no one thing. If you can trace all creation everywhere in all time back to one thing, you can look at that one thing, but as you go into it, you would discover that it is many things, much as your scientists examine an atom, discover its parts, then later suspect that each part is made up of different things.

That makes sense, because one of the beings talked about beings coming from everywhere, then somehow coalescing into those three seeds. So those three were made up of many, many beings.

Yes. In that way we can see how such a variety has stemmed from what seems to be a small number.

The Creation of the Explorer Race Threads

Where was this thread created? Where was this Adventurer when it was created?

It's hard to describe that, actually; I can describe it better in terms of moods and concepts rather than distance.

Is it a level? You talk about six levels.

Yes. The creation of threads that are available to creators takes place at the third level. This level allows such creations, and because it is at the third level, it is somewhat of a safety mechanism. If you had a creation of threads at this level floating freely about in this universe, it is very likely that those threads would be taken up by those who do not have sufficient skills to deal with all the consequences—and who could say what would develop?

So threads are created at the third level; they are not allowed to come to the second or the first level until they have proved their viability, proved that they can survive on their own and that they will be attracted to or propel themselves only toward a creator. And if someone does not have creator skills, the threads will do their utmost to avoid contact with them or will attempt to move beyond that level to get away.

All threads can't do that; some threads might have to do with attraction, for example, and a thread like that could not get away from anyone or anything. With that in mind, you might need a place where they can simply be protected as well as have mechanisms to protect others. The journey your Creator made with Its primary companion (I tell your Creator this at the same time I tell you)—although the Creator and Its friend felt it was at the third level, it was not. The thread connected with the Explorer Race was involved in attraction; the very root of the Explorer Race is attraction, you understand? How could someone be an explorer without being attracted?

So the thread was on the second level. I do not know whether your friend Zoosh or your Creator knew that their transit was through the second level until they started moving into the area of other creations. By the time they got to the area of other creations, the thread was destined to intersect with your Creator and *only* your Creator. There would be no intersections with any other beings close enough who were not creators, who would create a problem.

We didn't know about levels before, so you're broadening the whole story now.

If your Creator had for some reason *not* noticed (of course, that's not likely) the thread as it went by, it would have been returned to the third level. There was a safety mechanism built in there.

Where did they meet the other friends of the Creator? Was that on the second level, too?

No, it was on this level.

The first level, okay.

Yes, but the initial meeting between Zoosh and Creator—and their initial journey—was on the second level.

And there are creations on that level also?

Not the kind you would recognize with star systems, but there would be creations associated with feelings or what precedes creation that can be sensed with the senses you have.

When the Adventurer came here, when he came through the Mother of Love and the place where identities began, was that on the second level?

The Adventurer transited the third level.

So that's where and what those places are that create what eventually ends up down here.

Yes, and if the Adventurer started on the third level, what does that suggest? It suggests that that being is a creator or has that status. Now, that being has not exercised that status, but because it has that status, it will be exactly the energy that, when all of you come together to re-form yourselves as a Creator, will become the nucleus of experiential creatism, which will allow you to become a Creator in your own right. Without that being who wanted to be here, you could not become a Creator; you needed the nucleus of a creator to do that.

So that being came here as a creator, passed through your Creator, was colored by that experience, and lived a life, even though that life was ensouled by Creator. Since then he has been waiting. Of course, time is relative to such a being. But you see, then, how it works for everyone?

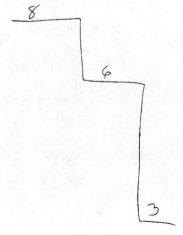

When I would talk to the friends of the Creator and the creator of the Creator, I didn't know about levels, and many things that I assumed were on one level were on several of the other levels.

We must recognize what separates different levels. This [draws], for the sake of illustration, is not a straight line, but something that often overlaps, not unlike the overlapping of a woodgrain, you understand, or even the layers of clay that an artist might make in a sculpture. There is a certain amount of overlapping in places, and those places are in constant flux, which allows the impregnation of what those levels contain into other levels. You can't just have doorways as you have here; you've got to have the capacity to move there at a moment's notice with whatever energy is needed, perhaps to the next level. This energy can't go whizzing down someplace looking for a door and come whizzing back; it might be too late then. You've got to be able to move rapidly from one point to another; that's why the moving, flexing, overlapping experience is not unlike what it would be for two clouds to meet, initially maintain their individuality, then seem to become one and then many.

That's a beautiful analogy.

Clouds, in this sense, are some of your best teachers on this world. They show the observer many things and illustrate many others. Because they are fleeting, they do not demand your attention but simply offer what they have to those who would participate.

I think somebody said that spirit beings play with the clouds.

They are allowed to. The initialization of clouds is as close as you can come to seeing Mother Earth's personality in its multitudinous faces. That's why children, in their innocence, are naturally drawn by clouds. I might add that the very old also admire the clouds, because there is a feeling, a recognition, of a loving, benevolent personality present within them.

What did you have to do with the creation of that thread?

There was not a personal presence on my part when that thread was evolving. But I have observed threads which will very often have varying degrees—here on Earth you spin different threads into yarn; there one might have a thread of a creation that spins itself into other threads more minute, different particles of potential creations. These particles then might take on particles from other creations to perform the creation cycle of variability necessary to attract those who would apply such creations, as creators do, and also attract other variable threads that might make the creational thread that much more interesting. I am more at that level—interested in the process of the bits of threads coming together rather than the individual threads or expressions of what they might become when applied.

So did I have a personal involvement with that thread? Not directly, no. But I did notice the being, the Adventurer; I did notice its participation in the creation. Fairly early on I recognized that the Adventurer would wish to participate in that. Not unlike the Adventurer's chagrin when he realized after the fact that he had already made a commitment to go the opposite direction, the Adventurer and I had a little ironic laugh about that. I bade the Adventurer good-bye and said, "You will make it in time, but you will have to make no stops on the way!"

The Initializing Being

There is a being on the third level whose responsibility it is to initialize or connect with all the barriers that you would travel through (in time to the nth [T^{nth}]) and also connect to the sixth level. I have checked, and the connection does not go beyond the sixth level.

But there is a beyond?

Yes, as far as I know, there is a beyond, because I once met someone who was from the seventh level. (More about that later if you wish.)

This initializing being is connected, then, through all these levels, and its entire effort is toward feeling—that's the best description. I say feeling because you can identify with that—feeling what's missing anywhere, from the greatest degree of something massive that's missing to the slightest degree of a missing nuance, then producing threads that fill in the gap. He emits these threads with a marker, like a marker that a geneticist might someday put within a chromosome of DNA to find its way to the gap it will fill. It might not go to the actual place where something is missing and needed; it might instead go to the creator who will build on that creation and fill that gap. That is what that being does.

Has he always done this?

Well, let me ask. A moment. He has always done this. The being passes on this message: It says that it did not know the purpose of its existence before there was existence. (That's its little joke.)

I love it! You show everything as expanding in all directions.

That is the intention of these books, is it not?

Your Creator and the Council

Yes. I just didn't know there were so many ways to go up and out! On what level does the Council of Creators sit?

The Council of Creators has, in my time, usually resided at the third level. This is very advantageous; for one thing, generally, material or beings or mass that exists at the third level is either a creator, part of a creator or meant for a creator. So the chances of there being distractions for this Council . . . the term "council" is perhaps a little strict; it is more a social organization than an arbitrating organization.

And you sit on it, right?

In a sense; my presence is felt there. It is the same with all creators; their presence is felt there. They can be where they are, doing what they do, but if it is necessary to commiserate about something, it can be done. It takes place at the third level, though there have been times when a more complete experience was needed, for whatever reason— usually the studying of individual consequences was necessary, in terms of allowing the creators to feel the individual consequences. Creators do not always feel them. They have learned feeling but, depending on their level of experience or the creation they are involved in, they might not be capable of experiencing all feelings at once. Your Creator, I believe, is not capable of that at this time—to Its advantage. I think that has been discussed.

We know He can't feel discomfort or pain or suffering. The reason I asked is because He had to go before that Council. They looked into the potential consequences of this suffering very thoroughly, didn't they?

Yes. For example, they didn't come to this creation, but once the Council sat briefly at the first level, where discomfort was just beginning to be experimented with. The degree of discomfort, compared to what you experience, is almost negligible. Your friend Zoosh gives percentages, so if you were to elucidate the percentage, it would be significantly less than a half of a percent, all right? To you that would be nothing. But since it was something new and something that was being experimented with, and since at that time it was only beginning to show a vast impact on individual personalities, the Council of Creators sat in that region for a short time to observe the effect of something new: discomfort on the feeling level for individuals. At that time the Council was adamant (me too) about never allowing discomfort to go beyond that percentage, especially for beings who were open and loving, cherished beings, not unlike babies on your planet.

I must tell you that it took a lot of convincing from many different sources to sway the Council of Creators to allow discomfort to become a greater percentage in this creation, to say nothing of other creations. And every single one of those circumstances was with the proviso that if something went seriously wrong, whoever was involved in that creation would have to, not pay the piper, but fix the circumstances, resolve all the consequences indefinitely for all the beings who ever happened. I might add that your Creator has been very creative in resolving the situation with what your friend Zoosh has termed the negative planet on Sirius, which no longer is in existence. I believe your Creator resolved the situation in the only way It could, short of simply having to stop and deal with all circumstances. Instead of the soul simply dying as a result of the destruction of the planet (to physicists, changing the mass of the planet), they simply moved en masse to the

3.0 dimension of Earth. I do not see any other way this could have been done. When you consider the minute timing involved, you had to be beyond 3.45. Now, think about that.

That's why we were kicked up higher.

Yes. Not only that, but recently you slipped back to 3.43, and during that time many of you began having strange nightmares. That was because you were just close enough to 3.0 to begin having nightmares or experiences that those beings were having at 3.0, which were left over from their difficulties on the planet in Sirius.

Why were they brought here? What was the point of bringing them here?

They could come only here.

Why?

Considering the level of negativity they were struggling under, this is the only place that had enough negativity for them to make the transition without destroying their individual personalities.

Your Creator is still under the same contract, because resolution has not taken place. But there has been an improvement. That was taken into account, and there is the intention of creating further improvement. There have been many beings who have volunteered to be involved in the furtherance of an improvement of your lives. So while your Creator is still a little bit on probation here, the outlook looks good.

If for some reason the experiment were to fail and negativity were to escape, isn't there a contract that calls for the uncreation of everyone involved?

Negativity escaping beyond boundaries in which it now is?

Yes.

Oh, yes, then it would have been necessary to uncreate this entire creation.

And all those involved, right?

Yes. That is, of course, why your Creator is being monitored so carefully, because mistakes like that are not really received well in the Council of Creators. If that were to happen, your Creator would be in big trouble.

And the friends of the Creator and everyone else?

And everyone involved—which tends to create a high degree of motivation on everyone's part.

Yes, and a lot of help.

A great deal of help, any help you need. It is a funny thing, you know . . . here's a challenge for you. Say a man is building a brick wall; the bricks are very heavy and it is exhausting. He has all the supplies he needs to build the brick wall—all the mortar, everything—but he needs help desperately. Spirits come from far and wide to help him, but they can't actually lift the bricks. It's like that. You can have whatever help you need, but *no interference.*

So we have to lift the bricks ourselves.

You have to lift the bricks and put them in the proper place.

Isis' Interest and Involvement in, This Creation

Yes, but look at how much help you've given. You were interested, you were on the Council of Creators, you were interested in the thread, and you said at one time you sort of babysat the Creator because He was so young. I'm trying to sum up . . .

He's *still* young.

. . . the extent of your overall involvement and interest.

Well, I didn't become that involved until I was watching the experience of the Adventurer. You must admit the irony of it all. The Adventurer is going to catch someone's attention—and he did. I think I became more involved when the Adventurer was on his way. I must tell you, I personally know of only one other being who's ever done that—taken time to the nth—and that being wasn't going to this place where you are, but it has taken a significant amount of time to recover from the episode. Your Adventurer, however, came right in, had a life and has been involved ever since. Think about passing through such experiences, then having to let them go completely and just have a nice life.

Would he like to talk to us sometime?

Ask; maybe he'll be available. He might have some interesting things to say, eh?

Right. He gave you the feeling of "let me look into this" or . . .

Not that; it isn't a mental decision like when something catches your eye and you think, Oh, I want to know more about it. It's not like that; it's more like . . . picture this: Picture that instead of your feelings coming up unexpectedly, they were like a garment. You could feel them all the time, but at different moments, according to the circumstances of your life, you would feel a feeling more strongly. Perhaps it would become a brighter color and you would notice it in the garment. You would notice it and become more involved when it was more active, and less involved when it was less active.

As it became more active, I was interested. When it went through periods when it was less active, when there was less drama, let's say, I was involved in other things. So I am not what you would call a constant companion, but more of the occasional visiting dowager aunt.

I know, but you have so much love for the beings here.

How can you not? Think what you are doing! It has not been done before, to my awareness—never. That is why so many beings pay you so much attention.

By the time you saw the Adventurer, that was really toward the end of this creation, right? This Creator had created this universe, which had gone on for most of its total time span by the time the Explorer Race came out, right?

Yes. By the time the Explorer Race came out, the vast amount of planets and suns and so on had been largely created. This is essential, because if you're going to birth something to re-create you, you want to have things in place so you won't have to be concerned with them. Creator has set things up to basically re-create themselves. As suns might spin out of the center of a galaxy, Creator does not have to consciously create galaxies anymore; it is something that gets set up and runs itself. Creator does not have to think and push buttons and pull levers. All of that needed to be in place before Creator could put the energy toward re-creating Itself.

But when you say the drama, the drama didn't really start until the Explorer Race was birthed?

Well, there were some moments of drama when Creator was beginning with Its consultants. It took awhile, especially when you consider the Master of Discomfort, with whom most of the consultants had had no prior experience. It took awhile to get everybody functioning smoothly together. There was some drama then—not what you would call high drama, but more of a gradual assimilation. Even then the Master of Discomfort had to create for itself a distancing mechanism, because he understood that if he became too involved with any of the other consultants, to say nothing of the Creator Itself, he would inadvertently (entirely inadvertently, I might add) send the whole experiment in another direction. So the Master of Discomfort had to be involved, yet distant at the same time. That's part of the reason this being is a master. Even though he has his own personal needs, he had to be able to let his personal needs wait for a while sometimes so as not to be served when it felt that too much mingling would cause his personality to have an effect on others—too much mingling with the other consultants, too much mingling with what was being created, too much mingling with your Creator. The Master of Discomfort has always had to keep a little distance.

What would have happened?

Well, think about it. Name another consultant off the top of your head.

Master of Plasma.

Now, the Master of Plasma has the duty to provide that energy—remember, we talked about love and plasma, about the fluid, and going back to what creates love and so on. If the Master of Discomfort were to become involved with that . . .

It would interfere with the glue that held it together.

Yes, because discomfort is a naturally repelling force, and since love is a naturally attracting force, it could have been a disaster. So even though the Master of Discomfort very much liked all the other consultants and they liked and admired the Master of Discomfort for having taken on such a difficult task that no one else would take on, they had to respect his distancing from them and love him from afar. That has created for the Master of Discomfort a necessary loneliness, which is difficult for him. So he is very much looking forward to that whole issue being resolved as quickly as possible—hopefully by you, but if not, by your successor.

Who's our successor?

Whoever you will birth to replace you. Do you think you will wait around?

Well, no.

Resolving the Master of Discomfort

You'll take over this creation, but you can't simply leave it. I think that you or your successor toward the beginning will resolve that for the Master of Discomfort, and it will probably be resolved to some extent through the use of velocity. Velocity has the most amazing capacity of transformation.

In coming years, your scientists will begin to understand how objects that appear to be solid are, in fact, not. The human body appears to be solid, but it is not. Objects such as the human body can travel at speeds beyond the speed of light and arrive completely intact. Once your scientists understand this, they will begin to grasp the value of velocity, which, for the human being as you now exist, is the ultimate curative tool for all disease. If you could move the body up faster than the speed of light, and if the soul and the conscious mind of the person is involved in a trained meditation or a prayer that is absolutely focused to change their circumstance and asks that circumstances become more benevolent, promising (you must absolutely commit; there can't just be a promise in a prayer) that you will apply that benevolence to your life (which means all who come in contact with you), all disease and discomfort, even if you've been born with it, can be resolved. Your scientists, physicians and physicists will all get together to do this, and in the long run medicine and physics will become married.

That is how the Master of Discomfort will probably be resolved, and that is how all discomfort for the human being will be resolved. You see many other races now that travel in time (which is beyond the speed of light, you understand); they know this, and that is why they have no discomfort even if they've been exposed to it.

What happens to beings such as the Pleiadians who in the past have come here? Occasionally they have unintentionally been affected by discomfort. They can't go back to their home planet without affecting everybody else, so they get in the ship and they become a unit. These beings have been trained in meditation (also called prayer here), and when they become totally focused in that meditation, the ship travels through light and time and all discomfort is resolved.

Something to look forward to!

Yes, it is also a safety mechanism, you see, to keep discomfort from places that are not really capable of dealing with it.

Isis in Our Universe

Okay, so you looked in, then, when the friends of the Creator were first bringing the work together. When the Adventurer got here, you paid more attention, right?

I paid more attention when the Adventurer got here, that's right, because I had had that interest in his path. And there were others that came from afar, but I will probably talk about those next time. But yes, when the Adventurer came, I started to pay more attention because it has a lot to do with my job to nurture, and nurturing is needed very much when people are experiencing the unexpected. When you are adventuring, the unexpected is a constant companion.

So the focus of your existence is nurturing.

Yes, here in your universe the focus of my existence is nurturing.

But not other places?

Not only nurturing, but also other things here and in other places. But most of what I do here is nurturing, encouraging, supporting, though not sustaining . . .

Teaching.

Teaching, guiding, showing but not leading.

Is there a representation of you anywhere? You're not physical, but is there any-

place that there is an energy or information about you in our mythology that is accurate?

Oh, I think over the years that a lot has been channeled. I don't think it's in general circulation in your time. There were some scrolls that . . . no, let me look . . . those were destroyed in a ship sinking at sea. I think that most of the information has been circulated through what you now call channeling, but the civilizations preceding you have simply referred to it, in one degree or another, as inspirational conversation. Many religions even in your now time utilize inspirational conversation to encourage their flocks to understand better. Obviously, if your preachers, your reverends, are going to communicate to people who don't necessarily speak their language or who perhaps use a variation of that language, they will have to use that version of the language. Let's say that the reverend is talking to all teenagers; he can't talk only Latin to them.

Oh, I see, they've got to talk teenage.

They've got to be able to understand teenage talk and occasionally put in a word of it so that he is not perceived as entirely anachronistic.

But you never started any philosophies or religions . . .

I use this as an analogy. I'm saying that I have been very careful to avoid becoming deified. As you see, the person I encouraged accidentally became deified, but that is not me. If I were to be seen, if I were to take a form of the body of a human being, a perceptive person might notice the ball of light above my head, but the average person probably would not.

Have you taken the form of a human?

From time to time, yes. Just as the reverend in my example has to talk to the teenagers, from time to time the individual I was attempting to inspire could not comfortably hear inspiration as a voice or be inspired to do something, but would need to be spoken to gently by a person. If it was necessary, I would do so.

For example, I once even took the form of a puma, a mountain lion, because the person I needed to communicate with was involved in shamanic work and in an emulation of the finer qualities of the larger cats—not trying to change shapes or anything like that, but studying the finer qualities of cats. By taking that form, I was able to demonstrate qualities not seen by human beings. No matter how much you study the big cats or any of the animals, there are some things in their behavior that you will never see. Like the objective observer anywhere, sometimes you see things, but even what you *see*, you don't see, because you don't understand it within its larger context. In the body of that bigger cat, I would show that person, in a way they could understand, things that would be understood only by all cats.

For example?

For example, I would show the man the way a cat walks, first in a way to be seen, because sometimes it's important to be seen; and at other times gradually blend into that walk, the walk where one is unseen, not just crouching close to the ground. There are means by which cats—even the big cats—can walk where they will simply be unseen unless a person is highly perceptive. This was something this person needed to learn, because it was going to be his job someday to understand and know, before other people said it, what they were feeling and trying to say. You know, most people have a lot of trouble, no matter what their language is, in saying what they really feel. It was going to be this person's job on the shamanic level, but really more what I would call a medicine chief level, to be the diplomat, to understand what other people were trying to say without their having to say it—which, as any diplomat knows, is a highly valuable piece of wisdom. So I was able to pass that on to this person in that fashion, since they were devotees of cat medicine, or what is sometimes called the cat clan.

It is because the animals are so evolved on this planet that I and other beings as well, are perhaps from time to time able to take that form or even occupy the form of a living and open animal to demonstrate such things as may be necessary. It is because of the evolvement on the feeling and creative level of so many creatures on this planet, from the vast creatures—whales and so on—to the tiniest ant and even microscopic creatures. Many of them are very, very evolved. The reason they can live in such a place where life is so uncertain is *because* they are evolved.

For the human being, living in uncertainty is very often terrible and difficult because you are separated from your total being. You don't remember who you are. You don't have that knowledge of your previous lives or your potential future lives, so the feeling of continuity is not there—except with your parents and your family, who come and go. That strong, absolute continuity is not there. But the animals who very often remember their past lives, who they might become and their total being, have that absolute continuity. They can come here because if something happens to them, they know for certain that they will go on, where you do not usually have that feeling. Another reason the animals come here is to support you. They're all around and about you so that you can be within a vessel of continuity even if it is not your own.

That's beautiful. What else do you want to talk about?

Since you are involved in this project to explain the dynamics of all life to the extent that you can within the time allotted for this project—books, publishing and so on, what you will receive will be beings who have a larger scope or some facet of the scope that will continue to stimulate a larger view. That is why we go on as we do.

Oh, I love it! How much of this will we take with us at the end of our natural cycle? Will this be stored or something so it goes through the veil?

It'll be stored, but you have to remember that some of you have this knowledge already, but without the continuity you temporarily forget it. When you leave here and begin to reassimilate your complete personality, it will come back to you. You've been exposed to facets; on the other hand, since you do not have all knowledge of all things, as some of you read this, it will be new, a fascinating new concept. But others of you will read different elements, different concepts within the Explorer Race series and have a personal feeling of, "Yes, that's right! It feels right, I *know* it's right!" There will be a familiarity that runs deep beyond thought and into feeling. At some level of your continuum, your total personality, you know that this is so. It will be different for different individuals, which is to be expected.

I'm very excited about it. I'm re-reading some of the previous Explorer Race *books, and they are just awesome.*

Good. Well, we opened the envelope a little bit more here.

Absolutely. How do you want to structure this? However it comes out, right?

However it comes out. And you will use it in whatever way you see fit. The interesting thing is that you see it, you hear it, you interact with it; it is really personally involved for each of you.

Thank you.

All right, we'll resume again.

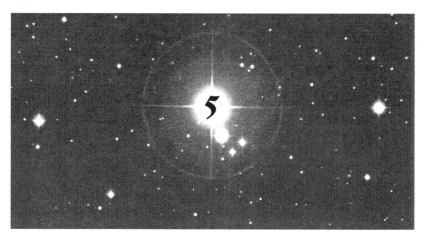

Soul Colors and Shapes

November 4, 1997

Isis here: So much of the differences associated with people are directly connected to the visual spectrum of colors. A certain range of personalities are discernible in people—not types so much, but what people would call types: "Oh, she's the happy type," "He's the serious type"—like that, regardless of race.

Color as Soul Food

These types are directly in alignment with colors. There are many more colors available than the ones in your visible light spectrum, but the colors you do see are intended not only to enrich and nurture the immortal personalities present here on Earth, but to be a backup source of food for these personalities. You know that your body must eat and drink; that is obvious. But what about your soul, also called the immortal personality. How does it sup? How is it fed while in residence within your body? It is not, as it seems to be, from the rays of the Sun or even the reflected energy of the Moon. These are beauties, but these beauties really feed the physical self, charge the mental self and to some extent support the feeling self. But what about the spirit self?

The color wheel I will use as an illustration, but let's speak of primary colors [of light] for a moment—red, blue, green. The personalities, the essences—the types, if you would—are fed by this, not a single color to a general type of person, but usually a specific color that feeds specific identifiable traits.

Happiness, buoyancy—the kind of person you can't keep down, as it were—is fed by gold, but without red it could not exist. Red is the energy that keeps these people up, whereas gold is the fuel. Red is essential.

What about people who are serious, studious, you might say? These people (their nonphysical aspects) are supported or fed almost entirely by blue, with a small amount of white. There are other character traits that are apparent; I have named but two. Can you think of other traits by which anyone might classify persons by type? Take your time.

Well, people who seem very anxious . . .

Now, that's a good one, anxious, nervous people. I am ruling out people who are anxious or nervous as a result of their lives. I am talking about people who seem to be born anxious or nervous. This trait would be apparent to mothers of a nervous or, as they used to say, colicky baby. These people are fed almost exclusively by red. It is an overwhelming color in many aspects, and because it is so overwhelming and because the planet upon which you are in residence has only so much capacity to accept overwhelming people, the planet requires the soul to integrate some green as well. This allows the nervous person to live longer or spread that nervousness out over a longer time. People like this, of course, will be fed and made to feel better when they are exposed to green. Nervous people really ought to walk in the green forest every day if they can; take a walk every day if you can in amongst the evergreens, especially pine trees. For these nervous people trees are excellent at extracting excess nervous energy while also providing extra green for them. That's what I want to talk about briefly.

I want to give you things that will help. I'm not talking about color therapy, which is meant for your energy body, but is primarily for the physical body. I'm talking about colors that feed your soul.

What about someone who is pessimistic and gloomy by nature?

People who are born gloomy, who have gloomy souls, are of green. One might expect that these people would have other colors, but green is a healing color. If a soul comes in with that bias toward gloom as a type of person, Earth is the place to come. Earth, being full of chlorophyll-based plants, allows you to transform. Gloomy souls and nervous souls come to places like Earth to transform because transformation can happen here so quickly.

So if a person is gloomy, it is good for them to be around plants. It is particularly good for them to have houseplants that are very hardy, that can take it—plants that are the toughest of houseplants even if they are weeds. Tending such plants even in a haphazard way attracts the green and reminds the soul that it is here to transform. The transformation color for such a soul would be red in small quantities; it might be good for such an individual, in the case of a woman, to wear a red belt or a scarf when going out, but not when indoors or all the time. If it is a man, perhaps a pink shirt. Different hues are acceptable; it does not have to be the color of a fire engine.

What about someone who's got a closed heart, who seems afraid to feel or doesn't trust feelings?

There are children who, inexplicably, are born apparently cold. I'm not talking about children who are that way because of some trauma. Parents of these children know what I'm talking about, children on whom love and nurturing has been heaped, but seem to be coldly distant and are perhaps unable to identify with the feelings of others.

These people are white; this color is intended. White, as we know, is a foundation or base. It is influenced by all other colors, so if these people feel the need to be fed, it would be best to be either in moonlight or in a place with white. Not necessarily wear it, but be in a white room or have a white rug perhaps—to be practical, perhaps white walls. These would actually be reassuring. If they wish to feel warmer or have a greater connection with other people, then something of gold (even the metal is fine)—a gold ring, a gold-colored tie or sash, something like that.

You're saying that the colors we surround ourselves with in our rooms and our clothing really feed the soul.

Yes, and in some cases can make the soul feel uncomfortable. But we have to recognize that the soul is in residence within the physical body, so the physical body and the feeling body as well might need certain colors that will cause the soul to sort of grit its etheric teeth.

Let's say you are going to work and have to deal with all the conditions there. It is probably best to pick colors that feel the best, meaning what's best for your feeling body and the physical body. But if you are going to meditate or pray, it might be best to pick colors that are good for your soul type.

In this way it is reassuring for your soul to have the primary soul-type color, with an accent color by which you wish to influence your soul. Perhaps it is a lesson for your soul. The potential meditator can discover this by having some idea of your soul color, then, rather than consulting a chart, use your feelings to go through your wardrobe and pick out something that also feels good—not necessarily wearing it. If you don't have an extensive wardrobe, you can get some pieces of fabric of different primary colors and drape one of them over you while you are meditating, removing it afterward.

This is not very complicated, but the reason I wanted to discuss it is that food for the soul is very often confused with food for the feeling self. Ultimately it is intended here that you make your decisions based upon understood feelings—what feels good and feels of love for you and as such cannot harm another. That is how you will make your decisions; yes, that's understood.

Nevertheless, souls need to be fed. It is not uncommon that if a soul is starving for its color, it will either stimulate conditions that will cause or allow the soul to be out of the physical self more, such as stimulating a need for more sleep. Granted, this can be caused sometimes by physical circumstances or spiritual needs or even feeling needs, but if it goes on indefinitely and is accompanied by a feeling of depression, this might be the soul needing food of its own color. Giving that food is useful.

Now, light itself can be helpful, different colors of light, but one cannot always do that. That is why being near useful colors can be helpful. Even a piece of paper that is colored a certain way can be helpful—to look at, for instance, or lay on your body is possibly useful. Looking at it can be helpful.

Autistic Children, Daydreamers and Color

What about parents who have autistic children? When the soul chooses that kind of expression, where they can't ask for something, could the parent give them a color that would . . .

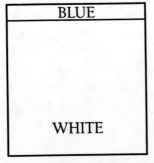

Autistic Children

Give me a moment. The average autistic child would have . . . illustration, yes? For the sake of simplicity [draws], what looks like a graph but is actually a box . . . I have included an arrow to show the top. White is the soul color, with a bit of blue—about as much associated with this chart.

. . . proportionately, yes.

Thank you. The child's soul could be fed by that. But with autistic children, who are primarily feeling beings and to some extent visual beings, if you can, present them with a selection of colors (of course, shapes are important too). If they are very young, dress them in white, with a little blue, and see how they respond. Or you might have their rooms painted—one wall only, because we don't want to overwhelm the rest of the child (the feeling body, the physical body and so on)—in white with a little blue on it, maybe a stripe through part of the wall. But as you can see by the drawing, the primary color is white. If the child doesn't like it, he or she will let you know; or she might add something to it if she has crayons.

What about a child who doesn't seem connected to his body? Who seems to be absent-minded and daydreaming?

Ah, the daydreamer. This is usually temporary, but it is a bias that runs through life. Often these people simply have good imaginations that need to be stimulated. But you have suggested it as a type, and it surely is one—sometimes a combined type, but a type. The color for the soul of such a person would be . . . another drawing, hm? [Draws.] Excuse the lack of straight lines. Green, with white.

This suggests, of course, that you could make a flag or a banner, or simply a square piece of canvas or what-have-you that looks like that. Then see how the child or the patient responds.

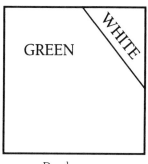

Daydreamer

There seem to be people who live mostly in their minds.

White. If I didn't respond to it, it means I've covered it. I mentioned studious; I'm allowing that to be mental.

So studious, serious, mental are all one.

Honoring Different Facets of Yourself

Yes. I'm mentioning this because in many attempts to understand personality is the desire to find some simple means to clarify, quantify and type individuals. The trouble with that is that some components of the individual are often contrary to their other components; a person might feel good wearing the color green one day, but his soul color is actually white. One cannot utilize only one method; one must honor different facets of oneself. One might conceivably even recognize that the feeling body has its preferences, which it will let you know if you respond to your wardrobe strictly on the basis of color. For those who wish to experiment, if you have a large enough wardrobe, discover a color that feels good to you, then try different patterns or hues of that color. If you don't have a big enough wardrobe, go to the fabric store and get some pieces of fabric (they don't have to be big) and look at or touch them to see which one feels best to you. You can discover a great deal about yourself, not as a permanent thing, but as a daily thing: how your feelings are nurtured by what you wear, what you see and even what you smell in some cases. This is not a psychological test, but something that is different from day to day. Knowing what your soul craves is helpful, because sometimes what is missing is based on some aspect of your personality that you're so used to, you don't really think about it.

I don't think anyone has thought about colors for the soul. I don't think this has ever been discussed before.

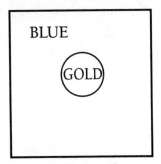

Multitalented

What about the person who seems to have the capacity to do many things at once reasonably well and finish them, the multitalented person? This person has an interesting soul graphic [draws]: gold on a field of blue. I'm sort of drawing pennants, as it were, because they are easily reproduced, are they not?

We'll call them multitalented.

Yes, there are people like that. Since we are fractionalizing a bit, what about people who have the ability to become very good at one thing, such as a profession or an expressed character trait? There are people like that.

Perhaps, for instance, a carpenter, a master carpenter. I don't have to be too precise [draws]; the artist can fix this (I erase with squiggly lines). A moment.

Carpenter

Please excuse the exception to the primary color—chartreuse on a field of green.

Using Colors to Pray or Meditate

Can we say that people might make their own and meditate with them?

Yes, even with squares of paper. I have made the effort in this case to draw such squares of paper as someone might easily reproduce. Even a child could reproduce it just for sheer pleasure. It doesn't have to be complex.

Do you want to just briefly draw the ones we mentioned before?

I can go back; for those who need single colors, no illustration is necessary. For one, I said red with a little bit of green?

Yes, the pessimistic or gloomy type.

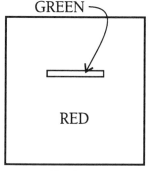

Pessimist

All right [draws]. I cannot write inside, so you'll have to understand that what's inside is green. If people want something new to play with, to see what their soul responds to, they might do this. In the case of the meditator who lies down, feel free to lie on such a thing or move it around different parts of your body. For those meditators or people who pray with their eyes open, have it near you and look at it while you pray or meditate. See how you feel; if you don't feel good or it's not comfortable, then close your eyes and set it aside or perhaps change the appearance.

It is not a fixed thing. For instance, since I just did red with a little green, I'll do a variation of that [draws], giving you the idea of how it could be. Red—we're going to use about the same amount of it.

It could be a different shape.

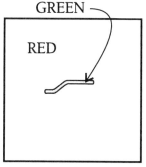

Variation of pessimist

Yes, it could be like this. So feel free to choose according to how it feels. And as another alternate shape [draws a spiral in lower corner], it might be something like this. You have the flexibility to change it yourself and play around with it. I think you will enjoy that.

Different ET Soul Shapes

I'm trying to look at the principles here. Does each soul have a particular shape that it's most comfortable with?

That is a very good question. I will give you generalities here. Here's a soul shape from Orion, since that has an amusing connection to our current interaction [draws]. Not an uncommon soul shape.

From someone who was first physical on Orion?

From someone who is focused through Orion, born and raised on Orion or who has a powerful connection with Orion, not as a result of something done to you or with you. It would be someone

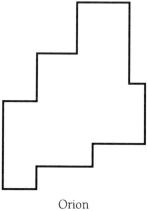

Orion

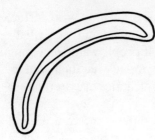

Pleiadian

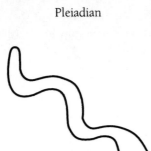

Andromedan

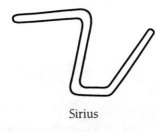

Sirius

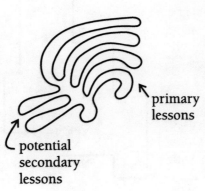

primary
lessons

potential
secondary
lessons

Arcturus

associated with Orion in some way, perhaps a lesson for the life born and focused through Orion.

Can you do some others? Pleiadian?

I will do Pleiades [draws], a typical Pleiadian soul shape.

Onward to Andromeda [draws], understanding that this is not fixed, but typical.

Is the energy of the soul that shape, or does the soul like to look at shapes like that? How can we understand that?

If we were to see the soul outside of the body, in transit, perhaps, from point A to point B, or if we were to see the

Andromedan variation

soul exit the body at the end of the natural life cycle, you would see something like this [draws]. A variation, perhaps.

What else . . . Sirius, hm? [Draws.] An interesting thing about the Sirius soul is that it is an almost perfect combination of masculine and feminine attributes. Here we have something that is squared off, apparently linear, with something that is more rounded, apparently feminine.

Arcturus?

[Draws.] Arcturians often have compound souls. This does not mean they have more than one, but that their souls are capable of experiencing more than one lesson in a given life—a primary lesson all souls tend to manifest. This tells you that Arcturus tends to express many different lessons, even primary ones. So we have on this side of the soul shape [writes label on the right] primary lessons.

And the two little ones on the other side?

The little ones are potential [writes label on left]. . . . This tells you that if you were to meet someone focused through Arcturus, they are usually complex and talented people; not infrequently they are people who can take on many, many different projects without becoming particularly confused, excited or upset. I might add, they are some of the most successful business CEOs or even political people on Earth.

This is a whole new thing. Can we assume that the more rounded is the more feminine?

Yes, you can assume that the more rounded is more feminine, not exclusively what it means on Earth, but also more receptive.

So they're all very receptive except the Orion. That's a very masculine . . .

But you have to understand that the Orion shape is about constructing, building, making, establishing. The Orion people you will find in the building trades, and they will create some kind of global business on the fundamental level, not the managerial level. At the managerial level you need to have someone who can relate to wide varieties of people in an unflappable manner. Orions are not famous for such functions.

How about Virgo?

The Virgo star system [draws]. Virgos are highly attracted to precise complexities. You will tend to find Virgo souls in professions related to complexities—code-breakers, in that sense. You will find them in the arts when a great deal of detail or precision is involved. You will also tend to find them in places where many different

Virgo

types of people come together to perform different or similar functions. Virgo souls have the capacity for enjoining complexity.

It would almost relate to the astrological sign, then.

Almost, but not quite, because in the astrological there is a need for observation, but not always the talent. People from Virgo . . .

. . . learn the Virgo lesson.

Yes, thank you, it is a lesson. They arrive here with such talents and abilities. You will also find these people in the diplomatic corps if they are successful. You will find such beings who will go into related positions or as negotiators, but only if the negotiation is complex. They will get bored if it is static or constantly repeating.

Tools by Which You Can Recognize Yourself

How soon will we get to the point here where we have clairvoyants who can help humans understand what they're focused through?

You are there now; it is only a question that needs to be asked of most individuals. It can be done now in any reading as far as I know, from multitudinous practitioners; the question just needs to be asked. For instance, "What is my soul shape?" or "Would this color benefit me?" You might suggest a color, then ask, "Would it be good for me to draw it? To paint it? To put it on a pendant, to wear it, to put it in fabric, to have it on my tie? To have a symbol for my hat?"

As humans are attempting to integrate parts of themselves from all over the planet and more facets of their souls come in, is there something like a core essence?

If we are talking about facets coming in, your foundational shape stays there and the facets connect, not unlike puzzle pieces; they might connect like this, askew as it were, two pieces. Or they might connect in a more symbiotic way like this [interlocking fingers]. They would touch, however, and form the complexity of your soul shape.

Now, in the case of the occasional walk-in (it happens now and then), the original piece would go on about its business, go wherever it needed to go, and would be replaced by the piece that comes in. But this is the exception.

Well, this is a whole new level that will allow people to learn about themselves.

It is useful because it gives you tools by which you can recognize yourself. Even when you are given the primary shapes as provided for various points in the sky, there are also the variations associated with the individual. I will give an example here [draws]. Recognizing that not all Orions have exactly the same shape, here is a variation on the shape. You can see there is a distinct similarity.

Now let me add a nuance, because I am drawing basic types. But here is a nuance that might enter it [draws another shape inside]. Let's take it to another degree. Let's say this individual wishes to acquire . . . whatever—say it is something material. You might make a shape like this and add it within the space here [draws a circle inside]—this is the universal symbol for benevolence, yes? While it is not in concordance with the Orion shape, it sets up a potential symbiotic relationship.

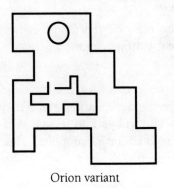

Orion variant

If the shape was this, for instance . . . let's create something that is more Pleiadian in nature [draws Pleiadianshape on the right] and say we added that. That might be a little uncomfortable, but because we have a complete shape that is the universal symbol for benevolence, at least in this universe [draws another tiny circle], it's compatible. If we were to take something that is strictly curving, not unlike the Pleiadian, it might not be compatible. So we use a curve, yes, but it is compatible and it might tend to attract.

Pleiadian shape

 Universal symbol for benevolence

Individuals have these shapes, and there are certainly potentials for psychics and other readers to get these for people. In some cases they will relate nicely to the drawings we're providing; in other cases they will seem to fly in the face. But it will give individuals something more by which they can utilize an image to not only support their soul, but also potentially acquire or even shed something.

For example, say you wish to shed something, something that is disturbing you; I will use the Orion symbol here. Then this would be the example, how you would write that [draws]. See, it's like a fragment being released.

This is really good to know. You're giving principles here.

Yes. If we wanted to attract a fragment, then we would put the fragment inside. Putting it outside is to release the fragment. You do not have to draw what it is. As the person, you know what it represents, and you can make the symbol and put it on your shirt or your cap or your undershirt so no one can see it. That's fine.

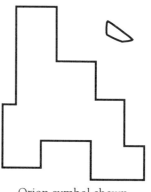

This could be presented as a principle along with all the other ones you give: If you want to attract something, you put it inside; if you want to release it, you put it outside.

Yes.

Orion symbol shown releasing a fragment

You're starting a whole new science.

It's fun, isn't it?

Yes! You're teaching us helpful things in a fun way.

Tools for Working with Children

We want to give the people tools they can use that are readily accessible to them, as well as more esoteric things to stimulate their imaginations. Here is something that a child can utilize. Get the child's shape—perhaps your neighborhood person who is sensitive gets the general soul shape—and the child draws that shape. The child draws the form that is attractive with crayon (or however the child draws), and then perhaps on a tee-shirt or some other item of apparel . . .

. . . that's the color of their soul.

That's right, the colors are associated with the child's soul, which is associated with its personality type. In this way the child has something it can use and play with, and create variations. [Draws.] Again, we'll do the Orion symbol, since we are utilizing that as an example. Perhaps we have an Orion child who would like to attract Pleiadian influences, which is this [draws tiny Pleiadian shape inside]—okay, something like that. How can we attract that?

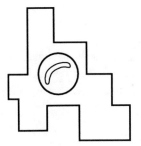

Pleiadian shape inside the circle inside the Orion shape, designed to attract.

This is what we do: We put the circle there first, the universal symbol for benevolence, and then we can put the Pleiadian shape inside the circle and it does not disturb. As long as it is inside the circle, it does not disturb the soul shape because it is surrounded by the universal symbol for benevolence. I mention this only because the child might be fond of the Pleiades or any of the other places.

So then as we grow up, you're saying, "All right, I am Sirian, but I want to attract the ability to build." You can intermix the qualities by using this idea.

That's right. You can be, perhaps, a person who has the Pleiadian energy, and if you wish to attract something, you draw the circle and put it inside your shape. Perhaps, for instance, you are a Pleiadian energy, but it is your time to serve your country in the military, in which case a little Orion energy of constructing, creating, making things—you suddenly have to put a bridge over this river, so a little Orion energy inside the circle would be very helpful. You put that in for a while and wear the symbol while you are there, or you carry it around on a piece of paper and look at it from time to time. Then perhaps you will attract some of that to you. It is not a guarantee, but it is worth trying; and it is much more effective if you make the symbols yourself. I'm mentioning children because it is something most children like to do. But it is helpful, though to a lesser degree, if someone makes it for you if for some reason you are unable.

More on the Question of Soul Shapes

Can we go back and just add more, as you did with Orion and Virgo, about the qualities for . . . you gave us Arcturian, but for Sirius, Andromeda and Pleiades you did not. Can you say a sentence or two about the Sirius personality, what it means?

The Sirian soul would have a great deal to do with personal flexibility and creativity within that context. It may not always have to do with societal flexibility, but it will always have to do with personal flexibility. For instance, an individual with a soul from Sirius might be able to more easily become a mother and serve the needs of her family while not abandoning her own. Certain other soul types might find it more difficult, more challenging, perhaps having more lessons, whereas a Sirian soul type would flow into it so easily that one would think she had been a mother many times already with families, yet it is apparent that it could not be.

So it isn't just nurturing; it's the capacity for personal flexibility. The person would naturally flow into it. It's like taking their personal routine and adapting to the routine of others without any apparent difficulty. To adapt to the routines of others is a requirement in society, but to do so easily and comfortably is not always seen—in fact, it is rare. Yes, and desirable, too. What were the others?

Andromeda?

With Andromeda you will always find the capacity for seeing over the horizon, being able to see or feel or, as a musician, sense, for example, what is coming next. This does not mean clairvoyance; for instance, someone with this soul shape might be able to play music spontaneously more easily than someone with, say, a different soul shape who requires sheet music, you see? Someone who is a draftsperson would be able to look at the front of an object and its three-quarter view, then sit right down and immediately reproduce it precisely in detail, enjoying it; it would not be work or a terrible task as it might be for someone else.

What about Pleiadian souls?

Pleiadian souls will always have the capacity to blend into large groups harmoniously if the group is already harmonious. Let's say you have a large group of children. Pleiadians make wonderful nursery school teachers, or first-, second- and third-grade teachers; they are natural at it. You see other soul types doing this, but if a Pleiadian person went to help out the teacher, as an aide, she would be able to do it so easily that the teacher would be envious. Or she would be able to substitute for a choir director, and because there is already a fixed harmony, she would just flow right in and be able to work with no difficulty.

They have some difficulty in fixed structures, but as long as the structures are flexible and harmonious or have the capacity for harmony, they are naturals. To give an athletic example, let's say there is a baseball team and it is working smoothly. But you are new to town, perhaps a youngster, and you want to join Little League and you are Pleiadian. You will be able to join the team and be good at what is done as long as you are given (by the coach or manager) the flexibility to do things your way. If you have to follow this step and that step, one, two, three, four, five, in that order, it will be difficult. But if you are allowed to try right-handed and try left-handed, if you are allowed to try this or that kind of slide (baseball terminology), then you will do well.

Can we back up a little? This has really not been explained. We don't actually come from those planets. We're way beyond planets when we plan our lives. Can you talk about how we focus our energy through those planets for the lessons we want to learn?

It is more that you have the lessons you want to learn. You have these lessons and you are automatically focused. You as a soul do not reach out to the Pleiades per se; the Pleiades reaches out to you. Since you as a soul are connected by lessons, talents, abilities—desires, even—the Pleiadian energy will feel compatible with you and will naturally reach to you. Normally someone born on the Pleiades would have the Pleiadian energy, and it would be natural, yes? But someone on Earth, which is an advanced school, who might be focused through the Pleiades, the Pleiades will have to reach to you.

For example, for the past three and a half years, when things have been getting a little more intense on Earth, not as many people were being born who are focused through the Pleiades—Pleiadian souls—because it is hard for the Pleiades (as a place, as a being, if I might) to reach into this intensity to support the Pleiadian soul. It is much easier for the Andromedan energy to reach in with its capacity for complexity and support the Andromeda-focused soul. So for a time there won't be as many Pleiadian souls manifested here; but that time will change. So there are different variables; that is how it works.

Your Point of Origin

To give something esoteric for a moment [chuckles] (as if this isn't), what about a being who's not a human being? What about a spirit that comes to visit Earth? What about me? Here I am speaking through Robert, and as that spirit, I am where I am; I live where I live now. But the part of me that speaks through him which has, as you might say, come to Earth, is supported by my point of origin. In that sense the levels above come and support me. What about a spirit being, meaning a nonphysical being, who comes to visit Earth in its travels? If there is some difficulty as the spirit being approaches Earth, then without having to reach for its own place of origin, its own place of origin will reach to that being to support it.

This, you understand, does suggest something: that your place of origin—even if it is your focus only in that life—will, because it has a personality and because you are a portion of it during that life cycle, have a proprietary interest in you, not as property, but as a child. It will be like a mother, and even if you are in another universe, it will take no effort in reaching for you and giving you some of your own energy for your soul, to support it. That is how, for example, an individual would come (in days gone by this was more common) from the Pleiades to an underground base on Earth to study, then become so enamored and involved with his or her work that perhaps she might come to the end of her natural cycle here. While the physical body may be taken back to the Pleiades for ceremonies, the soul is harvested. Pleiades reaches to that soul to support it, and the soul travels along that strand, which has reached to Earth, back up to the Pleiades. It gets there long before the body does, and then goes on about its trips through the veils.

The capacity for star systems to keep track of their own is limitless. This also suggests a question: What about the point of origin of a given soul, which may be far, far beyond this universe? Do *those* places give you energy? Yes, but they do not reach out the way a star system in a universe might. They will imprint you . . . let's create a depth picture [draws]. Here we have our example—an Orion soul shape again, a variation.

Now, this is the Orion soul shape, but what about the point of origin? The point of origin will be shaped as it appeared, was felt or could otherwise be sensed. For the sake of our example, let's say your point of origin looked like this [upper left]. This is just an example, all right? See these as two pieces; picture this one on top of the other [draws arrow]. A different view: Here's our side view of our Orion soul in the two dimension; this other will be back here [draws two vertical lines]. See?

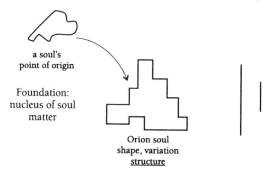

a soul's
point of origin

Foundation:
nucleus of soul
matter

Orion soul
shape, variation
structure

This one reaches for you, this one (pointing to the Orion soul shape.) But this one [your origin] is like inspiration. It is like tracks you leave behind you on the beach. It is something that is omnipresent that you do not have to reach for, that does not reach for you. It would be like a DNA code; it could be found if you know what to look for. And it would be behind you, in the sense that your parents existed before you. It is behind you, but on an almost linear level.

This would be the nucleus of that, meaning the point of origin would be the nucleus of the matter of the soul. It would support it, it would be the foundation, and the soul is the structure. You can write in such words as are useful.

Using Sound to Connect with Your Foundation

People who need this, what can they do? Do they say, "I'm focused in this life through that star system, but I'm from someplace else"?

Yes.

And if they want energy or love or something, they sort of focus within—because it's within, right?

It will be within; it would be identifiable, though not at your current level of technology. It would be identifiable through the resonance (sound that you cannot hear, but it is a resonance) that is diagrammed by the chromosomes in your DNA.

You know that there are 46 chromosomes in the average person's DNA. The space between the chromosomes would be like the wind blowing between the chimes on a wind chime, so it is difficult to describe what you can *do* about that to access it. The best way to access it would be to make sounds that are of a musical quality. See if you can find the sound that is most—not stimulating, but the most . . .

. . . comfortable?

No, comfortable would relate to your physical, your feeling body. It is more that it stimulates your imagination or your ability to think or to visualize pictures. When you find the sound that does that, you are probably connecting to the rhythm of your point of origin. Because you cannot make sounds that run the full range, if you cannot make that sound, then imagine what the sounds are and attempt to make them. Imagine you are making sounds above or below what you can do and try to hear them in your imagination, how they would sound. That might work; it's not for sure, but it might work. It will certainly work better than having the sound made external to your body, meaning by a machine, for instance.

Or by somebody else.

Yes.

Let's say you're meditating and you want to connect to that point of origin. You make or imagine sounds. Are you going to feel it in your heart or any particular place?

The stimulation of your imagination is what will happen, but you will have to be doing this for a while, you understand. In the beginning, as you begin making the sounds . . . and don't go up and down the scale like this [Isis illustrates vocally by sliding up the range of a few notes, then back down quickly]. Don't do that, but make the highest tone you can make, then work down slowly, or else sound the lowest tone and work up slowly, hm?

Initially there will be some resistance, meaning that your mind will want to wander, but try and stay focused. Once you get focused, you'll get in the rhythm of doing it, and it will feel pretty good. You will start to get imaginations, sometimes based on inspirations (imagining something you wouldn't have imagined otherwise, and it will be a benevolent imagination, not an uncomfortable thought), or thoughts that seem to come from nowhere, that are stimulating and benevolent and interesting. Once you are into the experience for a while, you understand, then this will be what you receive. Rather than try and create it into something, let it be what it is.

And it is not fixed. From one day to the next, the imagination might be different. Your point of origin may give you something one day to help you with something; it might simply give you a story, a facet or a piece of your existence or even stimulate your recollection of a talent you had forgotten. For instance, someone might be a good writer and feel or sense music, and be reminded that they may be musically inclined as well.

Choosing Your Focus

All right, so the point of origin would always stay. In different lifetimes our soul chooses to focus on different lessons, so we focus through different star systems through different lenses?

Yes and, of course, with different representational soul shapes. But your point of origin remains the same.

So in one life we might have this Arcturian . . . would you call this a lesson, a talent?

It's a soul shape, so I would call it a potential, meaning your capacities. A soul shape tends to refer to your capacities rather than a lesson. The example given for the multifaceted soul shape, a being that could handle many lessons, is just for that. The soul shape does not necessarily refer to lessons, but to the essential capacities of that star system.

That you choose to work on.

That you are focused through in this life on Earth—separating the being born on Orion from the being on Earth, but the soul shape would be the same.

To make it really clear, then, the Virgo soul who is focused through the Virgo star system would have the ability to be clear and precise and all that, whereas someone who is astrologically Virgo would seek to accomplish or learn that.

Yes, exactly. It differs from astrology, but complements it.

Once we know what our talents and abilities are . . .

It is surprising; one often does not know one's talents and abilities but must be told by others, because what you assume to be so for all is not.

Oh, this is wonderful! On what level are these decisions made? Our souls are so fragmented, then we have oversouls. On what level of our being do we decide to focus through a particular energetic system when we incarnate?

Almost always through the feeling self. It is an interesting thing. You have a feeling self beyond Earth, but here on Earth the feeling self is greatly heightened so that you can be more aware of it. It is the feeling self centered in the heart, the energy of the heart, that is that love warmth, which is heightened here so it can be more apparent, yes? It is that part of you that makes the decision where to go, what to do and how. So there is a progression, not necessarily associated with a straight line.

Imagine an orange; peel away the rind and there are segments. We bring all this. Each segment, perhaps, might be part of something that forms the whole of what you wish to learn, and a given life is a segment. We get all the parts with all these different lives and put it together, and suddenly we have the circle, or this universal symbol for benevolence. We have a complete thing.

The complete thing does not have to be linear. As a soul, a total heart being, your essence of yourself, you choose to understand compassion, hm? And then you might pick different places to be born, different circumstances; you might wish to have a nurturing life, or you might wish to have a life in which you need nurturing. You might wish to have a life that is challenging, or a life that provides for those who are challenged. Do you understand?

It's like a theme.

It is a theme, exactly. And you will follow that theme to put all the segments together until it forms a complete understanding of every aspect of that theme you have chosen to understand. I picked something like compassion because many people are involved in it at one stage or another right now.

What are some of the themes? Courage, adventure, creativity or . . .

Yes, but instead of creativity, in the case of an applied theme, I would call it creation, because creativity is a skill, an ability. But creation is something that might take a great many lives. You might also have lives of destruction so you can understand how things come apart—not meaning terrible, miserable lives. You might be the person who takes a house apart so that a new building can be put there. Or you might be someone who experiences being an artist in one life, or even a surgeon, in order to create new ways to assist an individual's process of becoming healthier.

So yes, all these types of things are themes, and themes on Earth are usually more active or proactive. You are involved in the activity—not only activity around you, as compared to themes elsewhere. For instance, if you are on Andromeda again, a place where a great deal of study and acquisition of knowledge and wisdom from other places takes place, you might wish to have a theme of lives there about integration, meaning how things are integrated, how that integration applies to the service you provide for others, understand? That might be a lesson here, but not as common as it would be there. It might be a theme where you might have more lives on other solar systems, other planet systems, other galaxies, and not so much on Earth, even though it is certainly an aspect here.

Explorer Race Theme

Look at the Explorer Race. For those in school here, how many themes are there? Is there an average number of lives devoted to each theme? Are there any principles that could explain how it works?

Almost any word in a dictionary (ruling out technical dictionaries) that can be described as being a theme, is potentially used as a theme by the Explorer Race. Perhaps we are talking of a thesaurus. But anything that would be a theme—anything—would be a potential theme for the Explorer Race. The things that are not in the thesaurus or dictionary would be hard-pressed, perhaps, to be put into your verbal language.

But they are basically qualities of consciousness?

But remember, the primary ultimate intention of the Explorer Race is to become a Creator. This means that thematics must be very much all-encompassing.

I see what you mean. Not qualities—it's everything.

It's everything.

You have to know how everything works.

You have to know on the personal level. And if you as a soul do not have the time to do it all, then somebody else in the Explorer Race must do it. When you re-form as one being, all these things must be understood on a personal level, not on a study level. Someone in your group must have experienced it so that you can all understand it personally.

So when we all come together, we'll know everything that each of us knows?

You will know, yes, on a personal level. You will, of course, have major themes that all creators must have, which you might call inspiration or imagination and, extrapolating from that, intelligence. But also you must have great and powerful compassion; you must know and completely understand consequences. So you see why this is such a wonderful school for you.

All the minor themes, then, are sort of divided up, and different beings do different ones?

Yes, and you have to have all the nuances of these so-called minor things experienced. That's why you need so many. I'm not talking about obvious nuances, but about nuances you can't even see but that are very perceptibly different though not obvious.

Like one is a degree off phase and another's just a little bit . . .

Or one might be one ten-millionth of a degree different.

Oh, I see. Just enough different so that you totally encompass the entire theme.

Yes, there is no exception to the rule that a creator . . . a humorous example [draws] . . . must be this, not this.

Mm-hm. [Laughs.] Yes, I understand.

No gaps allowed for a creator within its own boundary of creation.

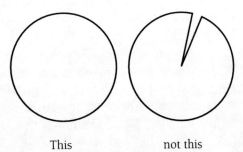

This   not this

This is interesting, because all the creators we talked to were born that way. How many times have souls like us gone through Creator School? This is the first time, right?

Not many times. It has been done, but not like this. When it *has* been done, where you go through Creator School, as you say, it is much different. It is usually done by beings who can experience all things at once, which is not necessarily a creator. There are even facets of your own being that can experience all things at once, within the context of your total personality. There are organs in your body that can do that. But to have all these people go through all these experiences—all these souls and so on—it has not been done like this before, which is part of the reason you're getting so much attention.

I tell you, when I come to Earth to look around (to be colloquial for a moment if I can), I see old friends here that I haven't seen in years. This place is a popular place to drop by and observe because it is so unusual.

Ah! Amongst the observers you see old friends—not humans, but other ones.

Amongst those who are coming by to say, "What's new?" we don't have to say, "We'll meet on Earth." I know they're coming, so I'll see them.

That's very good. How often do you come? I realize that part of you can come and part of you can stay someplace else.

Yes, but answering your question in the way it was intended, I will come during gaps and stops; there are times when I am not here per se. So it is here to measure. But I will simply say I'm not always here.

Is there an aspect of you that is one of these friends of the Creator?

I am not the Master of Healing.

Okay, but you didn't answer the question. [Laughs.]

Am I a friend of your Creator? I suppose so, after all this time.

Among the ones we've talked about, you're not one of those?

No, I am not. You see, you have to understand that these consultants or friends are all very precisely focused in what they do. One of the things you must know about me is that I do like variety. I like many things, I enjoy many things, and as such I need . . .

. . . freedom . . .

. . . space—is that what the children used to say? I need space. I need lots of space to go, places to go and things to experience. I am not perhaps the best individual to experience limits—though I have, in order to understand those who do.

Understanding Limits

Do you want to say more about that?

Well, once for a stretch of time . . . for a being such as myself in order to fully learn and be compassionate toward and understand an individual who would experience limits or be a function of limits would require me to invest a significant portion of myself—a millennia, for example. So I did this with limits for a time. Since I have other responsibilities and duties, I could not do all of it myself, so I condensed about one-third of myself into a square (with a couple of other angles in there) object or space, roughly the size of a golf ball. I kept 30 percent of myself there for a millennia. In that way I was able to understand the value of limits as well as the discomforts. Perhaps the most striking value is that within a limited experience, the chances of your discovering everything about that experience are greatly heightened.

But what was your experience? Where were you or what were you doing?

I was not attempting to do anything; I was attempting to understand beings who are experiencing limits, what it is like for them. So I had 30 percent of myself condensed into a small space; that was my experience of limits. It wasn't an attempt to do something in a limited way.

What did you experience besides limitation?

No, no, no, no, no. In order to understand limits, especially for a being like myself, you have to experience it. It's not what I did in there; I did other things as the part of me that was out and about, but the part that was in there experienced only the limit of that spatial reference, period.

It does not sound like fun.

No, but after that I understood it! If you are someone like me, you need to understand things in order to be able to relate to others who are experiencing it. How can I talk to an individual, even an individual soul, that is focused in limits if I do not have the knowledge of that experience, not only its discomforts but its advantages? I cannot communicate with them in a feeling or language or any nuance that would be common ground without having had the experience myself.

You have so much variety on Earth because you have variety of beings, variety of circumstances, and it is always possible in a given life on Earth to experience, at least briefly, what others have experienced and be able to relate to them better, hm? But you cannot always experience everything. For example, almost all of you have been to school and know what that is like: "School is this, school is that." But the advantage of going to school is that it gives you some common frame of reference, so you are not only learning about that experience (school, the common frame of reference), but you are also learning how it works—the mechanics of relating to each other.

The common ground, yes, but why the common ground? The common ground is so that you can communicate and have, for example, compassion and understand the consequences of not knowing that. Obviously if you have people sitting around a table to make peace because there is war, the more you can have compassion, not just from your heart and love, but from a personal experience of what the other person or side has experienced, the more likely you are to be able to make peace.

Isis' Duties and Responsibilities

What are your duties and responsibilities? What is it that you are responsible for out there?

Putting it simply, I am responsible for encouraging and nurturing.

Everywhere.

Yes.

You've given us a couple of examples on Earth. How would that work out in other areas where you do this?

For example, say there is a star field that is being created, many different galaxies. The star field itself in a portion of a universe somewhere has great joy in creating stars and planets and suns and all of these things, yes? But it does not know the best direction or shape in which to create itself; it does not know which way to flow. Should it be long and thin, should it be wide and stocky, hm? So I will give it my attention and allow it to use some large portion of me to experience a temporary scenario—you might say mentally, but in a star field's case, a temporary feeling that the star field can have in that shape.

"Here's how it works if you do it this way."

Yes. Say you want to spread out into a shape like this; then I give some of my energy and it temporarily feels that shape. "Does that feel good to you? Let's try this shape, then," for example.

Shapes have a great deal to do with feeling. Even individual feelings have general shapes, and (forgive the example) your cartoonists are quite good at reproducing shapes associated with feelings. That bonk on the head where you see stars; or the feeling of great love where we see the heart shape pounding. The cartoonist is quite good at this, and as the popular illustrator, they are actually able to teach the association of shapes to feelings.

Where you have a responsibility or a duty, do you feel the need of that star field?

Yes. I feel it, and . . .

It calls you, but it doesn't even know you exist.

It may not know that I exist, that's right, but I feel its need. And if I am feeling the need, that means that someone else has not responded. It's not that they have ignored it, but they were either doing other things, or it may be that I am simply the one who is intended to respond. So I respond. Theoretically, if I were doing other things, then someone else would feel it and respond. So needs are responded to. As far as I know, this is an absolute.

It's so precise. Do you have a creation someplace that you maintain?

No, I do not. If I had a specific creation such as your Creator has, then I would have to give them more of my attention and I would want to be available for a variety of needs, hm? [Chuckles.] That is my theme—variety.

That's why you like this creation.

Yes.

And the adventure of it. Do you have a home base?

No—you mean where do I hang my cape?

Yes.

I do not have that, and it suits me. I have discussed levels, and perhaps if I ever wanted to retire (which is not a concept associated with a being such as myself, but for the sake of illustration), I might conceivably go to the sixth level and rest. But since these circumstances do not apply to a being such as myself, I do not need to retire or to rest. [Chuckles.] It would be like that. Do I have a place to hang my cape? No. But that suits me; then I am . . .

. . . free.

Free, and able to serve in many ways.

Sounds like a pretty good job description to me.

I am very satisfied with it, and a surprising number of beings are doing variations of this to their own particular order of talent, ability or desire to serve.

What would you say your talents are?

As I said, my job is to encourage and nurture. I am reasonably good at this. My job is what I do well. And equally, perhaps there is an individual somewhere; I might go to that individual (I don't want to make it sound like I am working in huge systems only) and spend some time with a child or even a moth or a butterfly or with an atom or a proton, hm?

I have met people who seem to feel that they are connected with or are familiar with your energy.

That might very well be a facet of my energy. Most likely it is, because, as I say, I might spend some time with someone, and that someone might be thematic. They might go for many thousands of years with many someones within that theme. Or it might be to brush the hair and embrace a child in her moment of need. I may have a part of myself in most themes, yes? That is something you are all learning, and being able to do that is part of the reason you have children the way you do. You must be nurtured and you must give nurturance, and the good parent also encourages. Yes, you have to discipline sometimes, of course; but it is easier to encourage the child to learn something new and better rather than try to stop them from doing something. When they learn the new, better thing, they will just naturally stop. In my way I echo your friend Zoosh on this, hm?

How many people on the planet have touched your energy?

In the last week?

No, in this life. I realize that you might have known them and interacted with them in other lives, but of the people alive, how many of them have felt your energy in this life?

Perhaps 43 percent.

That many?

Yes. Some of them as groups, some perhaps as soul groupings, many of them as individuals. Lots of youngsters. I like children. Not to say I don't like adults, but I am particularly fond of children.

There's so much emergence now of the femininity, and they're calling it the God-dess energy. So is there a part of you that is refueling or investing your energy in this?

I would rather say supporting, because it comes under the level of nurturing and encouraging—encouraging, supporting, yes, certainly. It represents a whole segment of society that finds better qualities within themselves—again, it's teaching the child something that is better for him so that he does it. It encourages and nurtures, certainly, and to the extent that these groups encourage and nurture, I give my support.

And in a sense, then, your energy.

Yes.

When they call for the Isis energy, there is something of you they connect with, then?

Yes, certainly. We have to end soon, okay?

We can end right now.

Then we will continue soon.

November 6, 1997

I sis here. What direction shall we go in tonight?

I have a couple of questions related to the last session. We didn't talk about the colors orange and purple. What types of people have these colors? You said that color relates to a soul quality.

Purple: A Transitional Color

You understand, I tried to use primary colors. Purple represents the being who travels in many worlds and can be in more than one place at once. This is not a typical soul color, but is often found as a transitional color. This is a slight variant on the topic. You will find that souls might have specific colors, as indicated; but the individual with a lifelong color of purple is another thing. But first let's speak of the transitional.

When all souls come in, regardless of their color or shape (denoting point of origin), the presence of purple is with them even if they are not born. This essence allows the soul to be in more than one place at once—which is essential for the baby, especially inside the mother. The soul then is getting used to physical life, and will often need to be other places. It is perhaps understood that the soul steps in and out of the body to get used to it. The soul often needs to be inside its own body in mother's body, growing in mother—yes? But it may also need to be other places, receiving instruction and, most importantly, encouragement and nurturance. Even if you have lived a physical life on Earth before—within this time frame, perhaps—you still require nurturance and encouragement to be born here because it is school. Yes, there is recess, there is some fun and pleasure, certainly; but ultimately it is school.

So the transitional color is purple, even with the color of the soul. I would say that it is not superimposed, but there would be a tinge. For example, the auric field you might see around a soul or a body has a color or glow, but beyond that color (it's possible there is gold for some reason also) is the color of the soul itself, all right? When the baby is growing inside mother, the color of the auric field is that being's soul color. Now, the next layer will be purple, and even though there might be a radiated white or gold beyond that, the purple is transitionally in between to support that motion.

The other occasion upon which the transitional purple is available or present is in the passage to death, as it is called. If this transit is slow, then the sensitive person might see the purple. For example, say an individual is dying slowly, perhaps being cared for in some benevolent institution. The perceptive individual might at times see blotches of purple floating about. It is not at all unusual to find that the person might be phasing (if I can use that word) or stepping in and out of the physical body, even while alive, to experience the other side and get used to the transition. As he exits, regardless of soul color, he will utilize the purple to make that temporary transition to the other side, then return to the physical body with its soul color inside, the physical personality. Nurses and other individuals in hospitals or perhaps homes, convalescent homes or hospices you have known, will see this from time to time, and the color is almost always purple. I mention that because it is transitional.

Now, what about the sudden death, the traumatic death or the accident, as you say? Even if it is for a split second—most likely it will be a little longer—the purple will be there, because . . . it is like creating. Say it is a sudden death; sometimes the personality does not fully grasp that it has ceased in its physical body, so the purple acts as a kind of bridge. It slows things down.

Many people in near-death accidents talk about time stopping.

Yes, and there's a feeling of slow motion; regardless of whether there is death or even near-death, that slowing takes place. The purple does that. It has the capacity to perform this bridgelike effect. In cases where individuals do not realize they have passed through the veil and have to be gently led beyond, the purple makes it a more gentle experience. If they were to suddenly die with no transitional energy available to them, this is how it would work: They wouldn't carry their physical pain with them through their etheric state, but they would carry their emotional pain. And since you cannot experience pain, either physical or emotional, once you are beyond the physical body, what happens (this is an important point) is that you will immediately be physicalized again. Without even going through the veils and process, you would turn right around and become a soul within a physical body again.

Now, this is known only because of experiments conducted off-planet—meaning before Earth. These were not cruel experiments to let people suffer, but to follow the route and the transition of souls ascribed to such a scholastic life as this, yes? To see where they would go, how they would get there, and under what circumstances would changes, either subtle or dramatic, affect their progress. After that study (if I can put it that way) had been accomplished by all the participants, then it was concluded that only on worlds where there is strictly benevolence would it be acceptable to have no purple, because there would not be traumas as you know them. There would not be sudden unexpected death, and as a result, the soul would not require the purple.

In this way the circumstances of the soul passage through the veils was parted out, if I might say that. The purple experience came to Earth as a transitional soul color and to other places where there might be trauma—granted, there were few, but anyplace with a potential trauma. And birth here is a trauma, as we know. It can certainly be less of a trauma, but those years are yet to come.

That is the experience. I wanted to bring that up because although purple is perhaps not a primary color in terms of the colors that form the basis of your understanding of colors, it is an important color.

Purple as a Soul Color

Now, what about the soul who actually has purple as a point-of-origin color? And we've ascribed soul shapes to colors, yes?

Not colors; we've ascribed soul shapes to beings with different planetary origins, but we haven't correlated colors.

Now, the experience, the direction or the support system that is associated with purple is as mentioned: the capacity to do all these things. I have stated that purple is the great assistant, the benevolent support system for souls in transit, but interestingly enough, throughout life on Earth, if you have purple as a soul color, you might find that the spiritual professions will draw you. You might find that you are born with abilities to bring about great benevolent changes. This is usually seen initially in a child when the child can, for instance, touch mommy's forehead and her headache goes away. This is found with babies sometimes, because the baby will move its arms around, and when it begins to explore the world, it might very well touch mommy's forehead, okay? That is one experience.

I don't want to say that any of these are absolutes, but it is also possible that a soul being with purple as a color might find itself in unusual life circumstances, such as the so-called mongoloid child. It is not at all rare for the mongoloid child to have purple as a soul color because these children have the capacity to be in more than one place at once. They are adults too, yes? But they will sometimes have what I would call living dreams; if they are not disturbed and they have time to themselves, they might seem to be staring into space. Granted, the average individual has this experience as well, which is sometimes just called daydreaming.

Without commenting on so-called daydreaming, I'll say for now that these children and adults have the capacity to not only be in more than one place at once; they also have the capacity to function *with memory* in more than one place at once. This does not mean that you ought to grill the children to see where they've been besides in their bodies, but it does tell you that they have spiritual capacities that are not yet fully understood even by the spiritual community, though I know they have inquired and have been looking. I say, look more, because in time you will find that these children are not only wayshowers for applied unconditional love (applying unconditional love is different from consciously experiencing it), but they also have these unusual capacities.

Schizophrenics and the Color Purple

Another group of people that might demonstrate purple as a soul color might be what are called schizophrenics. These individuals are not always of the purple color, but sometimes they are. I will tell you which ones: those who find an avenue to benevolently express that so-called schizophrenia—meaning dual significant personalities. Schizophrenics who wind up in institutions, or develop schizophrenia (meaning they've become schizophrenics as a result of the circumstances of their lives) are different. But beings who are born with at least two distinct personalities are usually of the purple.

So you can see that the purple does have a significant spiritual and benevolent hue in terms of its effect on the individuals who experience it as well as those they touch.

Why would a soul choose to be born a schizophrenic?

It's very rare to be born a schizophrenic; it's usually acquired. But you might choose to be born as that because it would allow you as a youngster, as a baby, to experience more than one input of knowledge and wisdom as well as more than one application. When such children are born to spiritual people, they will almost always understand sacred practices (ruling out perhaps some of the more conventional religions) put into life, such as some native peoples. Such children will almost always be nurtured into spiritual applications for their lifetimes. They might become shamans or mystical people, though probably not medicine people, because that requires a constant recollection of all the knowledge accumulated. These are people who, when properly trained, especially by others who are practicing that calling, can easily step through the boundaries from one dimension to another—and I do not mean only in terms of the mystical sense, but physically. They are rare because they always draw attention, so it is necessary for them to be born into circumstances where they will be nurtured and protected.

Down Syndrome—a Teaching Life

What about the mongoloid, the person with Down syndrome? Why would a soul choose to be born that way?

It is absolutely the best way to experience applied unconditional love. As that type of child, you give it totally, absolutely, to everyone—unless you are taught over and over and over again not to. But generally the tendency is to give it to everyone until those people learn how to give it back to you and others. So it is a teaching position.

That needs to be known!

Yes, it is a teaching activity, a teaching life in which you are totally dedicated. Although you might do other things with your life—you might have other activities and fun things or even a simple profession, you would always show love and affection, with the intent that others learn that it can be a safe thing to do. Now, certainly it isn't a safe thing to do in all circumstances, but for any soul who has not learned unconditional love as an applied experience, it is the quickest way to learn it in a single life.

You could have had lives as a soldier or as a policeman or an adventurer, a mountain climber; you could have had lives like that where you learned many physical things and had adventures and did exciting things, but you never really had a chance to learn about giving and receiving unconditionally as a full-body experience, meaning spiritually, mentally, physically and on the feeling level. You knew that you were missing it and you needed it. So you might choose to have a life such as this wherein you would have the opportunity to learn all of that in one short life, meaning the average life span of one of these people. I might add that this is why it is essential that they not be eliminated genetically.

In the future it's going to be very tempting for your scientists and geneticists to begin attempting to phase out what are perceived to be diseases, and certainly some things are terrible experiences for people to be born with—so-called imperfections—but some things really perform a great service. Even though not everyone has understood the service yet, it does not mean that the service is not there. As a matter of fact, from my point of view, anytime one is born with a handicap (as they are called) or a challenge (as they really are), it is for a purpose, and it will inevitably serve the soul. Such things do not happen by accident even though one might say they do or say, "Here are circumstances that prompted this." But the soul has the ultimate choice to be born and survive. The soul has that choice. If the circumstances are so traumatic or perhaps if medical treatment goes awry, which happens now and then, then the soul still has the choice of whether it will choose to live or not.

I don't want to lecture you, but I will simply say, be cautious, geneticists, because it will be very tempting to eliminate certain propensities toward disease. What you might do is work on the genetic structures of the immune system—rather, let's call it the full-body protective system. This includes more than the biological immune system: the capacity for a powerful experience of instinct. You might say people are born with instinct, they do not acquire it. If you can work on strengthening the potentials there, you won't have to worry about disease, discomfort or even traumatic accidents so much. When one has a fully developed protective system (which includes the immune system, but is not exclusively that), accidents are very unlikely to occur. This includes even the unforeseen.

The Power of the Well-Developed Instinct

What else is included when you talk about instinct?

For example, one thinks of instinct as being a feeling. It is certainly that. Yet imagine this: Suppose the mountain climber had a well-developed protective system. The instincts, then, would be so powerful that the climber would know not to take one route up the mountain but the other; perhaps a handhold on the first route was not quite right, perhaps there would be an unexpected rockfall, or perhaps he would be stranded on an ice field—many possibilities. But the well-developed protective system does not *think* this; it simply delivers a message felt by the physical body—as you might say, a gut feeling. The individual with a well-developed protective system, having been nurtured to discover what instinct is about in benevolent ways (that teaching exists right now in various cultures over your planet), does not have to *know*. The person does not say, "Why?" when they choose route B over A. They don't have to say, "Why not route A?" It's just, "That doesn't feel right, whatever the reason." Maybe it turns out that on route B you meet someone you can help who is climbing down the mountain or someone climbing up the mountain that eventually turns out to be a good friend or more. Who can say? Sometimes it is a feeling to avoid a mishap, and other times it would stimulate a benevolence for you.

What I'm saying is that a well-developed protective system, or instinct, has the potential to change your future, which would make mishaps less likely and potentially create benevolence for you in your choices.

You're saying the teaching is out there, but can you briefly tell us more about this training to increase the instinctual nature?

Training Your Child's Instincts

For example, in cultures where one is trained as a child to develop his instinct, "develop" does not mean to invent or create, but to practice with your instinct and discover what things mean. You might simply play a game with a young child, a toddler or perhaps a two- or three-year old who has just enough physical coordination to understand things that are better and things that are not so good.

The game is something I would call parental observation. When the child is doing something that is safe and exploring his world, you do not interfere; but when the child is doing something that is not safe, instead of just slapping his hand when he gets his finger near the electrical outlet, you tap his hand slightly. If he reaches for it again, you tap it again very lightly and gently. Right after you do that, you reach over to his solar plexus, just above the navel, and gently make a little circular massaging gesture. Just above that, just pressing slightly, you make a clockwise circle, pressing gently.

If the child reaches again, slap the hand very gently and reach over and do that again. What happens is that the child is beginning to develop an awareness of his world, but at the same time the body of the instincts is beginning to blossom just above the [belly] button and below the rib cage. This is where it begins. What you're really doing is giving the child the physical message by tapping his hand away and at the same time underlining with the physical message (no spoken words) to the child being and accentuating *here*. It's as if you're saying, "*Here*, feel what is safe."

At the solar plexus.

Yes, feel what is safe. But you're not *saying* it. It's a nonverbal physical communication, which the slap is also. But since slaps also come at other times as punishments, this is not a punishment but a nonverbal physical communication, which is very important. A lot of older cultures—native peoples living off the land, of which there are not many left, as you know—have always utilized nonverbal physical communication, even though the child might have some rudimentary knowledge of the language and could understand the words for no or yes. But the understanding by the parents is, we need to encourage the child to know what is good and what is not good for him or her, *first* on the basis of what they feel and *second* what they are told.

That has been lost in modern society; now it is the other way around. What you are *told* comes first. But what you *feel* is not even given second place; it is usually shunted off to the side and denied. But the first line of knowing and the first line of the protective system of the instinct is feeling, trusting and acting. It is not feeling, then being told why. It is not mental at all; it is entirely physical.

What I'm suggesting to the geneticist, the scientist and also the behavioral scientists who will be working much more closely with geneticists in the near future is to join even more and remember the value of physical teaching that does not include words. The wonderful thing about that is it doesn't make any difference what language the parents or child will ultimately speak; this goes beyond language.

And it doesn't make your child wrong.

That's right, and at that level of his learning, the child cannot tell the difference between a slap away from a dangerous place (away from the electrical) and a slap because he has done something bad. Children cannot tell the difference, so they begin to identify dangerous places like sticking their fingers near the electrical outlet as bad.

It lowers your self-worth.

That's right. There is no differentiation. But you can differentiate if you use less talk and more gentle action. I'll tell you a little secret: We think of this with the child because it is obvious; people have understood this. But this technique can also be used with the adult. If the adult knows what you are doing, which is necessary with the adult, it can work very well. It is particularly useful when the adult is learning some new skill, and it is always done gently, otherwise the body will immediately interpret it as bad. It will be the genetic equivalent of canceling a chromosome; it just sets you back.

More on Soul Colors

You said that there are many souls who have purple who are not disabled. Are there any souls whose nature is purple? You mentioned the baby whose mother's headache went away when he touched her forehead.

I did say that the soul who has purple will be attracted to spiritual activities, but all people in spiritual activities do not have this. It is very rare, because the soul that is of purple will not be satisfied living in only one world—they wouldn't make a good driver because they'd be in more than one world at once.

But it would work wonderfully in spiritual professions—not just what is being done here, but certain duties of a minister. If you are ministering to people who are dying, for example, it would work excellently there. As your day-to-day personality, you could talk to a person who is passing over and reassure him with whatever faith and knowledge he requires, and at the same time his soul steps out, you can journey with him part of the way. You can form a wonderful connection and help his transition. This, I might add, will be done more in the future as ministers learn that it is all right. Some ministers have done this secretly, and it is very much all right. Ministers, if you have done this, don't feel guilty; it's a wonderful thing to do if you can do it easily.

When a clairvoyant sees the color of the aura, is she seeing the soul color or the etheric or feeling body or what?

If she is looking at the color of the aura of a resting or even sleeping newborn baby, it will usually be the soul color. If, on the other hand, you look at an acculturated baby even six months old, you might see things associated with emotions, feelings and other impacts of living. But you usually see the soul color in a new life, a baby. You might at times see it close to transition, around someone who is dying. Ruling out the purple stepping in and out, you might still see the soul color.

The other time you might see it is when you are looking at someone in sleep. If he is sufficiently out of his physical body (it wouldn't necessarily be a light sleep; it might be a little heavier, but not necessarily the deepest level of sleep), you might see the soul color also. But there might be other things coming into the body based on that person's personal experience or any so-called negative attachments he might temporarily have. You ought to be able to easily note and delineate these, because there are distinct areas, but certainly not a full-body impact of the color. So for the most part, in slumber the dominant color will be the soul color.

Is there a correlation between the color and the shape of the soul based on the star system it's focused through?

Yes, there is, but it is more of an infinite variety—some would have it and others would not. In terms of an applied technique, I want to leave this to psychics and others who might help you find your soul-color correlation.

Develop this as a technique.

That's right, because there are so many variables involved, we cannot give a fixed proportion by quantification of the population. We'd have to say it depended on whether a person had had this or that experience. This is more likely to be easily consummated, understood and applied by a psychic or sensitive or reader who can obtain the soul's shape and color and perhaps apply some of the principles and correlate them. I'm going to leave that up to the development aspect.

Does the soul color relate to the point of origin or to the experiences the soul has had since it's been individualized?

A soul will focus through a given place, yes, to learn something.

For one life.

For one life. But the soul color is a color associated with the experiences the soul has accumulated throughout all of its lives, which include future lives as well. Outside the context of time, it might not include the lives that could happen, but it will include future lives that are planned on and will in fact occur. Even though there might be variables, it will include some impact from that. But it will not include the impact of the *experience* of that life.

Imagine you are tuning a radio, and some stations are stronger and other stations are weaker. If we include certain notes, it sounds like one kind of music, and if certain other notes, it sounds like another kind. The acquisition of different instruments and the sounds they make would affect the color, so the color might change somewhat from one life to the next based on the actual impact of what you experience.

What about gold? I always thought souls were made of golden light.

They are, but that is what I would call the *stuff* that makes them up. Yes, they are golden light, but we are talking about the essence of the *personality*, not so much the entire energy body. For the sake of illustration, picture the gold lightbeing. Within the essence of that gold lightbeing is the color of the soul, but the gold lightbeing is still gold.

Is orange an important color? We didn't get to that yet.

Orange is a bit of a combined color, and almost always denotes exuberance. In that sense, it is a temporary color. It is not what I would call a typical soul color, though it might be one if the soul is having a particularly exuberant lifestyle, meaning that they are very physical or very passionate or have strong feelings about this or that and take action. The chances of orange being a soul color throughout the entire life is unlikely. It has been known, but it is unlikely.

White Light as the Point of Total Origin

Let's talk about points of origin for a minute. You're using that for the . . .

. . . for the individual life, yes. I want to make sure which system we're using so that we do not unnecessarily complicate it.

Is there nothing, then, that connects a person to his original point of origin, since we all came as the Explorer Race, from three soul seeds? We all came from the same place.

Yes. Well, you all came combined through that, yes. It is very typical to be able to say, "You as an individual came from this, and this is what it was like for you when you became aware of yourself as a personality," which is done with certain individuals. But in terms of points of total origin, to the extent that I know, I would say that the point of total origin would probably have to be white light. This is because one cannot have any capacity for energy to stick to any other energy—meaning to create any substance, whether that substance would be physical mass or an idea or a feeling or a wall or a dog or a cat or a human—without the absolute unconditional love of white light. My understanding of the precursor of every known thing is white light. Let's just say there is the mass of white light, yes?

The primordial white light.

Yes, that's nice, the primordial white light, that's nice. But the moment anything is applied or any action is taken with consequences involved, let's say that it's like cutting the butter with a knife. The knife or your hand, as it's moving through the white light, takes on a gold context because the gold is compatible with the white and cannot damage or injure it. The gold also has the capacity for motion/energy application—otherwise known as *doing.*

Experiencing Soul Resonance

I don't think you can talk about it in a way that people can read, but are souls also harmonic? If you were very sensitive, couldn't you hear the harmonic or the tone of every soul?

Without even being that sensitive, you can feel it. Harmonics are infinitely easier to feel than to hear. It is often assumed that because cats or dogs or some animals can hear ultrahigh sounds (and it can be proven), what they react to is based on sound, but this is not always the case. Almost everything they react to is based on a feeling that is trusted.

So a human being can feel that soul resonance from another individual without having to hear it. This can be practiced, and I will say how. The easiest way to feel the soul resonance (this would have to be done with someone who is loved and trusted on both sides) is to be with the person while he or she is sleeping but you are awake. You move your hand like this and position it precisely [see photo]. Go down to the bottom of the sternum, and just where the soft part begins (the person is lying down), you put the two fingers over that, at about a distance of an inch and a half or two inches, and see what you feel [see second photo]. Hold it there for a while. The person must absolutely trust you, because when anyone does that to anybody when they are sleeping, the tendency is for them to wake up. The moment the person becomes more conscious, it will be very difficult to feel it.

So you're reaching with your left, or receptive, hand (it is receptive even if you are left-handed), then you see what you feel. Now, don't try to assume or extrapolate what it might mean, just notice how it feels. If you have another person you love and trust and who loves and trusts you (this can be complex), then try it with the other person in the same circumstances and see if you feel different. The main thing is, your body is the instrument. It will be a physical feeling; note what you feel physically.

Now, certain suggestions are necessary. It would be good if both parties, the one who is feeling and the one who is sleeping, are as clear and pure as possible. You're going to want to clear any discomforting attachments in a way that works for you, all the different systems for this. If you happen to have a discomforting attachment to that part of your body, it would be very easy for the person to feel that. When he or she reaches over that part of your body and feels discomfort, he would not know what it means. So that is required.

I do not make it sound simple, but I want to say how anyone can experiment with this—compared to the sensitive who might use the same hand gesture, not holding it over the sleeping person but just pointing briefly at an individual to feel something. You will have to point in such a way that your connection with that person makes it acceptable: The person knows you're doing it, the friendship permits it, or you do it quickly enough that you are not invasive. Even though what you are doing is benevolent, who can say how it might distract the person.

So you might do it quickly, then notice the immediate impact—how do you feel in your physical body? Then try it with a different person. This is best done in some group setting where everybody knows everybody else, or at least everybody knows that you are the sensitive and you are doing this for research. You can either write it down if it's describable by words or just remember. I would say it is best to do this with at least four or five people, but not more than ten, because there are only so many physical feelings you can remember. Then if you want to build on that, you can attempt to correlate the natural talents or abilities of that individual with the feeling you get. Do you see where I'm going here?

Yes.

Ultimately, you will be able to know not only the soul essence of the individual, but because your own physical instrument, your body, registers this, you will be able to point to somebody else, feel a feeling you've already felt, understood and described at least to yourself or perhaps on paper, and say, "This is exactly the same" (meaning there are no variables), "so these people must have this in common." (I'm stimulating projects here.)

Although they're all absolutely unique and different, there are enough common experiences they've had that they resonate in similar ways, right?

Yes. As the researcher with willing and open subjects, when you're all as clear as you can be, you might be able to eventually suggest to individuals, for instance, compatibility in friendship or business or what-have-you. You might also be able to suggest to individuals the tendencies of certain types that might work better with that individual. When enough research is done, you might be able to suggest which types of individuals would be more suited as companions, or which types of individuals would be better suited to which other individuals. It is not an attempt to replace astrology, for example, to say nothing of good sense, but . . .

. . . it's another support system.

Yes, support systems. It will require extensive research, and I think the research itself will be fun. Eventually many of the researchers can get together. The interesting thing about this research is that each person has his or her own body or instrument for registering these feelings, and these feelings might not be correlated to another researcher's feelings. You will have to correlate on a different basis, and I will let you find that out. It won't be that difficult, though it seems difficult now. Ultimately it will be correlated by people discovering their similarities with somebody else. One researcher would be able to correlate on the basis of how their instrument or body reacts, and once the correlation is done, those who have been correlated will know that about themselves. Even if they go to another researcher, the chances of being correlated differently are unlikely. I do not wish to control the research. I'd rather you experiment with it.

The whole intention is to help you to find out more about yourself so that you can live better, that's all. The whole purpose is to *live better,* for yourself and ultimately others. That is the intention. Even though it sounds complex, as any new tool of analysis in some form is, it is actually an application that, once understood, is very simple and is a useful tool in developing everybody's instincts. Although it seems to be developing the instincts of only the researcher, when someone finds out more about himself (from the researcher's point of view), it will give the subject of the research a chance to experiment and see if there's anything to it.

That's all the questions I had about the previous material.

What do you see as the purpose and intent of this book?

Anything that adds to the understanding that humans have about you, about themselves, the Explorer Race and beyond the Explorer Race.

All right. It is my intention to give homework. Sometimes I might say, "I did this with these people" and so on, but I also want to give tools for growth. But I could, perhaps, talk about another interaction with some group of individuals just for the sake of interest, not necessarily having to do with the Explorer Race.

Creation Mechanics

The Magnetic Energy of Earth

I will talk briefly about the internal magnetic energy of Earth as is felt by the pole. The magnetic pole, as measured through the Earth, moves around somewhat in order to serve all of Earth's needs, yet magnetic energy is actually a substance in its own right. Granted, it cannot be picked up, felt or examined as other substances, but it is a measurable mass of energy. It can be quantified and described in various ways and has been. But rather than say, "What is this magnetism?" let us say, "*Who* is it?" When we know more about its personality, we understand more about creation mechanics.

And that is the ultimate topic of these books.

Yes. Since you are in Creator School, creation mechanics is useful. It is not difficult to correlate what is so for our planet with what is so for a physical being of any sort. Now, first the teaser: The planet has a pole that goes through its physical body, but *so do you.* Now let's explore who that magnetic energy is through Earth. I might add that just as one has cousins and aunts and uncles, there is a relationship between the magnetic energies through all planetary bodies or massive bodies, even stars.

You mean no matter where they are, they're all related to each other?

They're all related to each other in some way; they have a basic relationship . . .

Within a creation, not beyond creation?

From my experience, in *all* creations. That is why it is important to understand the personality of magnetic energy. It is the actual, quantifiable (certainly here on Earth) physical energy and substance of love. Now, love itself is a feeling, an experience—all these things, yes? But if you were able to understand transitions, it is like this . . . a moment. Here we have love [draws]—not a very good version, a poor heart, but love nevertheless. Here we have a pole [draws a column].

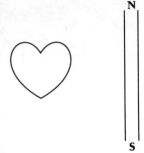

We have magnetism, which can be quantified. When magnetism is personalized, when it is occupying someone such as a human being (compared to a planet, who is also someone but on a larger scale), it transitions to a temporary mode of itself. If a person were feeling that love, that heat, that warmth, as has been discussed in previous Explorer Race books, and you were to put a highly sensitive magnetometer close to but not touching the body (we can't have it touching because the body would be nervous), you could measure that love as a *magnetic radiation*. It would be measurable beyond the magnetic radiation normally present within the physical person.

So when the person is feeling love, that is the transitional state of magnetic energy as personalized. Even though we know Mother Earth is someone, let's say that the pole energy of magnetism is unconditional, impersonal magnetism, whereas the condition within the human being would be unconditional *personal* magnetism, all right? This is important, because if you can grasp this about creation mechanics, you will realize *why* nothing is an accident.

Magnetism, then, is an actual substance that can be love. The personal physical being still has the capacity to be love, but it is not external to an individual, or a personality. It does not in and of its own right have the capacity to be the reverse of love, or unhappiness.

So, the creation mechanics level is this. As a Creator, you say (your Creator had to say this), "I am creating beings for my universe. Some of these beings are planets, some are people and some are plants and animals and so on down the line. I am creating all these things, yet my ultimate purpose here is to create some group that will replace me. How can I put these individuals into a world where they will evolve into a Creator with only a fixed physics? Not everyone in this universe is going to evolve into a Creator, only some.

"Now, everyone might eventually evolve into a Creator if that is their choice, but this is a stream intended at this time only for the Explorer Race. How can I prevent it from being a universal experience, so that everyone is not drafted into some cause they do not wish to participate in, yet at the same time encourage my Explorer Race souls to become this? I must build in a tool of creation mechanics by which they can find their way, reproduce the way they find, and ultimately re-create it. This will be not only love, which will be the universal experience for all beings in my universe, but it must also be something that, no matter where they go in this universe, regardless where they've been before and where they will go afterward, they will find and can utilize: magnetic energy.

"With magnetic energy they will be able to understand very early on. They will find an unusual rock, and the rock is attracted to other rocks, and no other rocks are like this. They will begin to think about that. As they become more thought-oriented, they will begin to explore scientific predictabilities and results. They will explore more about that. They will be greatly attracted to magnetic energy and will try to make it work for them in many ways. It will not work too well at first because they will be attempting to use it as if it were a product, not understanding that it is some*one* who wishes first, of course, to be asked; second, to be appreciated; and third, to be allowed to go away on its own when it wishes. This means it cannot be captured."

This tells you something about the poles north and south through the Earth; the magnetic energy that lives there comes and goes freely. Some of it comes out, goes around the Earth or perhaps even chooses to go to some other planets: That's fine as long as there is enough in the Earth.

Coming back through . . .

That's right, coming back through so that Earth has what she needs and that you, with poles through you, have what you need.

The Explorer Race Magnetic Body

The poles through you are a little different. You look at the Earth and you think of it as having a north/south axis. Your natural tendency is to assume that you would have a north/south axis lining up with *your* chakras. No, the pole through you is different. It goes here: We reach up to the breastbones and draw a line here—we're going to give you landmark, okay? We find the nipples here and draw a line across there, all right?

Granted, for some beings those drop when they get older, but you understand what I'm saying in terms of physiology; draw a line when you are younger. Reach about two inches below and two inches above, then make an oval, not a circle. The pole goes front to back, but not straight. It goes like this. [Draws side view of a body.] I draw a poor drawing, but you get the idea. Here's the front. That's the idea. Here we have roughly the oval, like this. This is the pole through the human being; the energy comes and goes. Do you think it goes out of there? It ought to, eh? It doesn't. If the human being were just here to do nothing, the pole would come and go out the back, but the human being is forced to *be*. Assuming the human being has legs [draws legs], it goes out the feet.

Through the spinal column?

Yes.

It splits and goes down . . .

It might go like this and then like that, okay [draws arrows up and down through feet]? But I'm not in the right place . . .

But it might go out the head.

It would come down like this [draws lines showing a tube through chest]. I must draw this very precisely, a little bigger in the back.

It comes and goes like that, hmm? It comes in at the back. It would go in like this (I draw a dotted line through the arm here) and up and down the spinal column and continue on down through muscles, bones, down through the bottoms of the feet. The bottoms of the feet are purposely designed to be areas of manifestation for the human being.

Explorer Race Person

Many native civilizations know that as you walk on the Earth, so you will create your life. This sounds to the mental being that what you do to others, with others and so on, accumulates the life experience and then the life can be defined. But native peoples know that "as you walk on the Earth" means *physically.* That is why very often native peoples will dance.

First they dance their cleansing dance. Just by being physical they will throw energy out, then they get cleansed. They know they get cleansed because they relax or get into a rhythm of the dance. The moment they do that, they are clear. In more evolved tribes (most of them are fairly evolved) you usually have someone who is the spokesperson or else all the dancers think, visualize, feel—whatever is their custom—what is good for the tribe, what is wanted, what is needed. Maybe they chant it, but they feel it as well, putting their feet on the ground. This is shamanic, but it is also practical, applied creation mechanics. It actually puts that energy into the ground; the Earth feels it when you are barefoot here. Because Earth is a creator almost in status (certainly in applied creation) and is doing creation, Earth knows what it can provide for these people on the basis of what is comfortable. "If I have it, here it is," says Mother Earth.

So all this is about how Creator will allow you to experience magnetics in a certain way so that you and only you become the Explorer Race and others are not drafted into this occupation.

[Draws another figure.] This is one of those concepts that is easier to understand when we show you another not-Explorer Race person, a person probably on some other planet, living innocently enough, eh? But let's say they look like you for the sake of illustration so there's some sense of common ground. Axis through the body, yes? Pole [draws two 2-way arrows, then the caption]—specifically non-Explorer Race person. But let's use someone specific: Pleiadian, since they are so closely correlated. Here we have an axis directly lined up with the heart, it goes into the body like this, then straight up like that. That's it. Axis does not come in the back.

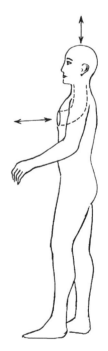

Non-Explorer Race Person

Or go out the feet.

No. This does not mean they do not have the capacity to do all that you do; it means they don't *have* to do it. Of course, it can go down and do things. This means the energy comes in, goes out up here, all right? This is a person living in a totally benevolent society. A person living in a totally benevolent society, then, is not required to create an action that will have consequences they personally will have to follow up. If there are some consequences, any member of their society may follow up on the action, because their energy is all quite interchangeable from one soul to the next.

If this makes any sense to you, this is how the Creator says, "In this way we make sure that the creation mechanics work through our Explorer Race individuals, because the Explorer Race individuals are forced to take action on the basis of what they do." Where does the energy go? It goes to their feet; even if they don't have feet, it goes to the lowest possible extremity on the occasional person who isn't born with such things. For the sake of the example, it goes to their feet, what they use to get from here to there—you understand? It is action-oriented. Action-oriented means that you are responsible. To put it more simply, you are allowed and trusted to take action based upon what you have done and the consequences it has wrought, whether it is good consequences or not so good. You are trusted at this stage of your spiritual experience, in your total experience of being. Since you're in Creator School, you are now trusted and held in such high esteem by Creator that Creator says, "You can do it yourself, and just to make sure you do it or make some effort to do it, the energy is run through you in this kind of pole."

What is the significance of the back chakra?

It's not a chakra; we've tried to bring up these systems not so much in concordance with other systems.

What is the significance of that area?

The opening, or receptive place, allows energy to enter in both directions. What do we know about magnetic energy?

Positive and negative; two poles.

Plus and minus, negative not meaning bad, polarity. In order to get that benevolent polarity, to be magnetic, we must bring the positive in one direction and the negative in the other direction—positive in the front, negative in the back [draws]. They meet somewhere in the middle and create magnetic energy. We could say loosely that regardless of your sex, the front opening is masculine, polarized positive, loosely speaking, and the feminine energy is negative—as a measurable charge, not as anything else. In other words, to keep it simple, positive (front), negative (back) come in and form the pole, which is an activating pole—you will want to move, you will want to do things.

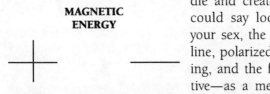

MAGNETIC
ENERGY

The Mechanics of Attraction

How does it correlate to the axis through the Earth? You have to ask yourself, "Is it only physics that causes the Earth to spin as it goes around the Sun? There are other bodies—asteroids, moons—that have orbits and spin in varying degrees. Some may not spin, but just wobble. The spin, which supports the specific gravity of the planet and also the experience of gravity, allowing life such as your own, is caused by the desire to take action, to create and in total openness to live with the consequences, be they good or not so good. That magnetic energy through the Earth is, in a sense, the risk-taker, the adventurer, the lover, the nurturer, hmm? It is also the child, the elder, the essence of nurtured life itself. It is nurtured and it nurtures; it wants to be alive and it wants to support life. It attracts life and it is itself a form of life.

Remember, I said that there are other poles through other planetary bodies. The magnetic energy reflects the essence of that planet and what kind of life that planet would choose to have, so the planet will attract only that. The magnetic energy that runs through the pole of such a planet is the actual mechanics of attraction. So the love magnetics that run through this Earth is the mechanics of attraction. It is how the soul finds its way to Earth instead of to Maia in the Pleiades, for example. The soul itself—regardless where it's been, what it's done, what its shape is, what color it might be more compatible with—knows what it's looking for. It's looking for a specific love charge, to be welcomed. It is attracted, just like any navigational equipment, and goes right to the place that welcomes it.

Is that magnetic energy Mother Earth's love, or is it someone else's?

It is Mother Earth's desire for certain beings to come to her, so it is her impact on the magnetic-energy being or beings, since they are made up of different bits. It is her impact on that magnetic energy. Even if that magnetic energy were to fly out, say, of the North Pole, travel around the solar system and go to Saturn, it would leave behind what impact and desires Mother Earth had on it, go immediately into Saturn's pole and take on the traits—the clothing, as it were—of what Saturn would desire in terms of beings, be they etheric or any form of being on or within her. While that magnetic energy is there, it cloaks itself in the Saturn-personality desires. If it goes on someplace else, it will do the same thing there. As it leaves Saturn, it might maintain that energy for a time in case it wishes to come back, but the moment it goes someplace else and becomes involved in some other planet, it will shed that garment, which will naturally find its way right back, as if it were attracted. It is attracted to its nature, to its own kind, and will go right back to Saturn. Then the magnetic particle (if I might use that term) goes on and becomes involved in the axis of some other planet.

So the soul creates this Explorer Race magnetic body when it incarnates here?

The soul creates what I would say is the opening for that axis, because it is not possible to be here without that axis. It is the rite of passage of the soul: If you're going to go there, you have to be open to creating a body that reflects the bodies there or are intended to be there in the beginning. In this way the body will have a passage through that; even though you can't stick your finger into the passage, the passage will be there and receptive to that axis.

So a Pleiadian soul, with that type of energetic body, just won't function on the Earth?

That's right, because the axis is not intended for such responsibility. Although they could visit and be here, they would have to have a limited interaction with you so that they do not cause too much consequences. They've been very cautious in the past, and other ETs also, so as to have the least amount of impact. That is also why most of them have had to cause you to forget they were here. If there were consequences, they as individuals or other Pleiadians would have to reincarnate on Earth as an Earth person to resolve those consequences. The Pleiadian people can't just come and resolve that because they would have the same circumstance: They would absolutely have to reincarnate on Earth to resolve those consequences. It is for their own sake that they have to cause you to forget at least temporarily, especially in the early years, so that there would not be sudden trauma. It is actually better for most of you to remember gradually rather than suddenly. When you remember gradually, the traumatic effect, or consequences, are less severe.

But even if there are consequences, which certainly have taken place, once the Pleiadians have distanced themselves (I'm using them as an example because of the association between them and you), once they have created enough distance, you yourselves are in fact working on applications and consequences. You yourselves have the capacity to work out the consequences.

If a huge Pleiadian ship were to land in the middle of Times Square, there would be major consequences, and there would have to be someone else who would resolve it. The Pleiadians could not resolve it—make everything all right; someone else would have to resolve it, and that would be complicated. So they have not done so, and rightly so. They were instructed that it would not be a good thing, and that when the time was right they would come and land, as we say, in Times Square or Red Square, if you would. Then you would be prepared to instantly deal with the consequences—you would be happy to see them. If you were frightened, fear would stimulate all the other fears you ever had in your life for whatever reason. That's why some people would be only slightly anxious and others would be terrified. If you're happy, happiness is felt the same by all people. Even if it is not expressed the same way, it is felt the same and the happiness itself resolves the consequences. The happiness is the consequence, and happiness is its own resolution [chuckles].

So we have to be mostly through the fourth dimension then before we can leave fear behind?

Mm, not necessarily. You just have to be able to feel comfortable with yourself and know how that feels, and be able to feel safe, to experience safety not only as something that outer conditions support, but as an inner experience, allowing it to project around you; then you will be safe. After that, no matter what happens, even if somebody moves in next door who might otherwise be frightening, they're not frightening to you. You know there is nothing to be afraid of because you are safe, meaning you are a projector of safety for yourself.

So it is a choice, a practice you need to work on. It is easy to create the *illusion* of external safety, but a little more challenging to create the *actuality* of internal safety. Internal safety makes external safety unnecessary. [Chuckles.] When you have internal safety, even if an ET crawled out and looked like an octopus (though this doesn't exist that I know of in this part of the universe and almost negligibly in this universe at all), you would say, "Who are you?" and "This is my name." That would be that. There would be no reaction, no fear. (In reality, not many ETs have tentacles, except for the origin of tentacled beings on this planet who may have some tentacled beings elsewhere.)

The Sperm, the Egg and the Soul's Involvement

Does the life scenario chosen for this life tie into the shape and the color of the soul? I'm asking how it works.

We tend to think there is this biological reaction, the sperm and the egg combine and start to grow, and when there is enough material mass, then the soul comes in. That is the assumption, yes?

Yes.

It's not like that. In reality, it is not like a store where souls go shopping, but they will often be present briefly at conception or even slightly before. Very often they will come with teachers, guides, advisors, even friends, and say (at that stage of their being, they're very realized), "These are going to be my parents," [chuckles] perhaps discussing it or saying, "Don't they look nice?" and other comments and visiting. The soul is not totally in the configuration in the total energy and shape that it will have when mother has actually conceived, though it is close. The soul can briefly enter mother if it is acceptable by mother (sometimes it is comfortable, sometimes it isn't), and might go in and say, "Here is where I will grow."

From my perception, the soul comes first. So the child is ensouled from the beginning, and the body grows with the soul. I don't want to say it grows *around* it, because that sounds like the soul is in the center; I'd rather say it grows *with* it. Regardless how elaborate the body might look, the first few cells are just as ensouled as what comes out looking like a human being. At the same time I do not wish mothers who have difficulty birthing or whose birth has not been a success to feel uncomfortable. Always remember that all souls have quite a degree of choice before they are actually born. [Chuckles.] After you are born, you still have some choice, but not as much.

Your Energy Tether

How does it work, the energy coming in the back?

Remember, the magnetic energy goes up and out; it comes into Mother Earth from the poles and out. It is constant; it is the same for the human being. Magnetic energy comes in—or what will become magnetic energy comes in—and goes out. It is constantly flowing in and out even while you are in mother. But that is not what you are asking?

No. The soul focuses through a star system that has certain qualities of lessons embodied in it. I thought it anchored that energy into the back (I don't want to say back chakra), and that certain energies the soul wants for that particular lifetime come through, and certain energies it doesn't want don't come through. I thought it was a qualifier or a . . .

A tether? Or a focusing device?

Yes, a focusing device for particular energies that relate to the planet or star system you're focusing through, the shape of your soul for this lifetime.

Remember that the function of creation mechanics is largely to create, support, nurture and bring along, as it were, forms of life. Creation mechanics at the basic level is not about *what* you will do; it's more about how you will *be*, how you will *exist*. The axis of the human being is there to allow you to exist; it supports and sustains the function of the physical self, that which supports lessons. Is that what we're talking about here?

Yes.

That which supports lessons for you will tend to come in in a different position. Reach around to the base of the skull at the point where the soft tissues meet the base of the skull, and come down about six vertebrae. It comes in there.

That's still in the area. So that's where the energy comes in from our point of origin for this lifetime, where it impacts us or connects us or . . .

That's why I'm calling it a tether. That's where you are supported and constantly receiving a sustaining amount of energy so that you won't go off track, so that you will learn what you came here to learn, so that you will have the talents and abilities associated with that origin or focus and also what you have acquired. These are not always called talents, but propensities—something you do better than others, but you need to be shown.

It keeps you on a certain track. It is not too specific, but on that track there are occasional meanderings allowed, yet you will from time to time encounter whatever it is you came here to learn. If you had wanted to learn it as applied to some specific experience, then it might show up in only one part of your life, such as in relationships; whereas if you had wanted to learn it generally, it would be a total life theme.

It's as if you are flowing in a stream and the stream had different thicknesses of liquid or even different—I'm disinclined to use the term *colors* because we have already done that—substances. Some are more viscous and some are thinner. The viscous element, which tends to stick to itself a little better, will be the life lesson, and the thinner elements are just experiences. Certain meanderings are allowed, but the main lesson will tend to stick to you better than the basic experience, just as honey sticks to the fingers, but water doesn't.

So the honey's going to get your attention [chuckles].

Yes. It will get your attention and you will have to do something about it.

That's a good one. I like this; you're making it very simple and unesoteric, not related to previous connotations.

That's what I'm really trying to do; I want to simplify. Simplifying creation mechanics isn't necessarily simple [chuckles]; that's why I'm trying to avoid the pitfalls of systems analysis.

I tried to give you certain basic foundational building blocks here so that you will have a general understanding of how things take place. I'm not trying to claim that I have given you a crystal-clear reason why some beings are Explorer Race and others aren't, but it is my intention to give you ideas upon which you can build rather than facts you have to accept. Good night.

I sis speaking. November 11, 1997
Would it be acceptable to have the book partly teaching and partly my adventures?

Yes, because you give us great teaching when you tell about your adventures.

Good. A moment.

Life as a Series of Arcs

I need to talk about something briefly. It is a portion of a shape, an arc. An arc is a portion of a circle, which is considered the complete shape in the world you now occupy, the shape by which all other experiences are often compared to—circles of life, cycles of seasons and so on. I'd like to talk about how shapes themselves, particularly arc shapes, are able to maintain their fluidity while having a bias toward the personal shape they are in.

We know that the flowing lines of an arc make up a circle, yet these same flowing lines make up many other shapes. When one looks at the human being, one can see the human being as segments of arcs, and one can look at life that way. It is true that some forms of life such as crystalline forms are better known for straight lines or triangles, yet when they find themselves in the flow of Mother Earth's cyclical rhythms, they will often be rolled from place to place, starting out perhaps as a great boulder rolling down a mountain, becoming rocks, then stones, then pebbles, then perhaps finding themselves in a stream and eventually becoming fairly rounded-off grains of sand. Although their internal structure might still be angular, their external structure has become quite circular, or at least resembles a sphere. One might say that this is obvious, that this is an apparent reference to the scientific rules of life on Earth. Yet one could also ask, "But why?" as the child might until he or she receives an answer that is perfectly satisfactory.

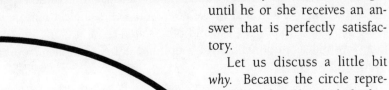

Let us discuss a little bit *why*. Because the circle represents the foundational rhythm of creation itself as you know it and are striving toward it here;

the structures of life, the cells in your body, the planets, the suns and so on are all roughly circular. We must ask ourselves, as students of such things, is this simply life, or is it different in other places? I can assure you, in other universes it is very often different. But since you are learning the fundamentals here of creation mechanics and also the responsibility that goes with such authority, you must have certain shapes represented not only symbolically, but as a literal part of your living existence. This is why the circle is such a predominant theme in your existence on Earth.

Let us consider for a moment the simple arc [draws], a segment of a circle—better known as the 45-degree angle. Putting such a fluid line on paper suggests it does not have depth, yet I'm going to talk a little bit about the life of shapes.

You know that Earth is a living being. You also know that certain geographical places, even though they might look like other places, have different impacts on different individuals, not only because of the circumstances of their lives, but simply because of the energy attracted to or disseminated by those places. Sometimes this is called geomancy. But is this the only circumstance of such apparent mysterious influence? It is not.

The shapes themselves (I will utilize the arc shape tonight) are, within their own being, constantly pulling to create a circle. An arc is a portion of a circle. The reason I choose the arc is that you can look at it and say, "This line, this shape, is seen over and over again in life." What if I told you that each portion of a circle has a tension within it to re-create a circle in its own right? The cells in your body, say, the blood cells and the fluid that runs through your body, when put under a microscope, are sometimes round or oval—but the shapes themselves *want* to be circular. When they are at least partly circular, they want to be circular.

What if I told you that all life in this part of the universe is struggling either to become circular or to maintain an angular shape (because it is required), although its natural propensity is to be circular or have the arc shape? If you understand that or can even accept it theoretically, it begs the question *why?*

The Sphere of Creation

You must understand something fundamental. We can talk about creation mechanics—how this works, how that works—but what *is* it? What does it look like? What form would it take if we could scoop up a handful of creation mechanics, hold it in our hand and say, "This is it; it is this color, it has this consistency, it has this shape." If you could scoop it up in your hand and hold it, it would very quickly reassemble

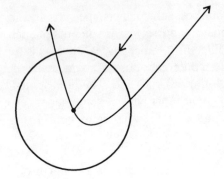

itself into a perfect sphere from whatever you scooped it out of, emanating and attracting light. In other words, the sphere itself is the *means* by which the light . . . the light is the substance of all physical life, and this condensed light, either expanded or condensed, is what makes up all substance. This spherical thing that has taken shape in our palm is not only attracting light, but it also has the capacity to transform mass from one shape to another. In the process, the light comes in and the light goes out from the sphere, but what's happening at the *center* of the sphere? Is the light simply turning around in the center and coming back out? Is the light that's being attracted coming in on one side of the sphere and going out on the other side, being sent out? No. The light that is being attracted, or recycled, comes into the sphere, goes into the center of the sphere and folds into another dimensional universe. Here's our center [draws]—I'll make it a dot. The light comes in, it folds and goes elsewhere [draws], and the light that comes out is coming from other dimensions.

It's like a black hole in the center of every sphere!

In the center of every sphere or circular shape, the substance that attracts and holds the light, that keeps all things together, is love. Yes, it is light, but it is like a magnifying glass, a focusing device that moves the light from one point of existence to another. Yet the intention is that all spheres or circles have the capacity to do this, and it is the *trick* by which creation happens quickly. You have heard of an optical illusion; it is truly the sphere (all spheres are like this) truly based on the assumption of optical integrity—at the center of the sphere (which we're using as an analogy), light, as it comes in, is recycled to where it needs to go, based exactly on its qualities. Maybe that light was once a part of a mountain or a sunset; it comes in and is recycled to someplace else on Earth even if it is light from a shooting star, someplace to the stars. Light that goes out comes from all these places all over the universe as well as here on Earth.

The trick to creation mechanics, then, is not putting things together one brick at a time, as in the creation of a brick wall; it's in the sphere of creation. Your Creator, for example, brings along with Itself Its own portable sphere. Your Creator takes the form of a sphere when It begins this universe; It becomes Its own optical instrument. Your Creator has a feeling for how the universe would look. Does the Creator take seven days to create it, as in the story? No. The Creator does not take seven days, including the day of rest. The Creator forms this optical, integral device. And having the thought and feeling and inspiration of what this universe would look like, your Creator quickly expands into that total shape, and within Itself, just like protoplasm, forms quickly (coming from light gathered from other sources and light recycled from within Itself). In a twinkling of time (much less than one second) does the actual, whole universe immediately take shape in terms of planets, star systems (not yet people, just the planetary bodies).

At this point your universe is totally spherical, yet over time, Creator becomes more enamored with this part of the universe or more interested in that part, spending more time creating in that part or this part. That is why your universe eventually takes on a more oblong or circular shape, but in sculpted roundness, arcs, not a total sphere. It will be your job, I might add, when you become the Creator, to let loose the cosmic balancing expectancy (which is a bias) of the natural sphere, which will allow your universe to re-form itself, without any harm to anyone, into the perfect spherical shape. That will be what you do to prove your ability as a Creator before you are allowed to go on. This is the exact duty you have been given. In order to do that, you must have the experience you are having on Earth where everything tends to evolve at some point toward a rounded shape, so that you are constantly being reminded, even the casual observer, that this shape has some mysterious meaning. I am often pictured with the sphere on top because I have given this teaching to other members of creation mechanics classes. It is the intention to show the importance of this shape.

Now, different shapes have different purposes, but this shape is the most important, because it *does it for you* rather than your having to place the bricks one at a time. You have a feeling, perhaps, when you leave here and re-form as your own Creator—you will go all over this universe, and it will be like a celebration—you will have a *feeling* for this universe after that. It will be such a celebration, such a happiness, such a joy, you will just let go completely. And when you let go, the experience of creation mechanics just automatically happens. You will become totally spherical in your shape, and being in charge of this universe, your universe can do nothing else but *emulate your shape*. The reason your religions show God as a human being is that it is natural to assume that Creator is the same as you in some way. This is not an accident; it is a bias of your souls to believe so, programmed in by Creator so that you would be constantly supported with hints that the natural spherical shape can, in its own right, reproduce. People who look at crystal balls, even though they might be like tarot cards or even some guessing thing to another person, know that it is the shape, not the crystal, that makes the difference. Those who have been practicing for a time know this.

I bring this up to you tonight briefly so that you will understand that the shapes themselves have a life of their own. Even though we might say a cell has its own personality or a nucleus has its own experience, the shape that that cell or nucleus is in will itself protect that nucleus— because the shape of the sphere is based totally on absolute structural integrity, which is the foundational element of this universe.

Now, I don't like to make things complicated, but if you can, think of it this way: If you can have a totally spherical lens, it will also focus, but in different ways. And when you *become* that spherical lens, you will lend your focus to the lens, allowing the lens to become personalized to you as you will be when you are a creator. When the lens then becomes personalized to you and what you desire to create, it will *show* that. Remember that things are referred to as optical illusions because it's what you see *with* the lens. Because you are here in this dimension, you see only so much with the lens; but when you become the complete sphere, including all the experience of all the beings within it, *you* will not only see, but others will see. All will see what you wish to create when they are in this universe. If they come to the universe to learn, as the Explorer Race has done, they will tend to leave much of their wisdom behind during their learning experience, because the focal bias of the lens causes you to see only what the lens wishes you to see (the lens in this case being the Creator). When you are no longer in this universe, you see what you *know*, and you are not limited by what you used to grow here.

What's a practical application we can make of this?

It is more philosophical at this time. Know that the nature of creation is intended to produce only that by which the light within it can learn and grow and sustain itself.

For instance, could we visualize the nucleus of every one of our cells as able to pull in fresh energy from someplace and release our stressed or aging energy by some process like that?

No, I am talking to you about what is happening, what you cannot see. You are learning how to put bricks on the wall one at a time so they will look good and be strong. But I want to remind you of what is happening all around you all the time, though you are not looking through the glass that way. It is as if you are on the side of the glass that shows you yourself, whereas the Creator is on the other side of the glass and can see not only you, but all beyond—like a one-way mirror.

The Accumulated Wisdom of the Explorer Race

There is some interference tonight, so the connection is difficult. The interference is not intentional. I will tell you what it is so you're not concerned. Your planet, in this specific time right now, is being radiated with a type of particle that will allow the memories you have accumulated as a result of all your experience here as the Explorer Race, be retained, but not on this planet. Many of these memories are causing some stress to Mother Earth in her regeneration process, but they are important to the accumulated wisdom of the Explorer Race. So right now the entire planet is being radiated with these small capsule-like particles that will accumulate the raw material of the memories and take them to a place of storage where the rest of the Explorer Race is waiting. In that way, the movement between dimensions will be made easier for you, since you will not have to retain the personal and collective memories of your experiences, some of which are difficult. In the coming weeks and months (I should think for at least the next four and a half months) you will have other experiences like memory loss. There will also be times when it will be difficult to read things that are conceptual, or if you do read, it will be polarized—you will either be able to read and absorb tremendous amounts, or you will only be able to read slowly, having to stop and think about what you have read. Then the polarity will switch. Others will have these experiences. For right now, that energy is slightly interfering.

Those particles are coming from the Earth, or to the Earth from someplace else?

They are coming from where most of the rest of the Explorer Race is waiting, serving you by removing the more burdensome elements of memory that tend to recycle both internal and external conflicts. Yet when taken in a total and complete experience (including all the members), they will serve the cause of wisdom well.

This will go on perhaps for the next three to four weeks, up to four and a half months. It will reach its zenith in about three and a half weeks, then in about two and a half more weeks, quickly taper down quite a bit, tapering off gradually for the next few months. Some people cannot release their memories right now, but they will within the total span of this time. It's been going on now for about six weeks. Altogether, the whole experience runs not quite six months.

It has affected my reading and understanding, so I must have one end of the pole.

Yes, you're on the other end of the spectrum, and it may not change for you. But for some beings, it will be difficult to conceptualize in some ways. People who understand through reading will be able to read well. People who understand through pictures will need to understand through pictures, and too much reading will give them difficulty. (I'm using this example of reading since you are so intensely involved with it.) People who understand by sounds, such as musicians or even parents with little children, will have that experience—compared to people who might understand by smells, such as animals. When I say "the collective memories," I'm referring not only to the Explorer Race as human beings, but partly to some of your consultants—plants, animals, parts of the planet herself which, when taken together with personal experience of individuals, lend physical sensations to the memories. Purely mental memories make little sense, but they make a great deal of sense when one can utilize the whole range of senses to understand *why* and *how*.

How does our project fit in, then? We're trying to bring back the memory of who we are?

It will be unhampered, because most of the memory being taken away are memories of difficulties or traumas, hard-fought-for wisdom, you understand? It will make it easier, but at the moment it's creating a bit of unintentional interference.

Do you want to continue?

Would it be acceptable to simply continue Thursday night?

Of course.

Then perhaps we will do that.

The Insect Form and Fairies

November 13, 1997

Isis speaking. Tonight I want to talk a little bit about peoples I have been with and perhaps will be with in the future.

The Explorer Race in Its Primordial State

I want to trace back a bit the avenue of the Explorer Race. Before the Explorer Race started coming into this part of the universe, you were working on your primary motivations. In order to do so, you were to go to places where planets and even solar systems were distinct, strikingly known for something, or where the cultures were predominantly known for something.

We know that in recent evolutionary time (time that allows change), Orion, in its not-too-distant past, was known for structure—society and organizational structures. Before that, the Explorer Race was in what I call a primordial state. This does not mean that you were a part of some soup of flotsam and jetsam, but rather that you were getting used to the expression of emotions, passions and feelings through physical vehicles.

There were also fewer numbers of you then. I don't know if you know this—perhaps you had surmised it—but the quantity of individuals in the Explorer Race has gradually grown, and the number now on Earth is its greatest number of individuals at any time. So when we precede Orion, we're really only talking about groups of individuals numbering fewer than 50,000.

In times preceding that, you were visiting galaxies farther away from your known universe as you now explore it. Some of these planets were experiencing natural upheavals, which means that the planets themselves had not settled into their benevolent rhythm by which they would support life. When you incarnated there ("you" being the Explorer Race), you would require aid and comfort from technology, for your bodies had to be able to conform to extreme conditions. Perhaps the planets, as you understand living planets to be, would still be expressing themselves in physical ways. On Earth it is volcanoes and earthquakes, but on this particular planet it was radiations. The radiations were not what I would call seriously dangerous, but the heat from the sun would get the temperature up to about 160 degrees during the day and the cooling-down period at night would drop the temperature to about 65 degrees. So at nighttime and in the early morning hours it was still relatively comfortable. But the heat of the day required either technological support (certainly for the young) or a shell-like body that could deflect such waves of energy.

The assumption, though unspoken, is that the Explorer Race is humanoid. But in reality, since you were just beginning to experience the physical application of passionate feelings, you were at that time expressing yourself in a form of life that would be closer, on casual inspection, to the insect world. You were generally not as small as they are here, but if you compared biological features, you would say, "These people remind me of the insect world." There was that hard outer shell and a body that, not unlike the turtle, could draw inside the shell during the extreme heat of the day and whose legs could extend far enough that if one had to beat a hasty retreat, one could suspend one's body above the heat of the soil and rocks beneath and run quickly to the nearest shelter.

This culture was established before you arrived there as the Explorer Race, and what you really did was superimpose your souls on one generation. The beings there allowed this, but said, "If this is going to occur, one *entire* generation must be this Explorer Race, not one group that is the Explorer Race and another group our natural selves. If we did that, we would surely stimulate polarity." So the agreement was made that it would be one entire generation, which was not quite 50,000 beings.

The cycle of your life there took, in terms of your now-Earth years, about 627 years. It was not strange because you were still getting used to physical bodies; it was just another type of physical body. The culture was not terribly aggressive. Violence against its own members was unknown; it did not happen. The culture was vegetarian, living off plants. Most of the plants were underground, but some of the mosses, as you would call them, grew on the surface under rocks and slightly above underground lakes and reservoirs, where the ground at the surface would be soft and moist. Granted, these were in sheltered areas.

It was at this point of your evolution that I paid a call, because the culture that so generously allowed you to be amongst them for a generation required a certain amount of assistance. It was not in their nature to express strong, passionate feelings about anything, yet they understood that that was the purpose of the Explorer Race's passage through their culture. They also wanted to be protected so there would be no residual impact or lasting effect on their culture. So they requested that a being come to give these Explorer Race members of their culture some task—some way to express passions, excitement, strong feelings and so on that would not involve their culture directly but would be a temporary experience they could easily let go of once the Explorer Race had passed out of their midst.

Simple Games for Experiencing Strong Emotions

It was my decision, therefore to introduce simple games, since these beings were not violent with each other and were never competitive, because they had to help each other in order to get what they needed. The goal was not games that involved competition with each other, but games that required a unity of purpose, such as, for example, rolling a boulder from point A to point B in the best possible way, causing no damage (which would be part of the game), and getting it there as soon as possible, hurting nothing. This would require a great deal of cooperation and effort and assistance by everyone and would amuse the older members of the culture that were not part of the Explorer Race, giving them something they could do together without leaving an impact on their culture.

This is what I suggested, and it worked quite well. As you know (you've played games your whole life in one form or another, certainly when you were youngsters), it is normal to get passionate, frustrated, upset, excited, happy etc. when playing a game, especially when accomplishing something that one person cannot do well but that many people can do better and better, especially as you get to understand the game.

That was my contribution in that civilization.

What do we carry in us now as a result of that? Was something added to our souls?

That's a fine question. As a result of that experience, you now carry not only the fun and the thrill of the game, but an underlying desire for some kind of resolution, no matter how strong or enthusiastic or competitive your game might be now—a desire that at the end of the game there be some form of resolution where everybody feels relatively happy with each other. That was the impact.

One can see that nowadays in versions of sportsmanship, even things that are not gamelike but that have qualities of a game—such as competition or wars and battles in which people always feel better afterward if there is some kind of resolution or treaty, some kind of acceptance of each others' differences, or a recognition of each other's value even if there is some great loss—I'd say that is the lasting impact. It preset a bias to seek resolution, and when you consider who you are as the Explorer Race, constantly involved with knowledge, wisdom, application, consequences and responsibility, seeking some form of resolution or consolation is very useful in that diorama as it plays out now.

How was it that you were chosen? Did someone call on you?

I was not so much chosen as the need was stated; it was asked. Because I've had a lot of experience with different groups of people at different stages of their experience or evolution (in terms of their evolving consciousness) and because I was available [chuckles], which is always the main factor, I responded. It is that simple.

Where was this?

It was in this universe, but before now-familiar things such as Orion and the Pleiades, when you were just getting used to the idea of being in physical bodies, the kind of physical bodies that could express feelings and passions. You were wanting to experiment with different forms of physical bodies in different conditions—what you would call today challenges, but in those days was really more about experimenting: what works where and why.

The Mystical Lemurians

Now I'd like to talk in terms of your more recent experience, being here on Earth. In the early days of Lemuria a culture was forming, the culture that would someday be what I would call the mystical people. These individuals were born with capacities much as children are born with capacities today—if the need for those capacities is not readily recognized, they will either go unnoticed or will sometimes be mistakenly referred to as illnesses or handicaps, even some kind of behavior problem. Often new and unknown gifts are diagnosed this way.

So in Lemuria the civilization at that time was very much involved with color, what has come to be known as liquid light. A color associated with feeling would be present. Feelings, once stimulated, would co-respond (respond with) the color: the person would be dancing or expressing themselves in some way in concordance with the color, the liquid light. What they were doing would also stimulate a color, and this would change the whole color. Then the next person who danced or performed in some way would be just that much different, adding her own feelings to it. This was not the mystical school I referred to, but something that is long established and is really in the background of what I would call the fairy world.

Dancing through Dimensions

The children being born then would someday be able to dance their way through all dimensions *while* retaining the physical characteristics of their own dimension. Now, you have to consider that for a moment. As you know, if extraterrestrials from higher dimensions come to your now dimension, they must use protective devices. They cannot just walk amongst you or they would be injured or might accidentally cause some sensation amongst you, which they wouldn't want to do. But these youngsters were going to learn a form of dance that would allow them, when dancing, to stimulate a portal they could dance through. Because they stimulated it, they would not have to find a way back to that exact place; their desire to return home could simply stimulate another portal to return them home. They learned how in this dance. They were doing this really before their parents (or older members, as they might have been called then) showed them anything. It was like watching children at play, not really understanding what they are doing, but being fascinated by it; this existed there also.

The children, then, were teaching themselves. I would place myself at the end point, as far as they could go through the dimensions, to act not like a target, but an anchor, so that they wouldn't turn off in some unfamiliar or unsafe direction. My energy was a desirable energy for them to come to; it would give them motivation to find different ways to dance—dancing different feelings, different colors, different sounds—until they could reach where I was positioned. It was not unlike walking through a maze in order to find your way to the inner garden.

In this way I would celebrate with them, energetically dancing with them, and show them how they could teach this to others. You must remember that they were born with this ability. Teaching someone how to do it when you yourself were not taught can be challenging; this goes with any talent. I would teach them how to pass it on and counsel them to be aware of whom they passed it on to.

This was a cultural experience I had that took place on a version of this planet in its past; I say a version because in those days, things were very peaceful all over this planet, and Atlantis as you know it was at that time simply an island that hadn't formed yet, though people expected it someday.

The reason I mention this civilization is that at this present time of your experience, children such as this are being born again. They are coming in with skills and abilities along the lines of the mystical. They are not being taught these skills but are being born with them. I will suggest to doctors and teachers, counselors and parents, brothers and sisters and all others who might be exposed to these children to not jump to conclusions about their different sort of behavior. You might see from them dances that are unexpected, or motions—something that looks almost like a form of sign language done with the arms and hands, occasionally with the body and legs. It will seem to mean something on one hand yet on the other hand simply look strange—even like some aberrant behavior. But this reeducation and reintroduction of these mystical skills to a group of children will happen all over the planet.

I'd like you to be alert to this because in time, once these children, intact in their physical bodies, learn to access other dimensions again and return totally intact, they will be taught (just like before—and with the same teacher, I might add) how to teach this to others. The advantage of this particular skill, of course, is that it can be used only benevolently; it cannot be used in any way that harms the participant or any of the individuals they are assisting. So do not be concerned about that.

The "same teacher" is you.

Yes.

Are we talking vast numbers? Hundreds, thousands, millions?

Oh, I'd say these children started being born about three years ago, and they will continue to be born for at least another seven years, perhaps a little longer, the total number in births not exceeding 250,000. A significant number, but not a preponderance of births.

Are they related to the souls who were born in early Lemuria?

They are the same souls.

How had they learned that first time? Had they learned it on another planet, were they taught before the life, or . . .

They had not learned; they arrived with the skill. The skill was visited upon them as they came in.

By you.

Yes. The intention here was to provide something that was not only needed then in a minor way but would be needed now. Once souls learn it, relearning it is infinitely easier. One must recognize that in these days the level of distraction is infinitely greater, so it would be much easier to relearn something than learn it as a completely new thing. To learn something as a new thing requires a minimum of distraction, which is not really available to most people these days.

Have any of those souls been born as mystical people in what you would call tribal situations?

Some, not many. There is not a direct correlation. Most of them have had very few lives physically between then and now. This makes the memory of what they have learned relatively fresh so that they can relearn it without much difficulty.

How will it play out, what will they do, who will they teach, what will be the result?

Understand that I am constrained; I do not wish to tip my hand so soon. But I will say that it is intended ultimately to create an avenue by which other people can explore potentials for Earth and its citizens and be exposed to teachers in other dimensions who cannot come here to teach you. By opening a temporary portal, you would be able to see them and they could see you. If not done in such an eyewitness fashion, it would give them much greater access to you in your sleep state and might make it possible for benevolent, philosophical and loving teachers to guide you through the challenges you face these days.

That's beautiful.

Some Thoughts about the Future

Now I would like to talk about a future time of my working with the Explorer Race. In the future, before you reassemble as a Creator and before you are fully engaged in space exploration—really only about 30 to 35 years in the future, during which time your society will be much more benevolent—society will still have some vestiges of the technology you are now experimenting with, meaning manipulative technology made of materials not desiring to be what they are forced into being and sometimes used for manipulating people as well. That technology will be fading out then, but it will still be there. It will be somewhat of a seduction to use it because the new technology will require permission from materials being used. When you have something you're used to using—say, for example, you're eating a meal and using your knife and fork as you've always done because it is so easy to eat a meal that way. What if you suddenly have a method by which you can eat the meal using utensils made of something that consciously participates, but you have to think and act and feel in a new way? You're very hungry and you're going to want to just reach for the knife and fork. But you will be encouraged in many ways to try the new utensils.

As I say, it will be a time during which old technology will still be seductive in the sense that you will want to use it because the new cooperative technology will be a little more challenging. It is then that I will come to work with you; many people will see me, not unlike they see Mother Mary these days and even Mary of the Magdalene and other well-known and beloved images. They will see me, and initially there will be a response like there is in your time now, a reaction to deity or potential deity, but I will do my utmost to change that into being an interaction with a teacher.

I will include humor, but not exclusively. If I must, I will even use god humor so that I do not look too, well, godlike. In this way I will teach the youngsters by the fun they can have interacting with the new technology, for that is always the easy way to retrain a society. The new technology is not really new, but it will be very much like working with the personalities of the stone, the plants and so on. The children will quickly learn how plants communicate, what feelings they have, what different motions mean in plants, yes? They have gestures not unlike your own, and even today if you learn these gestures, you will know what they mean. And there will be all manner of assistance. Let me give you an example.

Today, for instance, you take certain gestures for granted, such as nodding your head for yes or shaking your head for no. That is an obvious gesture you all take for granted, and I don't exclude the fact that you might be able to find some society that says such-and-such was the causal factor. In reality, this really began by mystical people or observant people who were looking at plants and attempting to get some communication from the plant—or conversely, by the plant's attempt to tell you something. If you're not getting it just right, the plant will move its limb from side to side; if you've gotten it, the plant will move its limb up and down. *That's* where nodding and shaking your head actually came from.

And the Children Shall Lead Them

In the future in that civilization I will work at length with children to show them these things. This will allow your society to be led by the children as it transforms from the old technology to the new, really traditional technology. Even today you are getting a glimmer of that. Your children go to school and learn all about computers, and the little ones very often come home, maybe seeing dad or mom struggling with the computer, and jump up and say, "Let's do this" or "Let's do that." It is a standard joke nowadays that the child is able to utilize the computer, being taught at school, but the parents are still trying to figure out what goes where and why. This is a precursor to the new experience. It is a situation in which you are not entirely comfortable, but because of your wonderfully developed sense of humor, you are able to take it in stride and accept it. It prepares you for being shown by the children this level of new communication.

Think about it: What if a plant could say, for example, "When I die" (or cycle in the autumn), "take this part of my leaf and grind it up and combine it with that other leaf over there from a different tree and perhaps some seed pods—not the seeds, but just the outer parts of the pods—and mix this up. It will be the permanent cure for the common cold." Now, plants are ready and willing to tell you this. It is really not best to gather plants when they are growing and attempting to establish life. It is so much better to accept what they have to offer at the moment they wish to offer it.

A plant might say, for example, that "such-and-such a day is the best day to gather this part of myself," giving you an exact day. You might go and talk to the plant every day and say hello. Then the plant says to you, unexpectedly, "This is the day. Do you see that limb over there where my needles are dying out? I have set aside that limb for you, and you can now, today, cut that limb off my body; I am prepared to deal with the discomfort. Take that limb, then I will tell you how you can use different parts of it to make medicines for this and that disease."

The children will be able to accept this very easily, just as you know children can be told about St. Nicholas and accept it because it is beautiful and loving. It is in the nature of children to be able to accept things, so it will be the children that will help that future generation get over all disease as you have known it and help you establish greater communications.

Some plants will even tell you things about your history that you have completely forgotten; this is particularly important in the case of family history. Think about it: Sometimes whole families grow up in a fixed area, especially during the time of farming or ranching communities where it is natural for the new generations to start up someplace nearby and where everybody helps each other. The same trees were there during that time, and it might very easily be possible for people to have forgotten why Grandfather did this or what Grandmother meant by that, or why is it that Uncle Ned is that way, or Aunt Sadie acts like that. They can't remember why, and they'd like to know. The tree, having been there during the entire experience of Ned and Sadie's life, will say (if not that tree, then another), "This is what happened and when, and this is why they act that way now."

Families can become totally reunited when their histories are restored. This is particularly important in the case of tribal peoples who have lost great parts of their tribal wisdom or people who have lost contact with parts of the family who have changed their names or moved elsewhere. It's surprising in this day and age how families and tribal peoples have drifted so much that you sometimes find that people you are at war with or at odds with are actually related to you. When you discover that, it will be very much fun. The children will tell all through the contacts with the plants. I will work with them to help them, of course.

When you said you would work with the children who would come in with these abilities to go through the dimensions, that will be all over the planet, not in any one particular country or place?

Exactly, all over the planet. Even when there's no apparent need, when the people are peaceful and everybody knows where their family is, there will still be an occasional child born with those skills—if for no other reason than to have some member of that mystical group of children exposed to that valuable and enriching culture.

They will be able to teach others to do what they do, then?

They will teach others to some extent, meaning they will teach some to do this and others to do that; they will probably not teach as apprentices are taught these days, where the master teacher teaches everything they can to the apprentice. They will probably have three or four apprentices and teach different ones different things. It would be intended that people will need each other in order to accomplish a single goal or multiple goals.

So much has happened in your modern times with your modern technology that people do not *need* each other in the same way they used to. This is why so many of your marriages do not last. On the farm or the ranch in times gone by, people needed each other to survive, but this is no longer the case for most people. As a result, the love in the marriage must sustain it alone, and if this is not possible, the marriage ultimately breaks up. What is necessary, of course, is to reestablish reasons to need each other.

[Laughs.] Sneaky!

Yes, but effective, wouldn't you say?

Absolutely.

That will really bring Earth people another step toward a universal culture, because on other planets this is very much the case. No one individual is taught everything about their culture. Everyone is taught different segments, so that it requires many to do one thing. In this way everyone feels they are participating in some one thing, and everyone knows that they are not only loved and cherished but, most importantly, *needed*. This is very important.

I'm done now. I wanted to give past, present (counting Lemuria as present) and future contact of civilizations.

You want a question?

Certainly, if you have one.

Isis and the Fairies

Zoosh said you once went to Venus and worked with the fairies.

I have always had a special place in my heart energy for the fairy world, because they have the capacity to not only pass through all the dimensions as these children did—that's why the fairies and these children will be such close friends—but they have also developed over the years the ability to amplify and create benevolence in communications on an interspecies level. If there are enough fairies around, it is possible for a horse to talk in the most benevolent way to a snake or, to use a more biblical example, for the lion and the lamb to communicate as equals, you understand? Because of the presence of fairies, their joy is so pervasive that it performs the function of absolute fulfillment in that moment, even lasting awhile after they are gone, of being totally fed, totally satisfied, completely loved. In other words, all species present there will have all of these benevolent feelings, and the idea or need to attack some other species for survival simply doesn't occur.

Fairies are, in that sense, the ultimate diplomats. They are able, by their simple existence, to create peace and harmony wherever they go. They are more effective in numbers than singly, but a single fairy can be very effective, given exposure to reasonably benevolent people, such as little children. For instance, if antagonists are together, human beings or even animals, it will require many fairies to be present.

So I am greatly involved with them; I have always been involved. I worked at higher levels on Venus with them only because that is where they chose to train in this solar system for the needs that would be required. I work with them a lot. I might add that as a group of individuals, or as companions, as they might describe themselves, they are perhaps the most effective and widely appreciated visitors that attend to the animal and plant kingdoms, as they're called.

They're not elementals, but something completely different?

They are a distinct species unto themselves. If you were to see one, it is surprising how much they look so much like they have been illustrated. I might add that there is a current motion picture [*A Fairy Tale: A True Story*] that is about a child's experience with fairies, but it also goes into the times when there was an attempt to photograph fairies. What the attempt really was, though, was to understand what fairies looked like. The child described what they looked like and the adult wanted to reproduce this in a way that the people of his time could understand. The adult knew that simply drawing them wouldn't do it, since technology as you know it today was just getting started then. That is why the sham of the photographs.

However, I must tell you that the photographs, even though they were not real at that time (there *have* been some photos), the way they were pictured *is* the way they look. They are anywhere from two and a half to three and a half inches tall (occasionally they are four inches tall, but that's rare). They have bodies that look very much like human bodies, and they have wings. In other words, the way you see them pictured *is* the way they look. So children and adults who see them are seeing real beings. Even today in your time, they're allowed to occasionally be seen, but never in such a way as to cause a problem—a sudden experience of seeing one could cause a traffic accident, as you know. They're not allowed to do that. But they are allowed to be seen occasionally, and will reveal themselves usually at the most unexpected time. For those of you out there who have seen them, I will simply say this: Yes, you have.

Where do they live? Are they out of phase with what we see? Are they in another dimension?

They're in another phase. With fairies, even if you have subtle vision and cannot see them, it's easier to know where they've been than to know where they are. They cannot be measured technologically, fortunately, but those who have subtle vision can sometimes see where they've been on the basis of a slight ripple in what you see.

Like a heat wave.

Yes, not unlike a heat wave but without the refractive elements of a heat wave, just a ripple. I will use dimensions for the sake of simplicity of understanding. The primary place where they live is in the fifth dimension, but here on Earth, and they can access everything from the seventh dimension through the third.

Are they ensouled beings?

Oh, certainly. Everything is ensouled, without exception.

I mean, individual souls. You can't be a human and a fairy.

A moment. *Everything is ensouled, without exception.* Think about that. What does that suggest to you?

Everything's alive.

Everything has an individual soul; if it has an individual personality, it must have an individual soul, because personalities are the demonstrations of souls. So every particle, every part of a particle is ensouled. That means that you have your soul, but you as a physical body are a conglomerate, you are within a physical being made up of particles and cells, of which there are trillions of souls. This prepares you as an individual soul to be a portion of some great vastness, which any creator must do. Any creator must get used to living in a creation that is totally saturated with different personalities. Simply being in your body accomplishes that.

But unaware of them.

Yes, unaware though you may be consciously. So yes, every fairy is individually ensouled.

But they're not interchangeable with humans, are they?

Would you be a fairy in one life and a human in another? Not likely, no, because the skills necessary to function as a fairy would be so elaborate and so focused (like being a monk, for instance, though I do not compare the two) that if they were reincarnated, it would require a constant state of being. In the case of fairies, reincarnation is unnecessary; they are immortals.

What are their skills? You talked about the love they radiated, but do they have particular duties?

Yes. It is their duty to be what they are. It's hard to say the beginning of a being that has always existed, but for an analogy to your own existence, in the beginning, a fairy would experience the joy of being and would carry that joy of being into the form of itself as a fairy, and would always maintain the focus of that joy indefinitely. This does not mean a fairy is required to be in places where society is joyless, but if it is allowed to visit such a place, it must maintain that existence. But if it is uncomfortable, as in a joyless place—a war or some place of great suffering—it does not have to go, because it can be a burden. If an immortal being such as this is drained of all of her joy because so many people are suffering and need it, she could be dissipated in her energy and need to go someplace for a long, slow recovery.

Thus they are not required to spend much time in a place that is joyless. That is why children have a certain amount of joy even in a joyless place. If there is a joyful child or a child that could become joyful, even in a joyless place a fairy could go and be seen by that child, and between the two of them they would sustain each other with their energy. The fairy does not take joy from the child to sustain itself, but the child can sustain the joy the fairy feels and projects in its own being, in this way creating almost a third level of joy between them.

I worked at a higher level of Venus with the fairies, training them to interact with the human race, as you are now known, before you came to this planet to become the human race. They didn't need training to interact with the plant world and the natural world, but they did need training to work with the human race, as expressed in the Explorer Race, because of your complicated natures.

Is that what you did on Venus, work with the fairy world?

Yes, that's what I did.

You didn't ensoul the planet, but just worked on that one level with that one group, then?

Yes. I didn't have to ensoul the planet; all planets are fully ensouled on their own [chuckles].

Well, Zoosh phrases it a little differently, so I gave you the wrong impression.

Every being has his or her own point of view.

So a fairy was generated by the Creator, then, from His area of joy in the beginning?

You are asking me how fairies came to be?

Yes.

You might as well ask how I came to be. You might as well ask how *you* came to be.

In the case of anyone coming to be, it is not so much that you are created; it is more that you become aware of your existence after the fact.

Yes, but they were created by the Creator in this creation?

No. They preexisted this creation.

Oh, they came here? They were invited?

They were invited, yes.

By the Creator?

Yes.

At what point during the creation?

Oh, I think that the word went out before the creation, but their presence was not really required until there were planets. Then they were invited to come, and they did.

How Fairies Work with the Planets

Okay, say more about that. What did they do with planets? They bring joy to humans, but how do they do that with planets?

Let's say a planet is formed. It doesn't get formed with trees and animals on it; it is simply formed, yes? It will celebrate its own existence for a time, but then it will, like anyone, wish to have company. The company might take the form of people, as you know people to be, or plants or animals or colors or sounds, musical beings—anything. Planets have each other for company in the beginning, but after a while they ask the question that you all ask at different stages of your life: "Is this all there is?" When any planet asks that, fairies—and other spirits, if needed—come and provide the example of company, then consult with the planet and suggest types of life that the planet might wish to have growing upon or within its surface to accompany and complement the planet, hm?

They don't create the plants, do they?

No, but the planet will then say, "Oh! That looks wonderful," and then it will simply welcome that form of life to come. It will first come as its ensouled being, as in any form of life; the attraction will allow it to come. Perhaps you would have a traveling individual who would come and plant something, or a seed would plant it, or perhaps you would have a spirit that comes and says magically, "How about a tree over there?" *Pouf!*—benevolent magic. There is the tree in all of its glory with the capacity to reproduce itself with seeds. "Let's have some soil," says the magical being. There is enough, and then the magical being goes away and says to the tree, "I will come back in a few million years and see how you are doing," for planets live a long time. That will happen with different forms of life.

I am simplifying it, because to tell you the complicated level would simply turn it into a dusty scientific explanation.

I'm trying to understand: So the fairies that are immortal and have been everywhere know all the plants that are available, so . . .

Why are you saying they have been everywhere? Your assumption is that immortals have been everywhere, isn't it?

Yes!

That's not true. I am immortal; I haven't been everywhere.

You've checked out quite a few places.

But not everywhere.

Not everywhere.

Never assume that immortals have been everywhere. That is a fallacy. Go ahead.

I'm trying to understand fairies. Do they come and picture to the planet what is available—is that one of the things they do?

Yes, they will picture it; fairies have the capacity to reproduce something as you might in a tableau, but with all of the expression. Since fairies have intimate connections to all plants, for example, they would show what the tree looks like, what it smells like, what it would feel like to the planet having roots going down in it, what the tree's needs would be, such as rain, so the planet might need to have water, then what water would feel like and so on. Fairies have the capacity (it's easier for many of them) to show a planet completely what would build up as an ecosystem (to use the scientific word) as a result of the plant's being there. And if it appeals to the planet, then the planet will say, "Yes, let's do this."

Different planets like different things, and the fairies might take years to show one thing after another to a planet until it decides, "Oh, this is what I like." For instance, some planets might like musical beings, beings that don't actually grow in the soil of a planet, but make tones when they communicate, delightful chiming sounds, and simply communicate to the planet that way. Because there is an effect with these tones and because the radiated energy from any vibrated tone will go through the planet, the planet must know what that would feel like—even, for instance, people who make drums out of something or sing songs, what that would feel like. The whole point is to show the planet what these things would feel like so the planet can decide yes or no.

In this way the planet is consulted. It's not like a window box that someone comes along and stuffs seeds into. Someone comes along and says, "There's this and there's this"—you know, the A to Z of life, as it were—"and there's this. Now, what do you think you would like?" And there's no rush; a planet has an eternity to decide what it would like to begin with. If after seeing everything, it decides that it is happy with the visitation of fairies only, it will say, "Then that's how it will be," and the fairies will put the planet on their visitation list and come by regularly. And if the planet should decide after a time that it might like to try a tree or something, the fairies will say, "Oh, well, here we go!" They will ask then for some magical being or somebody passing by or even the devic spirit of such trees, if it is available (if it's not close enough, it might not be available)—someone, anyway—to come by and create that tree. You understand? There are numerous ways to create these life forms.

How did it start? How did the fairies become aware of themselves with this ability? Do they go to all planets?

They go where they're welcome, and if they're not welcome in some place, they exit the area. But they didn't always work with planets; it's just something they *can* do. In the beginning they worked with spirits.

Fairies Assist Souls with Their Initial Journeys

Think of all the souls you have just on this planet. They all started *somewhere* and became aware of themselves. What's the first thing that happens when a soul (or an immortal personality, as Zoosh says) becomes aware of itself? It begins to define itself by the experiences it has.

Well, different beings must work with that soul initially so that it doesn't define itself in some way that could harm itself or other beings. It must have contact almost immediately with joyful spirits, because as it becomes aware of itself, one of the first things it will do is begin to create distance between itself and the larger thing that it was, in order to get on with its life. There will be that certain amount of separation nervousness even though at the same time the spirit of adventure and happiness about going on your voyage is there. So you need someone to encourage you, give you joy and perhaps even suggest places you might wish to go.

The fairies have the capacity to know the various places that would be good for any individual to go, and other places that are either not good for that individual to go or it's too soon for them to go there. Fairies would not be amongst the first beings that contact you, but soon after. In some cases they might be the second or third being (putting it in the case of individuals, even though it might be many of them) that would contact you as you become aware of your individuality. Because they are joyful, have been many places (but not everywhere!) and have seen many things (but not everything!), they can show a great deal. When you become aware of yourself, you are quickly aware of what's immediately around you, but being curious, you might wish to know what you can't see: "Is there something better?" you say. The fairy says, "Well, what about *this?*"

Fairies are very wise and joyful. They do not send you on voyages where you would learn something; they are not teachers per se. They do not send you, but they suggest things to you. They might suggest how to get there, for instance, in order to have a joyful experience in your life. But they are not teachers per se. They might have to teach as a result of something, but that is not their purpose.

More on the Fairies

Do they have some connection to the Pleiades?

Well, you have to understand that the Pleiadian culture, as it has existed until very recently and will continue to exist indefinitely, certainly amongst the children, is very close to the personality of fairies. Their culture is vast and contains many elements, but the Pleiadians greatly value joy, especially for their children. They guard their society so that their children have time to experience the joy of whatever they are learning. There is no slaving away to learn dates and aspects of culture and famous people to be tested on. The joy of learning is instilled, and as much time as needed is allowed for it.

You would certainly find more fairies on the Pleiades (let's use some modern term) per capita, for instance, than you would find on Earth.

A much more comfortable place.

Yes.

Do fairies move around at will? Are they regionalized? Can all fairies move around anyplace, or just around this creation?

They can leave this creation if needed, but they do not. There's plenty to do here.

So they move, they can flow around the whole creation?

They can move around, yes. When they move great distances, of course, they do not fly; they travel in light. For example, a fairy traveling in light might be perceived, as it comes into your immediate surroundings, as a dot of light. You might see it suddenly, very, very bright. It might even have that joyful feeling—it cheers you up all of a sudden. Then when they manifest in their form as they look here, the dot of light will no longer be present. There might be a residual joy, but you probably will not see them as they look here. But think about that now.

Do they look the same everywhere?

No.

Here they look like us, and like Zetas to the Zetas, and like insects to the insects.

Yes, of course. But to the insect world, they might take that form or they might not. Just because human beings are uncomfortable with the appearance of insects does not mean that insects are uncomfortable with the appearance of humans. It's not a natural thing to be uncomfortable with the appearance of other life forms; it is unnatural. In an underlying place of your responsibility, you know it is your job to care for them by learning from them. It's hard for you to consider as equals beings that do not have some similarity to you. How difficult it would be for you if your beloved deities suddenly came amongst you looking like spiders, glowing with gold light and speaking telepathically the great words you have come to know them by. What would you do then?

Is that what they looked like?

No, but suppose they did. They could look like anything. What would you do then, indeed? You do not have to answer that question, but it is something to consider.

Do all beings have that prejudice, then, or just humans?

Just humans. It is very unnatural to have such prejudices. But it is here that such polarities are allowed so that you will have experiences, consequences, responsibilities, results. You have to do things.

But it's only because of our ignorance, then.

It's because of your temporary limits. In other places, the appearance of any life form is assumed to be beautiful, regardless of what it is.

That needs to be said. That's really important.

I might add that to some extent, science is contributing to this by showing molecules and cells and smaller components in life in a beautiful way. It is a small step, but it is a step to prepare you to see larger things in the context of beauty when they are made up of smaller beautiful things.

Did you spend a lot of time with the fairies on the fifth dimension of Venus?

Quite a while, yes; the best I can say would be a hundred thousand years.

And you trained them to work with humans, you said.

I prepared them for what they would have to expect, so I had to go through lots of different potentials—"If this happens, then that happens" kind of things.

You say our timing is 50,000 or 100,000 years? How long do you consider that the Explorer Race has been on this planet?

As you know yourself to be, in terms of the actual experience here, I suppose the earliest arrivals started sprinkling in about 250,000 years ago, but the full-blown population of everyone being the Explorer Race, surely no more than 50,000 years ago. You had some early individuals come in.

Adventurers.

Oh, yes.

In this 50,000 years were the fairies here in the early time or middle time? Are there as many here now as at the beginning?

You are correlating their presence, you understand, to people. But remember, the primary beings they speak to are the plants, the animals—nature. Also, there were people here on this planet before human beings of the Explorer Race ilk were here. It was as easy for them to interact with those natural beings as it would be to interact with plants. You asked if there were more or fewer fairies then. No, there have always been the same number.

Were they able to show themselves? Is it only during the more technological time when they can't show themselves?

Fairies Show Themselves, but Most Don't See Them

They can show themselves; it's just that you don't see them. They've always shown themselves just as much as they are showing themselves today, but most people just don't see them. It helps to be in a reasonably good mood to see them, but it's not required. I know you want a simple explanation for how a person can see fairies anytime. You are not asking that, but you want it.

But I will not give it, because one of the greatest impacts and greatest benefits of what they do is to be unexpectedly seen. It is like suddenly having a vision of great beauty that is all the more pleasing because of its scarcity.

What I was trying to get at is, weren't we able to see them more then?

People were able to, yes. And there are still people today who see them with regularity. Certainly many people see the little dots of light a lot. Not all dots of light are fairies, of course, but some are. There is a way to know. When you see one of these little dots of light and suddenly, regardless of your mood, your mood is elevated and you feel much more cheerful for no particular reason, then you can be sure at least 95 percent of the time that it was a fairy.

Will we see and interact with them even more in the fourth dimension.

Yes, but not because they can show themselves better, but because when you are in the fourth dimension you will be more in balance. You will no longer be technological man; you will no longer be so unhappy or, as you say, polarized. And you will no longer deny what you see simply because your culture does not approve of it.

We will be more technological, but it will be a loving . . .

You will be much *less* technological.

Much less?

Crystals Are the New Technology

Oh, much less. You don't need the level of technology you have today. Look around; the entire house is made from technology and it is filled with technology. You don't need all that. Suppose you put a crystal on the ground, and it is a sheltering crystal. You ask the crystal in the nicest way possible, "Can you create a beautiful shelter for me that my family and I might occupy?" With the proper tones you sing and ceremonies and so on, the crystal creates it [snaps fingers], just like that. That is less technology.

The crystal creates a shelter?

Yes, a home. It would be a home of light. If necessary—"Oh, I need a bed to lie down in"—a bed would be there, you understand? When you didn't need the bed to lie down in, it wouldn't be there anymore. Why have something in your way? Why have some light make a bed if it is not needed in that moment? You won't have to make your bed in the morning! You just get up, it uncreates itself, and when you're ready to lie down, it's there! Isn't that nice? And that's less technology.

I'm looking forward to it.

Yes, the technology will be quite a bit less. Or you might have travel crystals: "We need a vehicle," and you don't need gasoline for the vehicle. "We'd like to travel in a group, the ten of us. We'll sit in a circle, put the travel crystal in the middle, and ask it to make a nice vehicle to surround us and provide a means by which we can travel anywhere on Earth, in the stars or wherever we need to go." Something simple like that. So the travel crystal creates something [snaps fingers] that works for both you and the crystal. And when you get to where you need to go, you don't need the vehicle because you're there. You go out and do what you're going to do there. One of you picks up the crystal, puts it in her pocket or in a little container the crystal likes to ride in, and when you're ready to go back or go on, you ask the crystal to re-create the ship. *Less* technology.

No one has talked like that before. Crystals—like these?

Crystals like crystals, yes.

So I might have a travel crystal here and not even know it?

Oh, yes. That is part of the reason it's important not to mine them too much, because they become what they will be the same way people do—by growing and being allowed to be cultured in their own colonies. But I do not wish to charge you too much; that is what your society is doing now; it is a step on the way to learning how to interact with crystals.

We are visited by the rain, yes?

Yes.

For the sake of the reader, there is a pleasant rain arriving now in response to the needs of the growing things outdoors, since they have stated, "Rain would be nice!"

Well, we're getting a lot more rain in the last year or so than we did before. Is that because the plants are getting better at calling for it?

Mother Earth, not unlike you after a hard day of work, washes herself more vigorously these days.

I didn't realize that crystals can do such things.

Even today people are talking about it, you know. Your science is using crystals for so many things. You will make mistakes; that is how you learn. There are people amongst you now who are working with this. They haven't arrived there yet, but they can imagine it. They can plan on how it might be, they can spread their ideas and art and literature. And once an idea becomes spread about that much, well, you know the old story—that yesterday's science fiction . . .

. . . is today's science fact. You're helping us by painting pictures to help us create this reality.

Yes, not unlike the fairies, I am suggesting ways of life, and if it is appealing to you, you might try it. But I am not imposing it, I'm just saying, here's how it could be; wouldn't it be nice to not have to make your bed in the morning? And not have to be bothered by having it in your way? Yes, as you say, not to have to wash the dishes! How nice. When they are needed, they are there.

All right, thank you.

Good night.

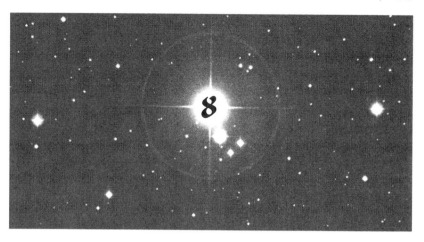

Orion's Transition and Its Application to Earth

November 20, 1997

Orion Transitions to a More Spontaneous Expression

Isis here. Some time ago some members of the Explorer Race were passing through the Orion system. There was a great deal of turmoil in those days in Orion because it was beginning to move away from an organized system of civilization to the more artistic or spontaneous civilization they have now. If you go to Orion now, the planets there, you will find artistic civilizations, not unlike the art you find here but perhaps with a different expression, because of the availability of cooperative technology (meaning matter around you) that participates in the art from its own desire rather than being manipulated to do so. You will find that art might be more colorful—liquid light and such as this.

Before this happened there was a transition from the more structured society (not unlike what you have now here on Earth) to that allowing place, and it was difficult. The people felt then that it was essential to have a structured society and that spontaneous expression be reserved only in certain very precise and allowable circumstances, such as between couples—lovemaking, for example—or in creative solutions for complex problems where people would have to dream up ideas that may not be the usual application if the usual application has not worked.

Isis' Emissaries Arrive in Orion

Those levels of spontaneity were there just as they are in your society, but their control mechanisms were more pronounced than yours are now. I visited there, or sent a portion of myself in the form of emissaries, to encourage the change in this way. My emissaries approached the more influential members of the society that were involved in control and in perpetuating the structure or levels of society into a future where they were no longer needed. I suggested that my emissaries arrive somewhat grandly, because the society would not usually change without being visited by beings that seemed larger than life.

Since in those days the warrior society was no longer as powerful as it once was, but was entrenched into the more political aspects of the day-to-day government, my messengers had to be very sophisticated—able to speak the language of the planet and relate easily to any member of society with a level of intimacy that would suggest that my emissaries knew everything about the personal lives of the individuals. This was not to upset them, not to speak of these things in public, but to make it clear that my emissaries were somehow larger than life without appearing overly godlike. There would be somewhat of a glow about them, but nothing so obvious that it would create a sensation. When I say glow, it is similar to what you say even today about the appearance of a woman with child, for instance, who takes on "a special glow." The term "glow" is the best we can come up with to describe a feeling more than a physical appearance.

My emissaries arrived in a ship that was fairly solid, but had enough qualities of light that hostile actions based on fear would not harm it in any way and those weapons would be transformed into something benevolent. This would tend to get the attention of the military and political authorities and also soothe them, showing that the approaching emissaries had no hostile intent. Also, for some weeks beforehand messages were broadcast on a personal level, not to governmental entities, but to all individuals; people there started having shared dreams (everybody had the same dream, and eventually they noticed it and started talking about it), visions or even daydreams that people were coming who were going to make a difference. The newcomers would make it easier for everyone to get along and would give teachings and techniques that would allow the people to transform themselves, their societies and their worlds into places that were more compatible with each other as well as other worlds from other galaxies.

Some people, of course, took it as a threat, but most people took it as some kind of religious experience. My emissaries were fairly careful to avoid being classified as deities, but they allowed themselves to be perceived as special because they needed to be influential. There were about 140 of them, and they went to different planets, different peoples and so on. They circulated freely for about 18 years of experiential Earth time, during which they talked to the children, the adults, the elderly; they talked to people in authority and people who were average citizens. They made their best effort to talk to everyone—or if not everyone in the conscious state, at least everyone in the sleeping state, with vivid dreams about how to practice individuality in a way that was nonthreatening.

What This Means to Your Now Understanding

This contact with the Explorer Race is vital to your now understanding of who you are. People here have a vague feeling that they need to be rescued or will be rescued from what seem to be overwhelming problems of society, because it has happened before, in terms of ships coming to get you on societies on this planet, but even more in terms of your travels on other planets, such as this example I am giving you.

That was allowed, you see, on Orion because you were continuing to move toward Earth. Orion was not the challenging school that Earth is. Orion in those days did not have wars; although it did not have complete freedom, it did not have wars, nor were there even pitched battles between individuals. There were no weapons, even ceremonial ones, and if people had arguments, they would not come to blows. There were similarities—arguments did occur, even heated arguments, but not violence in terms of a contact experience.

I mention this now because my emissaries stayed there for 18 years. After 15 years, for the next few years they said, "We are going to be leaving soon," so the people had to begin applying what they had taught them. Up to that point in time, most people were talking about it or had little groups where they would practice things, but they had not really put it into effect. But from the fifteenth to the eighteenth year of my emissaries' presence, there was a crash program, as you call it, to integrate the levels of what was being taught so that people could take a chance and lift controls to see what would happen. Of course, in your time now, this couldn't happen overnight. It was different there because there was no fear of overt violence, but there was an underlying need to create predictable order.

You see, the society you have now in the United States, where you say it is a society that is at least *intended* to be a society of law and order—the most attractive element in that statement is *law*, because it is, on the face of it, equally applied to all individuals. The seductive element is *order*, because order requires a certain level of control and, more importantly, creates or projects predictability into the future so that plans made today can be applied in the future with reasonable certainty that it will be safe.

In terms of Orion, they were removing that level of predictability and safety, and they had to become almost overnight (in their perception, although it was over three years), infinitely more flexible with their plans; things would blossom, and people who had previously been well-ordered members of society—allowed to be creative only within a narrow band of their job description or personal lives—would suddenly come up with solutions for all levels of society's problems. Although that seems constructive, when a society is very structured, it can be upsetting.

The reason I am bringing this up is that this is very much what you are involved with now. On Orion, as with you here, more flexibility is ultimately needed. When you make future plans, there must be contingency plans, not "what-if" plans like present contingency plans. Any plan will have to be rooted in sand rather than in firmer clay, because resolutions are likely to come faster than your plan might suggest. This is because the creativity level of the individual will be so amplified that by the time your five-year plan would come into practical application in your world here or on Orion, you would already have the solutions in place so that you can move the level of your plans, rewards, experiences or production well past any predictions for success.

When I worked with this society, I was really planting seeds for the future. They were able to adapt these things very well, much better than they felt they would, and it created a bridge to move from their ordered society into their more spontaneous and artistic society, which they have now. Many of you (not all, but many) had lives during that time on Orion or had wisdom in other lives that studied that time in Orion. Orion became a model for changing a society from something that was precisely structured to something that was more free and flowing.

As a result, in your time you will have the depth to be able to pull up some of this experience and, even in the polarity of your society, reconstruct your future plans in a more flexible way. I might add that the polarity you experience now requires a degree of flexibility in all future plans, but won't it be nice in the future when that flexibility will allow for greater, more immediate solutions? Instead of being at point 3 on the 1 to 10 scale, within five years you will be at point 9!

Is this the incident that Zoosh calls the daughter of God coming to the warriors on Orion?

No, this is later in time when the society was already in transit. As I said, the warriors in the time I am referring to had already entrenched themselves into the political bureaucracy and were no longer active warriors.

The Emissaries of Isis

What was your relationship with the emissaries? Were they women?

Oh, certainly, yes.

Were they women you had worked with and trained? Where did they come from?

They were portions of myself, literally.

Literally?

Literally portions of myself. As such they were individuals, but they were portions of myself. When they left, they came back and were part of myself again. They did not have linear lives, so they were individuated portions of me.

And you created bodies for them?

You have studied some shamanism; it was not unlike a shaman asking for volunteers of a portion of a plant. I asked the matter from the immediate galaxy of Orion (so that the beings could fit in) to volunteer to be portions of these bodies for the 18 or so years they would be activated and involved in Orion society—and the ship too was made up of this. When the ship left, the organic matter—the bodies, the ship and the objects they used—would return, if it chose to continue its life, to what it had been doing before. But the energy of the ship and the beings returned to me.

So you had a lot of fun—you made them young, old, all classes, all . . .

Yes, a variety that would fit in, but no greater variety than the citizens of Orion had. Some would be youthful and could relate to the children, and some would be older and could relate to the older beings. Some would be influential or have a conscious awareness of how an influential society works, and some would be craftspeople—simple people with a wisdom of how certain things would work. Within those structures and others, they could flexibly move about society with a personal awareness of every individual. Let's say a person approaches you who feels benevolent and you take a walk with the person. The person talks to you and brings up examples from your life you can directly relate to because the teaching relates to the exact experiences of your life. You would be certain to pay them extra-special attention. So they were very effective and attention-getting, and because of that level of intimacy, very unthreatening.

What was the population?

At the time of all of the associated planets? Let me get some numbers for you . . . a little less than a billion, about 950,000,000.

What percentage of those beings did your 140 selves talk to?

Everyone, every single one. They didn't have to sleep, of course, so if not in person, then in dreams. If done in dreams, they would have the same conversation; everything in that dream would be exactly the same for at least three nights in a row. It would be a vivid dream, so that after the third night the person would remember it almost exactly as if it were a physical experience.

Now, in terms of the percentage of those Explorer Race individuals who were in the Orion system at that time, about 15 percent of them were Explorer Race, about five percent of which have come to Earth and are here now. There are enough that the depth of that experience is available. As is typical with Orions, they are spread out all over on the Earth in all levels of society. One thing about Orion-heritage or Orion-focused people is that they always like variety. They don't like repetitive things; they can do them, but they prefer variety. They are spread out in all walks and classes of life, in all different types of expression of life, races, nationalities and so on. Every group of individuals all over the planet will have someone there—maybe several—who has the depth of that experience in their soul tree.

Do you plan to restimulate that now?

It is unnecessary. Just think, the feelings that so many people have been having for a long time—even before the "new age"—the desire for being rescued and saved. All of these feelings correlate directly to times when your society was rescued and saved and also to this experience. The need and expectation of being rescued and saved, tends to bring to the surface these lessons for reinvention in the form of stories, writings, entertainments, intellectual ideas, applications and inventions that will all lead to a much greater acceptance of spontaneity.

For example, think of education. In previous years, even 50 years ago, education was very regimented. There were certain topicsr—eading, writing and arithmetic, as they say—and these topics were drilled into the student with a religious fervor. In any school you will now find programs that encourage children to be more personally creative. Sometimes it will be in the form of problem-solving: here's a problem; how would you solve it? In other circumstances the social conditions of the school require the child to be able to solve the problem of getting along with this or that group of people when totally unprepared for such things from home experiences. In other words, flexibility in education is now absolutely integrated, whereas just 50 years ago education was very rigid.

A New Approach to Problem Solving

So you looked at the situation in Orion and said, "Well, how can I help?" Then you formulated a plan. What was the structure at that time? Was it similar to the one we had here? What was the structure you were dealing with?

The structure was an entrenched political bureaucracy. For example, if a new form of art—say, street theater (picking something that is popular, especially in other parts of the world, and in some places in the United States as well), as a new art form there—a bureaucratic council would apply rules about when and where the street theater could be, how many members could be involved, issue permits and so on. It was so structured that it was a bureaucracy gone wild. It tended to stifle art, but art is often the problem *and* the solution. Art tends to encourage people to be more. It very rarely discourages people from being more and almost invariably *encourages* them to be more, even requiring that you be more.

For instance, when modern art first came out, most people (the average viewer, not the artist) were utterly baffled. It stimulated an entire group of people who would interpret modern art. Even if the interpretation had nothing to do with what the artist was intending, it stimulated entire realms of intellectual thought. In your time there are mechanisms in place to stimulate not only the problems that will lead to solutions, but those that lead to solutions that will underline and expose problems you didn't know were there. Very often a solution will seem to be perfect, but will leave something out—it won't apply to all people equally, for example; or it seems to be perfectly suited to every individual, but it forgets children, or it forgets the needs of the elderly, thereby requiring flexibility in the future.

Yes, like airbags, which killed some people and could be dangerous.

Yes, airbags—exactly. It looked like they were going to be the fantastic solution, but now you discover that you have to reinvent airbags.

And be flexible about what cars you put them in.

That's right, and *where* you put them and how they are deployed and so on.

Back to Orion: You have a politically entrenched bureaucracy. What was your plan? How did you do it?

Just the way I said. We reassured the bureaucracy (which is people) that predictability was rooted in the past because it perpetuated all known things into the future, including all your discomforts—because they are predictable, you can count on them happening. In order to change that it would be necessary for people to discover what they had in common as well as be reminded of how vulnerable, how tender and how universal their experience really was.

When I sent these teachers to speak intimately to individuals, those individuals would speak to each other after these experiences, ofttimes to friends and family: "How did she know this about me?" and "You mean you had that experience, too?" It stimulated a vast amount of sharing of information that before this had been secret. If a complete stranger suddenly starts speaking to you about intimate experiences in your life that relate to their teaching, invariably a questioning process begins by which you start talking to your friends about it and experiencing a feeling that the isolation of your personal experience (in your time called alienation) is much more common than you realized. Because you were able to find a solution for this experience—or because some of these women teachers were able to find a more benevolent solution that worked for your problem—you didn't have to use the old system that perpetuated your familiar discomforts into the future. The new solution would apply not only to your individual problem, but as you talk amongst your fellow beings, you discover that the exact solution that worked for your problem seemed to work for other people with their problems even though their problems sounded different.

Then because you were a thinking being and not foolish, you came to realize that problems tend to be very similar and in no way as complex as they seem. You came to that conclusion quickly, because you realized that a single solution covered many different problems for many different people. That's when you realized on Orion that you could allow that system, once it was in place, to resolve problems. You didn't have to bring your past pain into the present and the future; you could simply use the method of resolution in more open communication with fellow beings around you, and the culture would assimilate these ideas. Problems could be easily resolved no matter how individual they seemed to be.

This is basically the formation of a culture's philosophy, in this case, Orion's philosophy. What it did was simply allow their philosophy to become more universal. Instead of having alienated or isolated individuals caught up in a huge bureaucracy that perpetuated their pain (but gave them predictability), you had connected individuals who were able to come together and resolve their problems, allowing them to trust each other much more and ultimately form greater friendships with people they wouldn't usually approach. And of course they were able to become more loving, more relaxed and more trusting of the way life tends to resolve any problem. Just as water flows through a gully, if it comes to a stop where it can go no farther, it will have to build up pressure behind the blockage until it can push the block out of the way or flow over the top, but it will resolve. In a very controlled bureaucracy, they might instead bring in dynamite and blow up the block, possibly causing problems in the future, because who knows what other damage dynamite will do? This is why in your time, the more complex society gets, the more methods of problem-solving that are invented, reinvented and, most importantly, applied.

Things Are Now Going Well on Your Planet

So do you plan to come and visit us now?

I am going to wait, because I think things are going very well. You are inventing this problem-solving and are being forced somewhat to become more sincere, but not from the mind. The mind can be sincere, say something that it absolutely means in the moment, but because it doesn't fulfill the heart's true desires, it can forget about that sincere promise. But when you make a promise based on your heart's desire, it is as if you begin doing work that is a pleasure and get paid for it. Then to fulfill a promise made from your heart's desire (work or education or simple relationship issues), you can easily fulfill that promise because you will be doing something you enjoy doing, and you integrate it into your life on a daily basis. When you see that person again, you are doing what you promised them you would do because it is your pleasure to do it. It is not work then, it is not struggle—it is not even compromise; it is being natural. Then you have made the choice to be the natural being that you are, with your individual gifts and talents that are centered in your heart, not in your mind.

So you are going to look around for a few years?

You are doing quite well. You do not need me to send the emissaries. If you need it, then I will send a few—not as many, because it is not many planets; I will send perhaps ten or twelve. I don't think you'll need them.

It's only one planet, right? You wouldn't go to the other planets in the system.

No, not necessary.

Well, that's pretty good. For a while it looked like we weren't going to make it, but everything's changed in the last . . . how many years?

Oh, I think the big changes that suggest that you will definitely make it (99 percent chance) have happened in the last seven years. A lot of it has to do with increased communication, because when people talk they discover how alike they are. But a lot of it also has to do with the increased awareness of your need for each other. In terms of the business community, the business community is totally interconnected, involved, enmeshed. One business might produce wheels, but they need to put the wheels on something, and another business produces parts but has no wheels. This is the way of business all over the world. So business has been forced out of necessity to become less competitive and more cooperative, shifting the experience of teams *against* each other to teams *with* each other—one big team working together. And because your business tends to gradually percolate into your community in the United States, what you have is a society imitating your economics. That's how you really get started.

Of course, you have these communication systems now that are getting more and more personal all the time. You can talk to people all over the world, not just by sending letters and waiting for weeks, but now you type something into a computer. Soon you will be able to easily speak into the computer and get the response back from your friend in Swaziland who will say, "Yes, and this is how I solved that problem." Your friend says, "Oh, I am having this difficulty with my youngster," and you will say, "I had that too, and this is what I did." Although the level of technology and economics may not be the same, in my experience resolutions of the heart always apply equally everywhere.

Just a few years ago it was considered acceptable to go to war and force people, but now it's not. This has a lot to do with the business community, because business has become more interlinked. When the United States says, "You'll do it because we say so" (I am not saying the U.S. is a bully, but that this has become an entrenched bureaucratic reaction), the rest of the world's businesses or governments say, "No, no. You can find a peaceful solution. We won't support you in this; we did before, but not this time."

As a result, the United States finds a way to save face and the rest of the world allows that. Then a solution is found. After all, you don't bring people into your system by sticking them with a sword; that destroys them. As they say, you get more with an olive branch.

Governments and businesses are often leaders in ways they don't expect, and they are also followers in ways they don't expect. I cannot tell you how often business leaders or leaders in education or politics have simply observed children, frequently their own, squabbling about something and then coming up with a solution that on the surface seems very simplistic—and their minds immediately apply this to their own problems.

That's why the increased level of communication is so necessary, so that people can see how things are really so much on an even footing. Once you apply other people's solutions within the context of your problems, they tend to work out if they are heart-centered—not just offered with love, but associated with what the individuals in that larger system really want to do for themselves. That's why someday people will be spoken to as youngsters (not unlike the sacred living tribal peoples of your time, some of which still exist), and the youngster will be understood—not programmed, but understood.

The elders will say, "He seems to be good at this," or "She seems to have a natural ability for that." This would be studied for a time without interfering with the child, without saying, "Why don't you try it *this* way?" but letting them just discover things on their own without giving them toys. And by the time the child is four or five years old, you as the elder or the observer understand completely what is the best avenue to encourage the child in—not to require, but to encourage the child so that he or she can blossom.

When the child is encouraged and nurtured this way, it will become a natural experience for the child to choose in the future what is naturally their heart's choice, as the generations come up. They will go into occupations they enjoy doing and have a natural ability for instead of one they have no natural abilities for and have to work very hard at— never discovering or working in avenues or applications where they have a great talent and could offer solutions and inventions that would be wonderful and needed by society.

And enjoy it.

And enjoy it, that's right, so that work becomes pleasure. As anybody knows who has begun or is involved in work as pleasure, there is no comparison; money doesn't make any difference. If you are doing something you love to do, getting paid for it is a bonus. I am not speaking impractically here, because very soon in your societies this will become an absolute foundation, a cornerstone. Polarities, challenges, problems, battles and fights constantly remind people that they are doing things they don't want to be doing, and that's why they are fighting. How can we help them do what they want to do in ways that are good for them and us? This is really what business is coming into now at the higher levels of its future planning, and as this perks down it'll perk into your society. At the same time, education and the family as a unit are coming to the same conclusions, to say nothing of what children are doing spontaneously on their own. So everyone here is very soon going to meet in the middle and discover that they are all talking about the same solution in their own unique language. [Chuckles.]

That's why so many people are on the planet now, because it is really quite a marvelous time to be alive. It is one thing to enjoy life; it is pleasurable. But it's another thing to see life that is complex—at least seemingly—and needs a great deal of assistance, then live through that and see the change. That is *exciting* and highly fulfilling, is it not?

The Veil and the Blue Portal

November 25, 1997

Isis speaking. The acquaintanceship of individuals with substances—meaning that which can be touched or sensed—is way down on Earth at this time. I'd like to encourage people to touch things with more contours, especially that which is still connected to Earth: rock faces, the soil, if you like, water—especially that which is running on its own accord through its own channels. The disconnectedness of the average Earth person with the planet upon which you are now in residence is a problem, because for Earth to let you know that something is amiss requires drama on her part.

Using Touchstones to Reconnect to Mother Earth

It would be much simpler if you all had what used to be referred to as a touchstone. A touchstone does not mean what it has come to mean. A touchstone is not something you carry with you or that is small enough to be taken into the house. A touchstone is something that is actually on the land all the time and is generally not moved. In times gone by in places such as northern England, it was understood that touchstones were not to be moved; they were to be touched. In more recent times this worked its way into Celtic religions and practices as holy or sacred shrines, rocks such as this. But in reality touchstones are usually quite large. They would not be convenient to move, much less would most people consider it.

The real purpose for the touchstone is simply to come into greater contact with Mother Earth. The more ancient touchstones are actually grooved because they've been touched so much. Sometimes it was to give Mother Earth an acquaintanceship with those who have moved into an area. People would go, lured by the shaman or holy person of their tribe or clan, and touch the stone with their right hand. Sometimes the shaman or holy people would use some other part of the body to touch the stone, but the average person would touch the stone either with their fingertips or their flat palm, leaving it there for a moment or two so the Earth could know they would be living in the area.

The other familiar use of touchstones was when a shaman or holy person would use his or her left hand, usually just the fingertips, sometimes not even touching the stone, to connect with Earth to see how *she* was feeling, what she could provide—or, more often than not, what she needed that the people could provide.

For those of you who live in a place where you can find a boulder or a stone that does not move easily, I suggest that you see if it is a touchstone. How will you know? You will know because it will seem to have been touched a lot, or it might draw you. You might look at it and feel you want to touch it, or you might simply feel that you want to know what Mother Earth knows there. Mother Earth's body is like your own: You have arms, legs, feet; Mother Earth has different parts of her body. Touchstones in Alaska or Iceland might relate to different parts of Mother Earth's body than in Chile or South Africa.

I mention this now because ancient peoples, some of whom have descendants living amongst you today, know these things, yet the more ancient tribal or clan customs do not usually come out to the public. Sometimes hints are given or illustrations, even ceremonies or masks, perhaps, that give hints. But nowadays in modern society, as you know yourself to be, you need to have elaborate explanations. Sometimes the explanations are stimulating and interesting; other times the words go on too long and you need to have a physical experience.

I suggest that you see if you can find the touchstones in your area. If they feel good to touch, touch them or come close to them—within three, four or even six inches, whatever's right for you. Touch them in ways that feel right to you. For example, if you wish to let Mother Earth know that you are there for a while or living nearby, touch the stone with your right hand. If on the other hand you want to know something about Mother Earth or get a feel about how she's feeling, then touch or come close to touching with your left hand.

This is a great experience for meditation groups or spiritual families to come together to do these things, because not everyone will feel the same thing. It can be a group activity. This is not news to you, but I am recommending it because the intimacy between you and Mother Earth has become so much less in the past 25 years that both you and Mother Earth could greatly benefit if you, as mobile beings, could take the first step.

Mother Earth has in recent times (the past 400 years or so) had to demand your attention, because the old readers of signs that suggest wonders are not in your midst much anymore, or else their visions get only limited broadcast, usually to groups of individuals still practicing the older sacred ways. The new shamans, as you might call yourselves, need to go out, find places to be touched on the Earth and bring people to touch them—either to expose Mother Earth intimately to you (touching Mother Earth with your palm is intimate for her) or feel something from her. So I urge you to begin.

That's very helpful. Do you have another anecdote or vignette of your experience with the Explorer Race that you'd like to share?

Let me consider that a moment.

The Explorer Race and the Blue Portal in the Veil

There was a time when the Explorer Race was passing through what I would call a veil. Before you came to this more difficult and responsible time of training on Earth, even before you came to this general part of the universe, you went through a time in which you did not incarnate physically very much. It's hard to put a time on this, but it was before your arrival on Orion and before any of you even manifested on the Pleiades or Andromeda or other places that have been allowed to have contact with you.

So you were in an intermediate time, really not sure if you wished to proceed, because proceeding would mean more drama, a greater testing of the skills you had acquired up to that point. There would also be responsibility, consequences and tests, and as you know, even in the spiritual world testing can be intimidating. So you were holding back, and no one in the Explorer Race had yet manifested a life through the veil that would require testing and responsibility to the extent you have it now.

I personally waited for a time; I felt that holding back for 50,000 years or so was not a terrible thing. Simply sharing amongst yourselves the mutual experiences would be worthwhile, and also finding out what some of the bolder explorers had been doing. Basically, networking (if I might use a contemporary term) would be acceptable. But after the 50,000 experiential years went by, I personally felt that it was time to encourage those who would pass through that veil to begin doing so. I could see clearly that the level of responsibility had intimidated you, so I went to the veil and illuminated a section of it with a blue light that was very loving. I created within that light an experience like a screen by which you could see potentials (not great dramas) for experiences, consequences that might evolve, teaching techniques, growth and also benevolent experiences that would be an outgrowth of a greater physicality of the Explorer Race.

Up to that point in time the experience of physicality and the affection that goes with physicality—as the simple exchange of physical joy between individuals, petting a cat or dog, enjoying riding a horse, getting your hands in the soil, seeing corn grow and eating it fresh off the stalk—all of these things had not really been experienced on the vital, physical level. So I encouraged the more adventurous members to pass through that particular blue portal in the veil to try lives on Orion and the Pleiades of times gone by, to consider lives on Andromeda and Sirius—and yes, to explore the more dramatic places where you would be.

This was, I feel, a contribution that *I* needed to make, one that perhaps only I could make at that time. Everyone who would energetically pass through the blue portal in the veil that brought people into greater physicality (or its potential) needed to know that there would be nurturing, not just drama. So at that time, as people passed through the portal I was creating, I touched their lives so that in their next incarnation (or even several incarnations) they would feel the energy of Isis that would carry them through the initial experiences of physical consequences and responsibility, the physical application of what had once been theories and hypotheses—in other words, the primary experiences of what you have moved through in your now time, that would prepare you for the lives you are living now.

Many amongst you today are still experiencing the Isis energy I placed on that veil; the threads that lead back directly to me allow my energy to be more amongst you without my actually interfering in your learning process, and they also allow the depth of my energy to be expressed through these individuals. Many of them have no idea that the warmth and nurturing that seems to be just below the surface for them, readily available for them and others through them, has anything to do with me. But many *do* know. And in my experience this has been largely beneficial for you.

Beautiful! At that time, how many had decided to come through?

At which time?

Before they went through the blue part of the veil.

At that time you really weren't physicalized. You stopped having bodies as you know them to be, even higher-dimensional ones. You weren't doing that. Many beings had already completed their Explorer Race experience and were waiting, but the ones who were set to go on had not moved on. There were populations all over this universe, but the Explorer Race was either waiting because they had completed, or the ones who were going to go on had not yet gone on. So at that time there weren't any Explorer Race populations living in a culture in bodies.

What was our fear?

It wasn't a fear; it was what I would call a reluctance to accept the responsibility of your own actions. Up to that point in time you were observing, you were experiencing; but you were largely led, or there were beings or people who guided you. Thus you didn't have to feel a great sense of personal, individual responsibility for your actions, which you have now. That might sound strange to you now, but then you were functioning in what could be called clans or tribes, cultures that were synonymous with hierarchies.

There were appointed members, usually born through a bloodline, who would be responsible if any individual caused an action for which there were significant consequences. You could interact somewhat with actions and consequences for the mass of people, but most of the people did not have to deal with significant consequences. As you know, hierarchies tend to be isolating because the same individuals tend to reincarnate in bloodlines. Basically, I felt the need to encourage you to broaden the responsibility.

The Wisdom Trackers

What about this group that was already finished? Had they leapt out and taken responsibility, or didn't they need the depth of experience that we had to go through?

That wasn't their job. Everyone in the Explorer Race does not have to do *everything* They had completed what they came here to do. They acquired a skill or an experience or an action or an energy, and they put it somewhere—they went somewhere, they lived, they walked there, they did what they did and they left behind the energy of having been there. If they had a physical body, that physical body stayed on the planet and then they were gone, but those parts of the physicality that made them up were affected by what they did and what they knew.

It's rather like a teacher going somewhere, walking amongst his or her students—teaching, yes, but also leaving behind the physical imprint of having been there. That physical imprint would give the planet or the land itself the knowledge and wisdom and potential to pass on to some other being who would manifest there, either another being of that culture or someone visiting—whoever was born there and was made up of that physical matter.

Many of them had done that already. They were, in a sense, what I would call the wisdom trackers. They came in, they had something to do, they learned a skill, they became wise with it (as in a teacher), they walked where they were supposed to walk, they left what they were supposed to leave behind and then they were done. But they didn't have to do everything; everybody doesn't have to do everything.

It seems that those on the planet now are doing more than the first ones.

Think about that for a moment. It seems, you said, that those on the planet (meaning Earth now) are doing more than the others, but think about that. What if those who came here first and placed knowledge and wisdom here hadn't come? How does a succession follow if there's nothing to succeed? I cannot agree with you that the people here now are doing more; it's rather that the people here now are doing *their part*. Those who preceded you either on this planet or other planets where you incarnated before you came here as a member of the Explorer Race, did their part so *you* did not have to do it. It's like having a factory; you can produce things in a factory, but only if others have produced the machines that you are using and perhaps trained the people. You can do because others have done before you.

If all these came from three seed beings, how did this division of who does what get allocated?

No different than how it happens now. Now you might have a life in which you do some one main thing in variation, and as a result you acquire a great deal of skill with that one thing. You might have several lives like that. It's no different.

When those beings were recycled through Creator and came out and fragmented gradually into more and more beings, more and more parts of the Explorer Race, some incarnated here, some there. They did this and that and acquired wisdom. Sometimes (this is important to understand) they acquired wisdom that they personally had no use for. This is very important because it's so relevant in your time. Even in your time you have people who acquire wisdom for which they have no personal use. Yet they go places—they walk, they step on the soil, they leave their mark, they leave a portion of themselves behind. They leave particles of themselves and integrate those into the Earth. Those particles will recycle through other beings, and perhaps those other beings will need this wisdom that they have never acquired in any of their personal experience. By having even a single particle in their physical selves that has been associated with another being who had that wisdom, they will be able to access it when it is needed. It might be needed by them, by someone in their family or group, or someone they are assisting.

Think about this. Some of the beings who finished before they had to go through that veil were learning wisdom; sometimes a whole life would be devoted to learning wisdom that they personally would never need in any of their incarnations (before they rejoined to become the total being of the Explorer Race Creator). You might say that on the one hand, it's a personal sacrifice; but on the other hand, they were doing something that would benefit others in the future.

Most of the time they had no awareness of this, and that is good. If you spend too much time doing things you know will benefit others in the future but for which you personally have no apparent use, you can sometimes get into a cycle of that and go round and round, telling yourself, "This is going to help somebody else in the future, so I will do it." This is how people will sometimes get off track.

So it is useful to *not* know; if you don't know, you can then acquire or utilize the best of that experience that does fit into your life, even if it is wisdom that defines the edges of the experience. When the experience itself has no personal application in your life, but the wisdom that *defines* the wisdom you had to acquire in order to get that wisdom—*that* you can often use. This is so only because you do not realize that you are acquiring wisdom for others and seeding it into the planet so that others can use it in the future.

If you think about this, it will remind you how much of a whole being the Explorer Race really is. Science has informed you (to the extent that it can understand your body) that you have cells and organisms in your body that merrily go here and there and do this and that in your body, performing a function designed specifically and only for something *they* do—not in any way designed to be consciously, directly associated with something that you personally want them to do. What you experience, then, is no real awareness of what your white blood cells or red blood cells or antibodies are doing; you are not conscious of their doing anything, but they are busy nonetheless. It is what they do; but in the larger sense, because they are doing what they are doing, it allows *you* to exist. What I've just said is a direct analogy to what I previously said: Because other beings have done what they did, because you do what you are doing, then others can exist, utilizing what you or others have done. In that way you are really one part of a larger organism that is constantly connected.

Birth of the Dream World

You don't usually think about this, but I'll give you an example that you (the reader) can identify with. Everyone takes dreaming for granted; people dream. There have been a lot of explanations for what this or that dream or this or that symbol means. I'm not going to discuss that so much, but what about the energy, the capacity to dream? I will tell you this: Creator understood that when you, as the Explorer Race, were going to come here, one of your most vital needs in order to *exist*—to just go on, to be yourself and to function, especially in lives that were full of tests and challenges, consequences and responsibilities—would require being able to dream *lightly,* to have dreams that would give you a context in your daily life; and *deeply,* to experience the energies of soul travel that would remind you of who you are and why you are here, and connect you to your greater self—all these things that others have discussed. Yet how is it that you can dream? What is the energy grid or thread? What is the smoke by which dreams can travel?

Fully three percent of the Explorer Race individuals who were parked, having completed before you passed through the blue opening in the veil to come here and do these things I discussed, were establishing the energy, the fuel, the substance, the capacity to dream from the lightest to the deepest depths before you passed into these more challenging times and experiences you find yourself in.

How did they do that? When they incarnated physically in one body or another (whatever was appropriate to the dimension), anywhere from the third and to some extent the upper second dimension, from roughly 2.7 to 7.9, they experienced almost their entire lives in some version of dreaming. In those days dreaming was difficult; it was a challenge because there was no matrix that would accept dreams. Dream symbols had not been established and there was no means to travel to the world of the fantastic. Whatever existed in your day-to-day life would not translate into the dream world; your day-to-day life, whatever it was, would be entirely separated from your dream world. There was no blending of the two worlds; there would be the dream world and the day-to-day world with nothing in between. This three percent of the Explorer Race literally established the clouds of experience that allowed succeeding generations to dream and draw the nurturance, the excitement, the energy, the knowledge and wisdom available to you now through your dreams, by laying down that basic dream groundwork.

I mention this as an example because it's a common experience for you all to dream, yet because it is common does not mean that it has always existed as you know it today!

Were they doing this in individual lives, not knowing how it connected to the whole, or did they have an awareness of what they were doing, as we do?

Depending on the dimension of their existence, beings in 2.7 to about 3.8 had no real understanding of why their lives were involved in this sleeping or waking dream almost constantly. If they were in a world that was not particularly evolved or was rigidly controlled, they would be outcasts. If, on the other hand, they were in a more advanced, spiritual world, then they would have an easier time of it. But many of them were experiencing life as the outcast because their society or culture did not know or understand what they were doing; they did not appreciate it.

The Wisdom of the Handicapped

For example, in your time some experiences are considered handicaps. These handicaps may be a handicap to function in your society as it exists today, but in other societies at either higher dimensions or alternate experiences in other cultures, what would be a handicap here might be perfectly acceptable or even make you a prominent individual.

For example, dyslexics here have a challenge, but in other cultures they might, for example, be considered great visionaries, having the capacity (if nurtured when they are young) to see or experience more than is physically present, meaning that dyslexics really do have the capacity to be able to sense beyond the physical reality—and if nurtured, they can be trained to do so. But in your culture, they are often considered handicapped. Another example would be individuals with Down syndrome. These individuals are considered handicapped in your culture, but in alternate cultures are often considered great teachers of unconditional love and joy, and many beings flock to them to be blessed or touched by them. They have, in these cultures, what you would consider in your time guru status.

Particle Knowledge

I mention these things because cultures do not always understand the completeness of what they are doing. Sometimes they are providing wisdom, experience and knowledge for either previous generations (outside the context of time as you know it linearly) or future generations. Those future generations might not exist in the same dimensional experience, but they will have at some time access to the space and physical matter that you currently occupy. That's perhaps why the Particle book [*Explorer Race: Particle Personalities**] of the Explorer Race is so profound. It gives significant hints about the flexibility of particle consciousness—and you are all made up of particles, physically and, to some extent, spiritually speaking. This is why, even if you are raised in a rigid society, no matter how controlling that society is, you have the capacity to be, as an individual, more or less flexible based on the particles that make you up as well as the acculturation you receive.

That adds a lot to our understanding. I had thought that earlier ones kind of skipped through the easy lessons, and the ones who are on the planet now are doing the hard ones.

Everybody has his own responsibility—your personal lessons and all of this—your gifts, your wisdom. You have, in short, your assignment, if I can say it that way. With this assignment you will at times give, at other times receive and at other times do both. During these experiences you will be doing things for the present, but very often—surprisingly often—for the past. This is not in the context of karma as you know it, but because people who have preceded you in the past might still benefit from what future generations do (from their perception), just as you in your time benefit from what future generations are doing, especially if those future generations are moving about in the soil of their dimensional experience of Earth.

Here you are in transitional third-to-the-fourth-dimensional Earth. But suppose in future times there are beings who are experiencing things personally or collectively that move them through third- to fourth-dimensional Earth from moments to moments in their own lives. Perhaps they have a high development of technology: they come here and land in their ship, get out, walk around; or they time-travel or simply develop some connection with Earth, perhaps touching a stone. There are many possibilities. And they have a skill or wisdom that is entirely unavailable in linear time. Let's say they're 2500 years in the future. They have the skill or wisdom that is unknown in all preceding times for the Explorer Race, yet that skill or wisdom is needed in your present.

How on Earth can we get that future skill or wisdom to your now time? Can it be done through mental telepathy? Perhaps, but it can be done more completely through physical contact. Remember, you are here to learn the lessons of physicality, and one of the ultimate lessons of physical mastery (also known as material mastery) is that physical

---

* See Book Market in back of book.

contact from one to another will very often bring you, or allow you to give, skills or experience that might never be learned in a given life. With even temporarily compatible substances, there can be exchanges of wisdom and beneficial experience without any conscious awareness from either party. This is done not only energetically through love, not only mentally through telepathy as you understand it, but primarily by the exchange of particles. You go down the street and shake hands with someone; you give them particles, they give you particles, some particles fall off and go into the ground. It cannot be underestimated.

So here's our skillful person 2500 years from now. Perhaps he knows, perhaps not. Perhaps he goes to the corner time machine and wants to experience Earth in a previous time; perhaps he wants to experience Earth at a time when there were many waterfalls on the surface. So he comes to a place on Earth where there are many waterfalls, perhaps a few years ago, perhaps a few years in the future, perhaps now. He walks around, enjoys the place; maybe he brings his family. They literally leave their mark and their particles there.

Those particles might be picked up by the stream, and water (being an active antenna) brings those particles all over the Earth in the form of running water, rain, snow, steam, gas. Eventually that particle enters, however briefly, an individual who can utilize its wisdom and depth, and at that moment all the inspirations that that individual's guide has been attempting to give him to solve a conundrum he's been unable to solve, either for himself or others, is made easier. It's as if the inspiration from the guide or teacher from whom you've been hearing a word or getting a feeling but it's not quite there for you—suddenly, with the addition of that particle even briefly in your body, the word is heard on a new level or stimulates a resonance within you that allows you to get it. You say, "I understand!" and from there you can suddenly develop the field of wisdom, even in its infancy, that was delivered to you unexpectedly 2500 years in the future from someone who might or might not (more likely, not) have known he was giving you that most important special delivery.

Could the technology we're using now that came from the crashed ET ships, some of which were from the future, be an example?

Yes, and even the lessons, because some of the technology being used is not benevolent. Because you are living in a world that is very much involved in responsibility and consequences and application and testing—testing all the time for you—you will have an almost immediate reaction. You or perhaps your society does something with an adapted future technology that is destructive, perhaps for military purposes, and the reaction is far greater than some older military technology developed in the past—not just greater in terms of its effectiveness, but the consequences are much greater. Then you must learn lessons faster; there are more tests, and you must pass them. I am not saying that these dramas are necessarily good or pleasant, but any technology used from the future, whether benevolent or malevolent, will have its effects, and you must learn from them, sometimes in spite of yourself.

Those Who Came through the Blue Portal

What percentage of beings on Earth now came through that blue screen?

What percentage is still connected? There are two ways to answer that question. What percentage, as you said, on Earth now (which is about half of a percent), and what percentage are still experiencing the connection to the Isis energy that are on Earth now. I can give you a number: 511.

You still feel these beings?

No, no, no. *They* still feel *me*; I feel all of you. Understand, I can feel you; I can feel you without consequences, since that is not my lesson. But the 511 still feel me. It is more important to put it that way. They might not know that they are feeling me; they will think that others have this same feeling, since you do not always communicate what you are feeling. Yet their feeling me often allows them to have some awareness of certain feelings, especially greater nurturing, and very often the capacity to pass on this nurturing to others.

Would you say that some of them are in some of the Isis/Goddess movements that are spreading?

Oh, certainly.

So half a percent of those who are on the Earth now . . .

. . . came through the blue part of the veil, yes. Quite a few when you think of it in terms of numbers.

Half a percent of six billion is 30 million. For someone to put something into the Explorer Race that our Creator didn't know about—which you did—you must be intimately connected to all of the Explorer Race because of whatever you can't talk about.

Yes. You came from elsewhere, but your Creator did something with you that He didn't do with the rest of His creation: Your Creator purposely created a portion of Itself that It could not relate to as well as It did the rest of the portions, because you were going to experience what your Creator did not have on the personal, intimate level. As any child knows, when a youngster has experiences his parents haven't had or can't relate to, you get a generation gap, as you used to say. To some extent the Explorer Race, especially today and in the last several thousand years, has a significant generation gap with the Creator of this universe because your Creator has not had such a personal experience with polarity as you have.

Your Creator needs so much assistance and so many consultants so It can understand you better, as a parent might go to a counselor to understand their youngsters, but also *you* need to have someone so you can understand your Creator better. Your Creator sometimes seems unresponsive to your requests, because many beings on Earth now feel an urgent need for Creator to give you, as is often said in religion, signs and wonders by which you can be reminded that the Creator not only loves you, but is visibly present and felt regularly.

Your Creator often does not seem to respond to these things because it is understood in the rest of this creation that items of beauty, such as rainbows, are signs of the Creator's love. Creator's point is that, "Well, all other beings in my creation know this; you must know it too, but you have to remember." Your Creator does not personally have the experience to know that if you are having a bad day or having extreme negativity (as you call it) or extreme discomfort in your life and you see a rainbow, you might not be as thrilled by it as when you see it on a good day.

Your Creator does not relate as intimately to you as It relates to other members in this universe. That's why you need someone to explain you to Creator and why your Creator needs someone to explain It to you.

Is that one of your tasks?

Sometimes, and there are also others who do that. It is needed so that you would be reminded that yes, Creator loves you and so that Creator will be reminded that yes, you love Creator. There needs to be an understanding of the communications by both, and sometimes an interpreter can be very helpful.

You are such an important part of the Explorer Race. When Zoosh talked about these eight friends of Creator and the Master of Discomfort, why weren't you listed?

Perhaps because Zoosh knew that we would be having this conversation at some later point. Why should he talk about me when I'm reasonably articulate and can speak for myself? Sometimes Zoosh skips over something he knows will be discussed later or will come up when the time is more appropriate. Zoosh might say, "That's not my job." [Both laugh.]

Even on that level we've got job descriptions. If only a half percent of those on the Earth now came through the blue veil, have many of them already completed?

Yes.

We didn't come through till later, or maybe we're slower?

Oh, no; it's not that. It's that you have to struggle out of the limits of time. You don't come through the blue veil and then start right after that in sequential time. You might go way into the future, way past this time, to have your first life, then come back into the past and have a life. The challenge here is being able to look at this as a whole place, as a circle, that one has a life at some point in the circle, where there is no linear time. If you superimpose linear time over the circle, as in a grid, then you can say, "Oh, this life that seems to be in this part of the circle actually happened in 1890," but when you take linear time away from it, it's just a life somewhere in the circle.

That's a good explanation.

Yes, it really is quite good. If you make a picture of it, it makes complete sense.

That's really the way it works. There are people who came through that blue part of the veil who haven't incarnated yet and won't do so well into the future. Perhaps many of them will be amongst those who begin to explore as the Explorer Race must, bringing with them not only their curiosity, but their unique personalities that will touch beings of other worlds.

Well, that's kind of unfair. It seems like those of us who have struggled through this time ought to be the ones who get to do that.

Remember, it is not a reward. How often has this happened, especially for people taking vacations? You're dreaming and working all year long, looking forward to your vacation. You can't wait for it to come. Then you take your vacation, and when you get done with it, you need a vacation.

It's very much like that. What seems to be work and toil and struggle now, in the larger context of your whole self, may not be quite that difficult. It's just that your day-to-day consciousness is separated from the larger context of yourself, so it seems like a terrible struggle. If you had the totality of your being here, this would be a snap. *This* would be the real vacation! There wouldn't be any problems you couldn't solve, and it would be so easy you would be bored. So those who will be doing these things in the future . . . well, it might be just as challenging for them. You might say, "Oh, come now! You mean one and a half percent discomfort would be challenging for them?" And I would say, certainly. If they have never experienced discomfort before, it could be very challenging. So this isn't about a payoff.

That's a good point because some of us think like that.

Yes, certainly, a wonderful point. It isn't about a payoff. It isn't about letters after your name after struggling through an educational process; it's about the process itself. If you talk to successful (as they're called in your time) or wealthy people, invariably they will tell you that the best part was getting there. Once you're there, you have it, but it is so much more desirable *before* you get it—as in the carrot and the stick, you know? That first bite of the carrot is wonderful, but after you get to the fifth and sixth bites, it tastes the same. So without a carrot beyond that, it really loses much of its grandeur.

Like for people who have all the money they can use and even more, it's the power and the glory and the thrill of it, you know.

It seems to give greater levels of the carrot; but eventually (this invariably happens to the truly wealthy, economically) they discover, usually in the wisdom years toward the end, that it's not the acquisition of wealth, but the careful distribution of it to various groups—or the redistribution, you might say—that gives them much greater satisfaction and pleasure. It's not power at all, but the rewards that they don't necessarily see, but feel. Yes, it is an interesting analogy. One finds that one grows mightily from any experience in such a testing ground as this.

For example, someday after the books have been out for a while (this book, too), there will be people who listen to the tapes. With future technology people can hear our conversations and sometimes get much more out of it than reading. You and I do not think about that so much when we are conversing like this, but future people, yes? They will perhaps experience the communication with full feeling, as we had it together, and in this way experience our conversation more intimately than words can provide.

Isis and Mother Earth

Yes, your words are very important. In a conversation a couple weeks ago, you started by saying that you had a personal relationship with the being whose energy was the magnetic energy of this planet, and you've never gotten back to it. Do you want to complete that?

I'll just say this: The magnetic energy of this planet is tremendously feminine, of course—magnetic energy being feminine—and I am totally magnetic. So for me to have relationships on the personal level with any magnetic energy is natural. The magnetic energy of this planet, although it is expressed in slightly different octaves, is still basically itself throughout all dimensions of this planet's expression, including dimensions that still exist in the galaxy Sirius. Even though that seems to be very far away, it is not far away within the context of the personality of Mother Earth as you know her. Her personality can easily be drawn upon in other places.

You, of course, have had lives in other places; you might even have other-dimensional versions of yourself in existence right now—your greater self and so on. It is the same for Mother Earth.

Mother Earth and I once had a very long acquaintanceship before she decided to manifest in any version of planetary expression. She came to visit me when I was passing through the second level and inquired if I felt that expressing oneself in a planetary demonstration of one's personality was the sort of thing one could grow from. And when she was talking about "grow," she meant that in capital letters—*significant* growth.

I encouraged her for about 150,000 experiential years (in the expression of planets) by our visiting planets in various universes all over. I told her that the common thread between all these planets was their benevolence. I said that although the expression as a planet in these universes was wonderful, growth would be in small letters; it would take a very great amount of experience and not be what she wanted. She wanted profound growth.

I said that in this Explorer Race time, however, in this coming universe, she would be able to experience growth in capital letters. She said, "How is that?" And then—this can only be said between friends—I said, "If I tell you now, it will limit your experience." Where have you heard that before? (Yes, from your old friend Zoosh.) "But if I let you discover it on your own, then I can tell you only this: If you want to have the growth in those capital letters that you want, you ought to consider being a planet in the Explorer Race times coming up far in the future in this wonderful creation-to-be."

She said, "I trust you as a friend, and I will do so." Then she began her very gradual motion, since there was plenty of time, toward the space that eventually became the universe you are now in. She arrived in plenty of time to take up her position in Sirius and eventually come into the Explorer Race experience as described in previous books.

Water Is the Physical Carrier Wave for Love

What is the relationship between the water on the planet and the water in our bodies? Zoosh said we could not do this without the water. What is its significance?

Water is the universal particle that can communicate between all portions of your personality and all other portions. Water takes so many different forms in order to remind you of its versatility and flexibility. Even if it does not tell you exactly what it does, it catches your attention—and you must have it to live. You as beings cannot function without water; you can't drink dehydrated water, though you can eat dehydrated food. Think about the different levels of your existence. You know there is the mind, the body, the spirit, the feelings, the instincts, which are made up of portions of the others. There are the different expressions of you, the multileveled experience of you. In physical terms water is the closest you can come; it is physically the echo of love.

Love is the universal energy that connects all dimensions, all experiences, all times and so on. There must be a physical counterpart to love so that there is, as electronic people would say, a carrier wave by which love can be experienced and taken everywhere for all beings. Water is the carrier wave for love in the physical reality. Is that not a wonderful gift?

That's why we have to be on a water planet.

Yes, you must; with the challenges that exist to you, love in its own right is not enough. Because of the polarity you are living through, you must have something of love that is physical so that no matter where you are when you are physical, you will experience it. It will be within you, around you. Sometimes you can smell it or what's in it. You must be immersed in it, or it must be immersed in you. You utilize it as the physical carrier wave for love. Those who work on their spiritual selves can feel love without water, but water carrying love is "louder." [Both laugh.]

Has Mother Earth ever come to you in the way that the Master of Discomfort went to the Creator, and said, "You know, it's just really too much"?

No, but you must remember that Mother Earth wanted growth, and she is experiencing massive growth, although some of it is very difficult for her. I was talking about water. It's very difficult for her to experience the complete connection of love with water when water is polluted. But when water is made pure by running through her body—that's how water is truly purified—then it can be more saturated with love in its many different forms (remember that love has different forms). When it is polluted, especially with certain kinds of pollutants . . .

Such as?

For example, solvents.

What does that do?

It makes it more difficult for Mother Earth to carry love in her water. I'm picking that out as an example.

Do you see that in the time most of us are on the planet, maybe the next 20 to 40 years, that water will be cleaned up?

I think you will begin to clean up the water in earnest—that is, having very strict international rules that are in the beginning rigidly enforced with an iron fist, really uncomfortably enforced—probably within the next five to fifteen years. That will get it established. Many countries will say, "This has got to change *immediately.*" One of the things that will happen is that dams will become more controversial. Even though water is used to generate power, it makes the water feel trapped, angry, depressed, upset. Water tends to acquire feelings like this more when it's trapped, so that even when it's released and goes downstream, it does not do as much good because it is love turned in on itself, which sometimes is anger and upset. It takes the water quite awhile to purify itself.

One of the first things people will do (and they're doing this to an extent now) is run the water through significant filtration processes before it runs through the turbines. Some of that is happening now. But rather than dumping the filtered products somewhere, they'll be very carefully burned and the smoke will be cleaned very carefully. This will happen for a time, but eventually dams will be slowly and laboriously removed as new power sources that are much cleaner and much more benevolent to the planet are integrated.

This is beginning in the western United States, they're taking down several dams.

Yes, and in the future that will become much more common, even though there are some huge dams being built now. But they will be a short-lived phenomenon in terms of history in its larger context. There will still be dams around in forty or fifty years, but not as many.

Wonderful.

We'll stop now, I think.

The Goddess and the Natural Feminine

December 2, 1997

Isis speaking. Perhaps tonight we'll talk a little bit about the future. The time line is a little obscure, given the changing measurement of time because of the change in vibration on this world, but in the future the calendar will also be different. It will go back further and go forward further and become a little more esoteric scientifically. But tonight I want to talk about the reorientation of both men and women to the natural feminine.

Reorienting toward the Natural Feminine

The natural feminine is that which is nurturing, encouraging, supportive and also stimulating in some ways, yes? This middle ground, as it seems to be, between the feminine and the masculine is the natural feminine, but there is more to it. In the natural feminine there are ideals and at the same time great practicality. The two do not always seem to be compatible, but in the feminine, ideals are *made* practical.

This might be because the feminine being is known to bear children, and when she has children she'll have ideals for them—wishes, hopes and dreams, yes, but ideals—how she would like them to be. So she will do what she can to prepare the children for these ideals, not filling their heads with impossible dreams, but preparing them, for example, for a public life. The mother of your now president, William Clinton, the woman who raised him, did this. She didn't fill his head with impossible dreams, but she let him know that he could be president someday, and she prepared him as best she could to have the capacity for and interest in world events.

The average mother does this as well. She might give her children the proper training in etiquette so they will know how to get along in public functions. She might encourage her children to make friends with other races and other nationalities so that they will be able to get along with anyone. She might encourage her children to be curious, taking them to the library and showing them how to fulfill their curiosity with the ideas and answers of others.

There are many things she might do, but the main thing I am pointing out here is that she does not separate ideals from the practical. She literally instigates the ideals (*infuses* would perhaps be a better word), into the practical, day-to-day life of her children, so that ideals (this is most important) are never out of reach. That is the important thing.

In your contemporary society, men, unfortunately, are not often given this unless they receive it from mother, because men in your recent times have been held to a standard that is not practical. They are often held to an ideal standard in the form of an admired individual—a soldier, a statesman, for example—but they are seldom given the practical means of expressing those ideals while being themselves. Rather, they are given this ideal and encouraged to emulate it, to be like that ideal no matter what their personal desires call for.

This is why I am discussing tonight the model feminine in that sense, because in the future the model feminine, the benevolent feminine energy, will be applied more equally to male and female children. This is something that I think you as a reader can begin to do for yourself. As a mother, look to see whether you are raising your children equally. Do you give the boys a chance to cook? Do you give the girls a chance to fish? Do you give the children—not in overly feminizing ways for boys or overly masculinizing ways for girls—the same opportunities?

I speak to father also: Father, you have probably not had as balanced an upbringing as you would have liked, so you may often need to defer to your wife (in this case, mother), because it is a possibility, especially in contemporary society, that her upbringing has been a little more balanced. I would like you to take a look at the men you most admire and the qualities they have or seem to have. Then I'd like you to look at your children, both male and female. Notice what qualities they seem to have. If you can encourage qualities in your children that are similar to the qualities you admire, that is fine. But if your children do not have qualities like the ones of the people you admire, just let them know that these are the models you look up to, but these models do not have to be theirs.

Also, mother and father, if you are spiritual people or even if you are performers or actors or have an interest in such things, you can, of course, play Let's Pretend. All parents play Let's Pretend with their children, even if it's just in reading them stories from a storybook. You can make up a story, or if you have difficulty, I'll make one up for you now. And I'd like you to act it out with the children or let them act it out or all of you act it out.

A Family Story from the Future

Once upon a time there was a wonderful family. The children and the parents are happy, and because they enjoy differences and variety, the grandparents live with the family, too. This is good for mother because sometimes she needs a little help, and it's good for father because he likes to have his father and his wife's father around, too. These people live in the future, about 3000 years from now.

One of their favorite pastimes is to watch their version of television, in which they can look in on relatives and ancestors from the past. When they do this, they play a game. In this game they imagine being you, in the time you are living in now. They imagine living in the most uplifting, encouraging and supportive way, regardless of how you lived. In order to win the game, they have to do so with everyone as a team. It is not a competition. They need to be a successful team, so they will act out different members of the family they are studying in your time, and they will have passed the test or won the game when they can convince each other that they *are* you. [Chuckles.]

That is the story. What I would like is for you to try to do the same thing. In order to be like them, you will have to be more like a team. You will have to pick roles, and in order to know that you have won the game, you will have to convince each other that you are all members of a benevolent future family that has an interest in you. You can play this by pretending to be them or by using the qualities you imagine they have, pretending to be you. I think it will be fun.

Playing the Future Game: Transforming Past Traumas

You mean the future people would be able to look into the akashic records or look back into this time spiritually?

They actually access the lives of people in this time. One of the purposes of the future game is to change the traumas and struggles and unhappiness of this time into something more benevolent. Now that they have had some influence (though not changing everything) in this direction, when they play the game again, the circumstances, the traumas and so on that existed in this time and this place will be less. In this way will the future family know they have had an influence, because it's changed the past—which is your present. They'll keep playing it with that same family until it is benevolent. When it's benevolent, they'll move on to another family.

So this is the beginning of our uncreating the discomfort.

Yes. People in the future do this because it is entertaining and pleasurable, and at the end of the evening they know they have done something worthwhile. Sometimes they can't totally change an extreme tragedy, but they'll make steps, and the next night they'll make another step, until eventually it will all be transformed.

I mention this in terms of the benevolent feminine, because this is a practical example of integrating ideals—changing the traumas of the past. How can you do that in *your* time? What I suggest is that you play the game of the future family the way the future family plays it.

If you wish to play it in traumas that occurred in your own family, okay. It is a family game played by mother and father, and if grandmother and grandfather and the children and all the family members want to participate, that is fine.

Each person takes a role and acts through the past tragedies or things you'd like to change for the better. Pick a time and a scene, as they would say in the theater community, and act it. If this happened in your life or the life of your family, you will know how well this is working because every time you do the performance, you will begin to feel better and better. And someday you won't feel like acting out that scene or that tragedy anymore. This means that you have resolved it; the pain around that tragedy has been resolved. That doesn't mean the tragedy will not have taken place, but it means the residual pain will have been resolved. Then you can go on and try another tragedy in your family. If you have achieved all of that and there is nothing further to change, then you can try it for another family.

This is something you can do for other people, and it does not harm them or interfere with them in any way. I recommend you work on your own family first. If there are not enough members of your family to do so, then you can include your friends. Tell them as much as you can; acquaint them, like a director or a writer might do, with what different members of your family were like so that they can act that role. Then go through the scene just like rehearsing a scene in the theater, changing things slightly for the better each time you do it until you no longer feel any tension. When the tension or discomfort associated with this time dissipates for the family members, then you can go on to another incident—perhaps in somebody else's family. The rules of the game are that you perform your character as best you can, allowing your character to grow and change.

This can be a lot of fun; it's also a pretty good actor's workshop.

But with a purpose.

Yes, with a very benevolent purpose. You'd be surprised at the degree of discomfiture being carried around in your own bodies from things that happened years and years ago, things you have come to peace with mentally, but not necessarily physically or on the feeling level. You can often transform the physical discomforts, and also the feeling discomforts—not always, but do try. It will be fun. It's a uniting thing to do, and I think you will make the world a better place.

The Masculine Polarization

How long have we had this expression, where we are more masculine and mental than feeling? Was it when we came down to the third dimension?

Much shorter than you think. The focus into the out-of-balance, in terms of both male and female being out of balance to the masculine, has really been only in the past five or six hundred years.

Before that time it wasn't like that. Even in the five or six hundred years I refer to, it was not everybody on the planet, but the people involved in what you would call the modern age. It really began right around the time when books were being produced, though before the printing press was widely in use. I am not suggesting that intellectual pursuits corrupt people, but that sometimes people can become acquainted with the cultures of others before their choosing, as in the case of wars, when whole groups of people are conquered by others and then influenced by a culture that is not their own. Or it can happen when a youngster finds out about somebody else's culture before he is fully acquainted with his own. And there are other things; I have mentioned just two.

The polarization toward the masculine is fairly recent, which is why I think you can change it without too much difficulty.

Do you feel that the impetus was the Renaissance?

Yes, it is around the time of the Renaissance, when more people were learning to read and when the middle class started developing—

people becoming go-betweens. Before that, the farmer would sell his crops or perhaps pay in taxes some of his crops directly to the landowner. But around that time the middleman began to develop: the shopkeeper, who would do business with the landowner and with the farmer. As a result, education needed to be spread more widely. This is not strictly an economic analysis of those times, because also during those times there were passionate causes being fervently striven for. And the roots of exploration were also going out much farther than they used to, past your own continent to other continents where the desire to transform native peoples into thinking like yourself was more than a simple need—becoming a literal obsession.

Would you say it had been balanced from that point backward in time? At a certain point it was almost unbalanced toward the feminine, wasn't it?

I wouldn't say it was *ever* unbalanced toward the feminine in your societies. There are some societies on other planets where you might say that the masculine is sublimated, but that has not been the case on this planet, no.

Even when there were matriarchies?

Even then. Yes, even then. In order to survive here, it has been necessary to hunt and gather. When you gather, you incorporate adventure. About 70 percent of adventurousness is masculine, 30 percent feminine. Given the nature of survival and its required necessities on this planet, I'd say that you have never had a society on this planet that was out of balance toward the feminine.

Even Lemuria?

Yes, even then, because in Lemuria they had responsibilities. The responsibilities would sometimes cause them to have to do things they would not normally wish to do, things not of their culture. Today you have statesmen and stateswomen who relate to other cultures; they are like middlemen, like a middle class between those other cultures and yours. But Lemuria was different. Since everyone was totally united, if one of their members related to somebody on Atlantis, everyone on Lemuria would experience that relationship. There was no middleman, no middle person, no middle class; everyone was not only the same class, but of *exactly the same vibration*. So if one of their members experienced a vibration that was, in the case of Atlantis, more masculine, everyone would. That is why Lemuria eventually had to rise up to a higher frequency. Experiencing the polarized masculine was becoming a little more than they could comfortably accommodate.

Atlantis was polarized to the masculine in about the last 60 percent of its existence, but at the beginning, even Atlantis was fairly balanced. Atlantis did not begin polarized to the feminine; it began balanced.

The Lemurians Will Begin to Assist You

So at some point as we move up the ladder of frequency, are we going to run into the Lemurians?

Very possibly you will. They will probably contact you first because they have so much to speak of. They will remind you of your experiences; they are very good at dancing anyone's past to them. When they dance your past, something you haven't been able to see, feel or understand or even be aware of as influencing you, you will then be able to feel, see, sense—use all of your senses to remember that experience—and understand your life much better. The Lemurians will be able to open a greater communication of the portions of yourself with your current conscious mind.

You said they are on the fifth dimension?

They range from the fifth to the seventh. If they wish to be more relaxed, they will let their society drift to the seventh; when they are more active or proactive, they will be in the fifth, because in the fifth they can easily influence the fourth. Since you are moving into the fourth, sometimes they will do that [chuckles].

So they are part of what's pulling us?

I would say yes. They are proactive in that sense.

You are smiling—why?

They have waited so long that they felt, "Perhaps we don't need to be here anymore." But now that they are able to begin to work to assist you, they are so happy.

Isis and the Goddess Groups of Today

The first thing you told me about was your interaction with the student who started a mystery school and the Isis legend. Are present day Goddess/priestess groups now starting another mystery school?

Yes, but to make it more encouraging, not exclusively my own, it is to encourage a coming together of the best your culture has to offer with the best the ancients (I might include myself in the ancients) have to offer, yes. But it is not to replace your culture (that is never a good idea), but to add things to your culture that might be beneficial to you now.

So you are actively interacting with these groups to bring back the best of the old and the best of now?

Yes, and encouraging them. Sometimes I am not acting actively but latently; I will interact with some of the members of these groups in their dream state, in an inspirational state or even on the feeling level to encourage them to take action on their feelings instead of keeping them to themselves. Women in your society have for some time been encouraged to keep their feelings to themselves, whatever they are. So I have been working to encourage them to bring their ideas and feelings and suggestions into the mainstream, to tell others and to try them and so on, rather than just keep it to themselves—which is all right, but not the best.

Are there things you can discuss about these mystery schools that can make them more available to everyone?

Yes; they will ask questions, in some cases to clarify things they already know and in other cases, I will speak of things they don't know about. Sometimes I will speak of things they already know very well, but this is to incorporate the reader.

Those 500 beings who came through the blue veil that are on the planet now, are some of them involved in these Goddess groups?

Some members are part, but they are not all a portion.

Would you like them all to be?

Oh, no. I am not seeking to create a following.

Bringing back this teaching is extremely important.

Yes, but the most important teachings to bring to the surface are ones that are with you now that are not getting the attention they need. This is why I think the Goddess/priestess/Isis book will be useful. It will bring the ideas of these groups to the acquaintanceship of the reader. By the way, I'd recommend that there be an appendix in this future book, and that each group have, perhaps, six or eight pages in which they can briefly discuss the nature of their work, if you are open to that.

Of course.

In this way the reader can consult the appendix to understand the nature of what is being examined.

Is this interest mainly in the United States, or the world?

It's becoming quite worldwide. The current interest in Celtic and other ancient English and Germanic philosophies—associated with the white race becoming more cognizant of its own cultural history—is perhaps more international than you fully grasp at this time. It is something wider in scope than is understood and appreciated even by the journalistic press. It is all over the world; in some places it is more and some it is less.

The Feminine in the Next Twenty-Five Years

You have pretty much been interacting off and on with humans since they've been on this Earth, right?

Yes, when needed [chuckles].

When needed. Is there a time that you look at as one of your favorite times, when you look back and say, "That was especially wonderful"?

Do you mind if that time is a little in the future? I think one of my favorite times is in the next 25 years or so when little girls will start to be raised with integrated spirituality, honoring the feminine rather than imposing what have come to be known as masculine values, which are really adapted from authoritarian texts. Within the next 25 years, little girls will be encouraged to bring forth the feminine more—and I might add that boys will also be encouraged to speak more about their dreams, to talk more about having seen grandma and grandpa even though they might have died a year or so ago. And when the children talk about their dreams, the parents will say, "Oh, tell us more!" rather than "Oh, that was just a dream, honey."

The next 25 years is really my favorite time, because *the children will be made equals.* For so long in your societies, children have been second- or third-class citizens, if that. It's fine to acknowledge that children need the care, nurturance and support of adults, but this does not have to separate them into a lesser class of being; they are not. As a matter of fact, the visionaries you seek to be inspired by are really all around you—but they are usually seven years old or less!

Of course there are others who are older, but the ones who are seven years old or younger are much easier to find.

That is wonderful! Everything we have had to experience, they won't have to. Why won't they have to live through it? The 93 percent of the Explorer Race has come and gone. All of the humans here now on the Earth comprise only 1.5 percent of the total Explorer Race.

Unfoldment of the Explorer Race

What does that suggest? As time goes on, there will be fewer and fewer Explorer Race people here. What this means, of course, is that you are resolving all your lessons. In the next 25 years or so, fewer and fewer Explorer Race people will need to be on Earth. This means people who are not the Explorer Race will start to be born on Earth.

That is a new one! They will just have a life and leave, not getting caught up in the cycle of reincarnation.

Yes, and the people who are still of the Explorer Race will no longer have Explorer Race lessons to learn, so you can let go of a lot of that polarity.

Wait a minute. That is 94.5 percent who will be gone. That leaves 5.5 percent of the Explorer Race—until you said it I didn't know it—that haven't even incarnated yet!

Not that many. Remember, something is going on now that is very controversial. A lot of youngsters, a lot of Explorer Race individuals, do not have to live a complete physical life. Many of them have to experience physicality slightly, meaning that they begin to grow in their mothers, but they do not go to term; they are not born.

They are abortions?

Either abortions or, more often, miscarriages. I am not saying miscarriages are good or fun, but they happen. Most of the time these days, aside from the obvious medical causes, miscarriages happen because Explorer Race souls who need to experience physicality but do not have to be an individual, will do that. In the next 25 years many children will be born who are not involved in the Explorer Race, who are simply Earthians.

For one life and then leave, or two lives or whatever they choose?

Whatever they choose.

Five and a half percent of the Explorer Race are not here now. Is it because they are not on the Earth in the third dimension or because they are not with the 93 percent? Some of them are on other dimensions and are going to reincarnate, and some are going to come in who haven't incarnated yet?

We need to update that 93 percent figure. It is much closer to 94.5 percent now.

Okay, 94.5 and 1.5 is 96 percent, so 4 percent are either going to reincarnate or incarnate for the first time.

Yes, and they'll be coming in some form over the next 25 or 30 years at most. But coming in at the same time will be other souls who are not members of the Explorer Race, and they need to be served also. A lot of their needs will be more balanced to the type of lives they would have on other planets, so society will necessarily change to serve their needs and will not need to be as polarized.

That is wonderful! We made it!

That is right; you are just about there.

What do you feel you contributed the most over the time you have been interacting with the Explorer Race?

Love, nurturance, support and insight. Very often I have been able to help individuals in their dreams, including what you call daydreams and moments of inspiration, to link inspirations together, which creates insights. Something pops into your head, then other pieces come together, and you suddenly understand something completely. These insights can be very beneficial to yourselves as well as others, because it will often change not only how you think, but what you *do*.

It might interest you to know that one has insights even in completely unpolarized societies. That is how those societies grow; so though they grow slower, they do grow.

Little AHA!s are there, the means to expand.

That's right. Things that hadn't been thought of together, or things that are together that hadn't been thought of as separate, will very often become the AHA!

Is there anything you regret? Anything you wish you could have done or done better?

No. One of the requirements to function at this level is to be at peace with what you do. If you have any regrets at all, it is an anchor and then you are stuck there.

Self-Violence and Self-Love

March 4, 1997

Isis and the Explorer Race on Maldek

Isis here.

Welcome. You've talked about the Explorer Race on Orion and on Earth. Did you interact with us on Maldek?

There wasn't that much interaction between us in that place. I'll tell you why. I always perceived that as being something that would be uncreated at some point anyway, and I looked at that experience as being what you might call a blip in your graph, a short and perhaps not such a good experience, certainly not for the planet and its other inhabitants. Since I could see what was inevitably going to occur there, I connected with individuals only when they requested my presence. Other than that, there was negligible contact.

So we went there with very high hopes, but you knew it wasn't going to work.

Well, you were still trying to impose predictability based on control, and you had been through the Orion system where that seemed to work. It wasn't making everybody happy, but the general principle seemed to work. You didn't realize that, depending where you are geographically, some things work and some things don't. Obviously, if you are at the beach, you can go swimming; but if you are in the desert, well, you should not expect an ocean. It is also true for different star systems, certainly, but even different planets within a star system. Some things work in one place and not another. So you tried to do something that was not intended for that place.

That place was actually always intended to be a place that nurtures the beginning of things—anything. And that once those things are under way, whatever they are—ideas, thoughts, beings, anything—and are able to sustain themselves, they move on. So the planet was like a nursery school for all life. Once it is able to take care of itself, it moves on. It would have been nice for it to still be there, but that will be corrected in time—by you, of course [chuckles].

Are you interested in giving us just a little overview? We have so little information about the Maldek experience.

Remember what I said about what you tried to do there, to create predictability with control? You are doing the same thing here, but I think there is a chance that you will get through that here and recognize that predictability is less desirable than balance. The reason everyone is tiptoeing delicately around this issue is that if you knew the details of what went on there, you would be riled up sufficiently that you would want to perpetuate right here what caused the battle in the first place. Let's just say this: Because of what happened there, the less you know about it at this time, the better. When you are less violent and less involved in reaction, then it would be safer for you to know about it.

Are we looking at 25, 50, 100 years before we will be in a position to be beyond the violence and can know this?

It is a flexible answer, that; it could be as little as three and a half years to as much as a hundred years. It is hoped by most beings that it will be no more than twenty years, but who can say?

It's still up in the air, right?

Ets Gauge Violence against the Self

Do you know how violence is measured by beings beyond here?

No.

It is not measured by what you do to each other, for that is sometimes capricious; it is measured by how violent you are with *yourselves.* That's the best and most accurate way, because the extent to which you are violent with yourself is the measurement by which you have the potential of being violent with others. This means, for example, going on reading or working past the time that your body desires to stop and rest; starving yourself because of some mythical image you wish to attain; running or exercising past the point that your body says stop, because you believe in someone's theory. To the extent that you do these and other things, including reckless behavior that could injure or kill you, this is how violence on this planet in your society here is measured. That is how we have a pretty fair estimate of the level of violence.

If we were to gauge violence based upon what you do to each other, it is not so accurate. This is one of the things that extraterrestrials measure; at least they have in the past. When they take an individual on board, one of the things they do, if they have the proper "platform" (they call it), is lay you on it. The platform will examine not only what you have ever done in that given life, but what you have considered doing and what you have the potential for doing. This is where you go first, to some kind of device that measures that. That is how extraterrestrials know who it is safe to communicate with more directly, and who is simply led off the ship when the examination is over. If they find that your violence toward yourself is less than 25 percent, they might be more inclined to communicate with you. But if it is more than 50 percent, the chances of their communicating with you are almost nonexistent.

That is revelatory. What are some other behaviors that show our potential for violence?

Consider how you abuse yourselves. Your physical bodies give you messages constantly, and sometimes you think they are just discomforts, not knowing what the messages mean. You might eat food that is actually not good for you. Let's say you pick something up and get a sudden pain in your body, but you eat it anyway. There might be some repercussion from that. That is violence to oneself. You are not at this time capable of accessing your unconscious in a conscious fashion, but let's say you repeat to yourself and create a dogma out of cruel things that were said to you by insensitive or deluded people. When you were growing up, perhaps they called you a name, perhaps they said you were foolish or not very smart; then maybe sometimes when you make mistakes, like everyone does, you say to yourself, "Oh, that's because I'm not very smart." That is self-violence: perpetuating the myth of cruelty that was perpetrated upon you.

Beginning Your Responsibility to Yourself

So those who believe themselves unworthy of what they want—the whole issue of self-worth—is included in this violence?

Oh, certainly. This is why consciousness, as Uncle Zoosh has stated many times, begins at home, with yourself. That is why the exercise originally given by Speaks of Many Truths about the heat in the heart and so on is designed to begin your responsibility to yourself [see appendix]. Once you start giving yourself love and discover that it feels better than giving yourself pain, the chances are you will give yourself more love. It is easier for you, in a world where you have so many choices, to discover that something feels good and do more of that than acknowledge that something feels bad and do less of it. It is always easier to do something new and better. It is given to you in hopes that you will enjoy it and come to feel the "home" of it.

There was never this explanation before. It makes so much more sense.

I will grant that Zoosh is a good teacher, but he does not always give you all the background information. But I am available for such things sometimes. So the issue is, how do we help the human being move toward what naturally feels good and is benevolent to you and encourage you to make choices of those things? How do we help you become conscious that what feels bad to you—even an inner feeling, as you say, an emotion that has a physical feeling—is a profound message that deserves attention? The best way, of course, is *not* to point out each and every discomfort—that would make you feel like you are more wrong than right—but to give you the methods and tools (the heat/love exercise, for example) that would help you stabilize yourself, come into the body (you have to be in the body to do that exercise) and discover how good it feels.

This will give you a basis of comparison to know that when something feels bad, it ought to be avoided at that time. Perhaps there will be another time when it is acceptable. When you have the heat, which is the physical evidence of love, then you know, "Oh, this is good for me." But with some discomforts or a pain, you know "This is not good for me right now." If you begin to make choices on the basis of what feels good, then you say to beings at large, "Look, see: we are ready, not just in our mental pronouncements, but we are taking the actions to improve our quality of life on an individual basis."

As more people take this action and there is more heat and self-love felt, not only does it work for those individuals, but on the cumulative level it will tend to trigger that heat/love feeling in others even if they are not focused on it. They may not be able to maintain it because of exposure to others, but they may notice it and ask someone. If it happens often enough and if they ask enough people, eventually they'll ask someone who knows how to do it. Someone will show them how to do it and then they will join the group that is doing it. If enough voices say, "Look, see: we are doing this thing," then beings who have been isolating you will open the veils a bit to allow others to come and visit you benevolently and allow you to visit them benevolently, according to your true desires, not just your momentary desires.

So where are we now? There's a full spectrum, but if they measured everybody, what is the average of violence to ourselves?

Not every society is unconscious, but allowing for a fairly unconscious society such as, generally speaking, the westernized world, you are at about 40 percent of violence to yourself. Let's take the average individual in a fairly unconscious society; their self-violence will range anywhere from 37 to 57 percent. Although they will rarely express this violence toward others, the potential is there.

You might ask, how do we know if someone is very violent toward themselves? If you are fairly open and in reasonably good balance or even just relaxed and feeling comfortable, when you come into contact with this person, even if they're not talking to you, *you will feel uncomfortable.* Maybe a little nausea will pass, but it will be a familiar feeling of discomfort that will remind you that you are someplace but ought to be elsewhere. You will often get this feeling if confronted or exposed to something that is a known risk or a known discomfort, yet you can tell if someone is pronouncedly self-violent if you feel uncomfortable around them. This is not an absolute, you understand. It works only if you are reasonably relaxed and reasonably balanced yourself; otherwise *you* might be the self-violent person reacting to the benevolence in them and feeling envious, becoming sick with envy. There are varieties, so there's no absolute law. But a reasonably balanced and spiritually secure individual can tell that way.

How Other Planets Deal with Self-Violence

This is used on other planets to isolate self-violent people from society—not to send them to some prison or cruel home, but to send them someplace where they can receive the therapy they need to express things physically and with feeling—passionately, one could say. They might benefit from the dance of the self; one dances one's feelings, and in the process the dance gets more and more vigorous until eventually one has pushed off all the discomfiture of feelings and eventually begins to feel only oneself. That dance then gradually turns into something more graceful and gracious, perhaps even gentle, but also possibly adventurous. In any event, it turns into something that feels good to you if you're exposed to it, because they are dancing themselves. That is the dance of the self.

The Newer Work Ethic vs. Older Cultures

That is very sad when you look at the population—the children of alcoholics, workaholics . . . you know. We are taught that working hard and striving and succeeding are virtues. It's part of the work ethic we grew up in.

You may have grown up in it, but you must remember that the people who established that culture were, if you don't mind my little joke, kicked out of Europe. Remember, the cultures even in Europe, which is a relatively young culture, are much older than the cultures here. For instance, you can go to countries like Spain or Italy that have older cultures, and the people may not be as self-violent. If they are tired during the day, they might take a nap. If they want to have a fun dinnertime with family or friends, they don't sit down and bolt their food down in a half hour or twenty minutes so they can rush off and do something "constructive." They take their time, they enjoy, they have many courses, they talk amongst themselves, they share their opinions. It is a social gathering, what would perhaps be called a happening over here. Do you see what I'm saying? Those who had the rigid, authoritarian work ethic were not accepted over there, and many of those individuals came to this country, not to establish a work ethic where none existed before, but to establish rigidity where none existed before.

In the history books they call it religious freedom.

In a way you could say that that is so, but only if rigidity and authoritarianism are considered desirable ways of life. Religion has become something that is of thought and consideration in your society, but in older places in the world—China, for example, which is a fairly ancient culture (granted, they have gone through some changes in recent years)—the religion is intended to be the day-to-day philosophy, yes. And one finds this in the Middle East in some places where the religion is a practice that one lives by.

But in Western societies one could not live by the ethics of religion because it interfered with commerce. So the religion was transformed into commerce-friendly religion. When religion is commerce-friendly as its first priority, the needs of the people on a daily basis—their lives from day to day—are not met. This is how you can have people with great wealth and people who are starving and suffering within a society that considers itself free. Free to be what? Self-violent, because you are all one; if one amongst you suffers while the others are happy, there is a part of all the others that is suffering. To the extent that you learn how to have the loving warmth energy within you and to treat yourself more benevolently, when others are suffering you will feel it immediately. And as a society you will rise up immediately to assist the party who is suffering because you will feel it as a *personal pain.*

This is how societies on other planets were able to establish a culture of benevolence for all beings, because people became loving as a physical experience, not as a thought. Thoughts are always interpretable, but a physical experience gives physical evidence and is felt very much the same by all beings. So the societies became physically loving with the heat and the warmth of love, and then they felt quickly the members in their society who were suffering and needed assistance, and gave those people the assistance they needed until all people's needs were served. The culture came into balance and was able to maintain itself as a loving, benevolent culture, nurturing the best out of all individuals and coming quickly to the aid of those in pain, not only to serve their needs, but to keep that pain (also known as self-violence) from spreading to others.

That's brilliant! That's wonderful. I don't think this has ever been talked about.

It is time, yes?

One Tool: The Heat in the Heart Exercise

You know, for years now, beings not unlike myself have viewed the Earth and wondered, "What can we do to ease their suffering?" We have always come back to the same thing: We must give them tools so they can choose benevolence. That is why the exercise with the heat in the chest is perhaps the best place for you to start, because it gives you a benevolent feeling that others can experience. The extent to which you choose to bring up that feeling in yourself will be a measure that you can consider, even with your thought, of how kind you are to yourself compared to how cruel you are. And cruelty is self-violence. But we cannot step in and say, "Stop that!" with the self-violence; we can only give tools and allow you to choose. If you were not in Creator School, we could step in; but because you are, we have to stand back.

Let's go deeper into this. What I thought was innocuous—this work ethic and workaholic thing—if that is so detrimental to our being, how do we reach those people who are seriously into drugs and real violence and terrorism?

For starters, you set a good example. Very often people do such things as a last resort. If you have the awareness of your own tools, things you were born with, you can find the trouble spots and help in ways that are desired rather than in approved ways of help in your society. Your society has many good qualities, one of which is that you have mechanisms in place to feed the hungry, clothe the shivering and shelter the suffering. But over the years you have established such levels of procedure for the people to obtain these needs that they will sometimes shun what you have to offer because of the requirements they must fulfill.

The Empath's Approach

Almost 60 percent of you on Earth at this time have the capacity to be the empath. Any individual could stand on your front porch and point over the horizon or even across the street and say, "Is anybody suffering over there in a way that I or my friends or family or town or city or culture could assist?"

When extraterrestrials come here, they pick places where there is the least self-violence and suffering. This is why they have frequented old societies in the past that have had to establish very disciplined balance, meaning no extremes one way or the other, no self-violence tolerated; they have often landed in isolated or mountain communities. They have people on board (yes, they have instruments, too) who can point at the planet, moving their fingers back and forth and ask, "Where is the place where the energy is the most benevolent for us to land our ship, get off and meet with the people?"

Where the empath feels the greatest heat or love, he or she knows, "This is the safest place for us, and the people will welcome us. They won't be afraid because they are not utilizing the discomforts of fear to punish themselves." The people are not self-violent, in other words. So that's where they land. Equally, if they point to a place that feels very uncomfortable, they know, "Avoid this place at all costs; there is great pain and suffering there, and the people have a high level of self-violence."

How Self-Violence Is Passed On

Did you know that if self-violence in an individual rises over 60 percent at any time, the chances of that individual becoming violent with others is almost guaranteed, because the human body is set up in such a way that anything over 57 percent is intolerable for a person to maintain on his own. This is why you will find people attacking innocent individuals. Someone might have done something to them that causes them to suffer, but their suffering is perpetuated. Perhaps it was done when they were youthful, and now as an adult they are perpetuating their suffering with resentment and anger and so on. When their self-violence and discomfiture goes past 57 to 60 percent, they cannot hold it. They must strike out, become violent with another person, whoever is handy, whoever is nearby, even if it is someone they love or someone who loves them, because they need another person to hold some of their self-violence.

This is how self-violence is passed from one to another. This is also why a perpetrator harms an individual who has done nothing to harm him. As time goes on and the wound heals but the inner wound festers, then *their* self-violence builds up and they pass it on unconsciously to someone else by being violent with *them* because they too have gone past their capacity to maintain their self-violence.

Say, for example, that an individual holds 60 percent self-violence, where he is strict and difficult and harsh and cruel to himself in every way. Then he must share his self-violence with someone else. He attacks someone, and in the process of the attack, whether the other person defends himself or not, even if the victim beats back the attacker and he suffers, that participation drops the attacker's internal self-violence anywhere from 10 to 15 percent for a time. But it will rise again if you do nothing to change your ways of being. That is why repetitive attacks take place; it is the mechanics of how these things work. This is how violence is passed on from one generation to the next in a family, for instance, or how old feuds are passed on in clans or cultures, or why individuals are attacked simply for the way they look or act, or simply because they are handy.

This is about the judgments people have about themselves—the guilt and pain and regrets, the really deep feelings they have about incidents in their lives, even if it wasn't actual physical violence. This could be emotional violence, all kinds of things.

Yes, it could be all kinds of things. It could be things said to them, as you suggested. These things all have an effect, and if people do not have a tool they can use, such as the heat/love tool, they will continue to do what they are doing. It's true they know no better, but it is also true that they don't have something else they can do that is physical. You are in the time now when you must *physically* begin to do things differently. To the extent you are able to do that, your society will change.

Kindness to Yourself and "Selfishness"

Many of you have come to this conclusion and are doing things together in groups, but even some of you in groups have not yet realized what you must do on your own, as an individual. Yes, many of you, as you say, lightworkers and religious and philosophical people as well—goodhearted people, good citizens, kindhearted people—will do acts of kindness for others as an individual or in a group. But you have been raised in your cultures with many false beliefs, and one of them is that to do a kindness for yourself is being selfish or is a sin or is something to be ashamed of. It is that which holds you back.

Zoosh said once that people should be more nurturing to self, and I immediately felt, just as you said, that "I can't pay attention to that; that's selfish, and I don't have time for it." We have been raised on a lie.

Yes. This is why from time to time you will hear about individuals who have been exposed to some great truth, and at first they are thrilled and excited. Then they get angry, because they realize that they have been raised, as you say, with entrenched lies. The idea is to not seek out individuals to blame, because those who raised you with lies were themselves raised with lies. The lies were not given to them by conscious liars either, but by those who lied unconsciously, not realizing that they had been lied to.

Using the Heat/Love Exercises for Yourself

The way to change that is to change individually, choosing on one's own to feel the love, the heat, and then act from that. For instance, while you are feeling the heat, say things to yourself out loud. As Uncle Zoosh has said, this might simplify your vocabulary a bit, but it will tend to create words and sentences that are permeated with love. You will discover, while you are feeling the love/heat, that you are incapable of being self-violent or hurtful or critical in any way. Centering into the heat and love and speaking it—and while you are speaking, the heat/love stays there—you can only be benevolent. It is not possible to do otherwise. It is a great teaching tool.

One says things to oneself out loud; you don't have to look in a mirror, you can just say it out loud. When you get good at doing that for yourself, you will know that you are in self-love because the heat/love will stay. But the moment you get critical or question your own value, the heat/love will fade or become significantly less. So you practice until you can talk for a long time, saying nice things to yourself about you. When you can focus into that heat and love physically (not just in a vision or meditation) and speak from that center to others, you will find yourself saying loving things to others. Most likely, unless they are in a terribly self-destructive, self-violent place, they will feel the love of your words—not just hear them, not just think about them, but actually *feel* them. This kind of truth felt in that way is rarely forgotten.

Well, I look at it as part of this plan to make us deal with the consequences, so it's not to be looked at with judgment or anger. That was part of the class. It's over now, and we need to come back to our own natural loving state.

That is why these truths can be offered to you at this time. Not only is it time to come back, but more importantly, it's time to *choose*. Will you embrace self-violence and self-destructiveness as part of your nature, or will you expose yourself to your true nature, which is loving benevolence with inspiration and application? Make your choice. You cannot make, as they say in schools, an informed choice without having a *real* choice.

So many supposedly aware, educated, conscious—even lightworkers don't . . . this has just not been brought out, you know.

Then I will bring it out now, because so many need to be reminded of who they really are, and these exercises with the heat/love can be done by anyone. It matters not your language, your religion, your nationality, your philosophy; you can do it without discarding your religion or philosophy. You can do it without discarding your personality. It can only enhance your true personality.

The Dance of the Self—Another Tool

It does not mean you must give up *all* your anger or outrage; it is a foundation to discover the true you. If you are still filled with anger and outrage, the next step is to dance the dance of the self. This will throw off the parts of you that need to be discarded. It will also throw off the parts of other people who spread their violence to you because they could not maintain it all themselves and needed your assistance. Eventually there will be nothing left to throw off because there will only be the you. Then your dance will change and become less vigorous. It will become a dance more of symbols and postures that express who you really are. You can do this to music, you can do it to drumming, you can do it to internal sounds of drumming and music, as you wish. But doing it will take years off the couch in the psychiatrist's office, because such physical discomforts are best and most speedily dispatched by being physical.

You will know you are at your true self because you will no longer feel as if your dance is so vigorous as to be almost out of control. We want that a little bit; it will slow down a bit and you will begin to feel relaxed. You will feel the heat naturally without really bringing it up; you will feel *safe*. That is a physical feeling most of you obtain only by setting conditions outside yourself. But when you are at the core of you, the total you, *safety is your natural condition. It is the primary emotion and radiated energy of immortality.*

How It Will Affect Others

When you get to that place, as you go out amongst people and radiate that, it's going to be communicated even though there is no context or words.

Yes.

It will stimulate that in others too, right?

It may or may not. It is not the intention of such self-responsibility to interfere in the timing of the lives of others, but it *will* be felt as clarity. If you are feeling clear, others might notice that you are clear, or else what you say is understood without much description. They understand what you say completely. If they are very cloudy or self-violent or destructive of themselves and others, they might not understand. But if they are reasonably balanced, they will understand what you say with very little comment on your part.

The Creator said that we were broadcasting devices, that we broadcast our experience all over creation. Are we broadcasting this self-violence?

Yes, and this is why your planet and culture must be veiled, amongst other reasons—not only to set up conditions for you, but to protect those beyond this creatorship school so that they are not impaled on the pikestaffs of your own personal challenges. Why should they have to suffer if their lessons are not those of creators? Only creators in training such as you are have those experiences, though not necessarily in the way I described it at the extremeness of self-violence. You must understand not only the external consequences of your actions or inactions, but the *internal* consequences of your actions and inactions.

Self-Violence Ultimately Causes Death

For example, at the end of your natural cycle when you pass through the veils and are shown the meaning of your life, if you had died from a self-violent disease such as cancer or some other disease that might have been transformed had you known about self-love and the dance of the self, then it will be shown why and how this took place. And that the disease of the body was really the material mass of Mother Earth (which makes up your body) saying that it cannot tolerate the physical experience of such self-violence and must return to its native state of being as soil or dust, which will then reflect Mother Earth's true love and will not feel *any* self-violence. That is why people die of disease.

Can we say that all disease is the result of a lack of self-love?

We can say that wasting diseases have to do with such behaviors, to the tune of at least 79 to 80 percent, but we cannot judge individuals who die of these diseases. We can only know that they have not been shown these things in time to prevent damage that may in some cases be irreversible. Certainly there are some diseases that are caused by mass events, meaning war, for instance.

But you still choose to be in that location, though.

Yes, in the larger sense, one might say it is an inclusion of self-violence. But the fine line here might be that you choose to be there because that's where your parents or your wife or children are or for many other reasons. Or if you are a soldier, that's where your buddies are, where your unit is and so on. We cannot say certain things unequivocally as if they are an adamant dogma, but we can suggest or allude to possibilities.

But we can say that this heat exercise and the dance of the self are powerful anti-disease actions on our part, right?

Yes, but it would be better to say that these are pro-health, pro-love, hm?

Pro-life.

Yes, if you like, pro-life, but perhaps with a more benevolent meaning, taking it out of its current political context. Although I must comment that those who wish mothers to go to term really have benevolence in their hearts. It is only when it becomes a destructive thing and people are killed, injured or made to suffer for their stance that it is not good.

To those who these days consider themselves pro-life, politically or religiously speaking, keep a fairly constant awareness of your heart's desire. If you wish the best and will work for the best for the mothers and the babies—and yes, many times the fathers—this means you are truly pro-life. But if you wish to harm or do violence to those who perpetuate causes that are against your beliefs, then it is not a cause of the heart, but a willful action of control.

That's what we've done. It's a sense that the body is like a tool or a vehicle to be controlled rather than a living thing to be cooperated with.

This is why shamanism, as it is called—or mystical actions and spiritual behaviors—perpetuates itself throughout all societies. I can assure you, in ancient times African people did not come over to teach Native Americans, and Native Americans did not go over to teach African people. They developed the knowledge with their visions and teachers and so on, but even a relatively observant man or woman can develop the knowledge of the sacredness and value of all life and that everything is alive—by observation if nothing else.

The challenge today in your modern world is that science has been extricated from shamanism. Shamanism contains science because science at its root is largely observation and noted results. But when you extract science from shamanism, it can lose its love; it can be lost. Anything that does not have the love and respect of the sacredness and value of all life will become, almost immediately, self-destructive because it cannot tolerate its own personal pain. This is why science has been able both to cure diseases—bring wonderful technological tools and entertainments to people—yet also to create horrible, monstrous devices that maim, kill and perpetuate suffering. If a practice such as science can be this polarized, is it not obvious that it is missing something? Put the heart back into science and recognize that shamanism is science with a heart.

Controllers

It's a revelation that the controllers from Orion through Maldek to the Earth end up controlling themselves.

Is it not the best way to learn?

Yes. That understanding is very powerful.

If you can never escape from that which you must know and understand, you will be immersed in your lesson. To the extent that you are unconscious of your lesson, you will continually repeat behaviors over and over again, to the chagrin of historians and political scientists who have warned against such behaviors. Yet this is the only way to understand that these conditions of self-violence and self-destructiveness are not true roots of your true selves, but apparitions associated with your lesson that control is based entirely in fear of the past, present or future, but is not in any way based in the heart. The heart feels and demonstrates pain, but it does not create pain; it only gives you the message that pain is present. The heart produces, generates and disseminates only love. And when you know how to work with your heart, as has been demonstrated, then you discover the wealth of goodness it can do for you and others. To the same extent that you choose to really live up to your pledge to the stars that you are ready, you will choose to work with your heart and be of love for yourself. And since love naturally radiates (we know heat naturally radiates), this will not be a secret for long!

Once we discovered that there were controllers on Earth (the sinister secret government), then our attention was on those who were controlling us. The point we have reached now is the realization that what we perceived out there is a reflection of what we're doing to ourselves?

First, when you see outside of you, it gives you a model by which you can analyze the events in your life, and it makes sense in a linear world. But the next step is to discover what goes on *inside*, which is patterned on a similar model but requires a true change in lifestyle and dogma.

This is very powerful, at least for me, anyway.

I think some others might find it reasonably interesting.

So all humans have to choose for themselves. The more models they see and the more communication there is about this, the more it becomes a possibility.

Yes, it is a cumulative effect, meaning that the more people who feel the heat radiated from others, the more likely they are to ask someone someday, "What is this?" Eventually they will find the right person. They might not become obsessive about asking, but as they feel the experience more and more often from others, gradually more and more people will do it. In time it will become a cherished pastime, and as you get good at it, you can do other things while you are doing that.

What Maintaining the Heart/Heat Will Do

If you get good at feeling the heat, you then begin to conduct your life differently. Maybe you discover for yourself that repetitive motion is something you enjoy, so you begin to wash the dishes in a new way. You wash each dish exactly the same, rinse it off exactly the same and put it on the rack exactly the same. Or maybe you notice that spontaneity and doing things differently is for you. So you wash the dishes in a different way each time or a different time of day.

Or you put them in the dishwasher.

Yes, perhaps you put them one way this day and a different way that day, or maybe all over the place. The main thing is, as you are feeling the heat generated from your heart that is self-love (and is felt anywhere across your heart or your abdomen, as you know), to the extent that you are doing things that are *not* love for you, it will be more difficult to maintain the heat. And to the extent that you are doing things that *are* good for you, it will be easy to maintain the heat. In this way you will discover what is truly good for you, or what is truly *you*. And you will discover what is truly not so good for you—which does not mean it is bad; it only means it is not for you. Maybe it is for someone else.

Remember, we cannot create ironclad rules of behavior known as dogmas, because everyone represents a portion of the One. And while there might be similarities between this portion and that portion—if the One were modeled on the human body, then there might be similarities between different parts of a kidney, but each part is unique. And so we have a unification with our differences. Some people might like digging for coal or chopping wood and other people will not like it, but there will be something they do like. And they will know because as they feel the heat, as they do things, it is harder to maintain that heat if it is not right for them.

How Technology Will Change: Volunteer Particles

In this way you will rediscover what is right for you on an individual basis. And while it might seem on the surface to conflict with commerce, ultimately it will be the best thing that ever happened to commerce, because instead of having to dig and search and search for the things you need to maintain your technology, your technology will become a manifestation of love. Your technology or life around you will manifest on its own. When you hold life to be sacred and treat it as if it were, including yourself (perhaps most especially that), so that you can know that something is sacred, meaning you feel the self-love in yourself and can feel it in others whether they be a frog or a bird or a rock or a tree—what occurs is that in time the particles around you of air and dust and so on are there not to simply be invisible, but because they make up a profound network of available energy that will, on an individual particle basis, *volunteer to be a portion of living technology.*

In the case of advanced ETs, when they need a lightship, they wi[ll] down in a circle and ask for energy and particles to form up aro[und] them to create a lightship. In this way the particles volunteer and come living, sacred, honored, respected and loved technology. To [the] extent that they are finished, other particles will volunteer eve[ry] flight. In this way technology never wears out; it never is absen[t be-] cause parts are unavailable. This means that even if a country do[es not] have enough chromium, it can still make stainless steel. It means [that] particles all around and about you—dust, light, anything—will volunteer temporarily to be a part of some technology. They don't have to be that technology forever; when they wish to go on, other particles will be available as long as someone requests that the technology be there to serve human beings.

That is your bridge technology. In time you will not need technology as you now know it, but that is a bridge, because it still gives you the opportunity to express yourself artistically in commerce. Those who have experienced commerce well know that machines are ultimately art as well as craft, because sometimes they seem to be created out of thin air to fulfill a need that would otherwise have been unfulfilled.

By analogy, our bodies never have to wear out either.

No, and certainly beings who are lightbeings such as yourselves have the capacity to temporarily manufacture a body, meaning to ask particles to come and be a body, going and coming as they wish, not unlike what happens right now.

As with the particles that come and go within us now.

Yes. Only the difference is, you will be conscious of it. Then you won't have to eat, you won't have to sleep. But right now you have to do all those things and serve the needs of your body so you can *be aware* that particles are coming and going. If you have to eat and release things after eating, you are consciously aware that particles are coming and going. In time you can make the bodies by asking particles to volunteer. Then when they are volunteering entirely on their own and doing it for their pleasure as well as your own, you don't need to eat or drink, you don't need to sleep, you don't need to release anything. And when you look at some spiritually advanced ET bodies, you will see that their bodies reflect such things. They don't need to eat.

We have a very few people on the planet right now who can do that. Is Babaji one of them?

Some individuals are given the gift of such wisdom with the intention that they show others in a sacred fashion how they can do it, too.

Sometimes they build up long philosophies to show this; other times the philosophies and teaching take so long because *they* were exposed to such philosophies. But ultimately it is always intended that these things be shared with others, to the extent the teacher knows *how* to share them. Sometimes they do not.

Sometimes they can do it, but they can't talk about it.

Correct.

Can you name any names? Have you heard in history of beings who could do it?

I won't do this because it separates one individual from another. As you can see by my whole talk tonight, it is my intention to encourage you toward unification, not separatism.

I think we have finished our theme for the night.

It's brilliant.

Thank you. On that note we'll say good night.

The Concept of Mutual Benefit

December 9, 1997

I sis here.

Welcome! I'd like to get a little deeper into self-violence. I thought about what you said. There are so many times that we have to work when we're tired. If you have a baby, you have to get up whether you're tired or not; you have to feed it. If you have a commitment, if you're on a team—there are so many times when it seems that we can't be self-indulgent.

When you are self-loving, it is not self-indulgent. It is good you have used this word, however, because that is the attitude of many individuals. We have to help you see how you can restructure your lives. When the individual is conscious of self-violence and there are still things that must be done, then there needs to be not only a negotiation with one's physical self, but one needs to follow up on that negotiation: "I must do this now, but later we will do this," and then you must do it. This you know from psychological and counseling techniques, but there is more.

If you need to do something, it is possible to do that something in a different way that might be more pleasant for you. For instance, once you have learned how to feel the loving way, once you have learned that the experience of all beings being united is real, you can have the strength to do what must be done (especially when it is unexpected) by connecting to other beings—not taking the energy of people, but sharing energy that is available for you. Sometimes you don't have the energy to go on and do something, you know, but you drag yourself through it.

To use this house as an example, what if you had such a good relationship with the elements that make up this house—the stone, the wood, the furniture and so on—that these things would give you the energy they have to spare so you can do what you need to do and don't have to exhaust yourself so much. For example, how would they wish to do so? The same way others would wish to do so—by mutual benefit.

Homework: Make Friends with the Elements in the Home

Homework for the reader and anyone who hears this: When you are ensconced in your office or in your home, take a time, preferably when other people aren't around so you can feel relaxed and comfortable, and go around to the different materials in your house and make friends with them. These materials are stone, wood, plastic and so on, but they also are alive in their own way. Their life is different from yours, but it is nevertheless life.

How would you make friends with stone, for example? Here you have a fireplace of stone, and in the fireplace there are different stones, yet some are similar or alike in material. You might go over to the fireplace, reach out with your right or left hand, whichever works best for you. Generally speaking, since you would be giving something to the stone, use your right hand (for right-handed people, okay?). When you wish to feel from the stone, to know perhaps which stone to touch, then you could use your left hand. This is not absolute; some left-handed people will be different, but maybe this a general rule.

Now, go along and pick out a stone, then picture in your mind's eye the type of place that stone might have come from. Maybe it was a mountain, or in the case of this crystal here, it was a crystal vein in a mountain or somewhere on Earth. So you picture it, and as a sensitive spiritual person, you become that crystal vein or that mountain as much as you can. This is a shamanic technique that we're going to build on. When you feel that massiveness, it will tend to create a different physical feeling in your body. Then reach out and touch the stone, saying nothing. The stone will be reminded of who it is and where it came from. Since you cannot bring the fireplace back to the crystal vein or the mountain, you can, as spiritual woman, feel it as best you can, then touch the stone and remind it where it came from and who it is. Do you understand?

After that you go around and touch other stones in the fireplace if you think they need it, or ask that stone to pass it on. If there is other stone in the house—here, there, around everyplace—and it is also crystal or at least stone, you expand that feeling of being the crystal vein or the mountain so that it passes all around and about your house, you see?

To all the other things that . . .

To all the other crystals or stone. When you feel you are done, pull your hand away slowly. If you get a sudden uncomfortable feeling, the stone has not had enough, so put your hand back on and do it a little longer. Eventually you will be able to pull your hand back slowly and you won't get the uncomfortable feeling because the stone will have had enough.

Then repeat the process with the wood. In the case of plastic, it is chemical manufacture, but part of it might be oil or derivative of oil. You can picture oil underground as it might look, then try to feel yourself as oil; then touch the plastic and so on. Same thing with wood, trees, any other materials. Glass would be sand on the beach or quartz, something like that. Usually it is sand that becomes glass. You go around the house and do that as much as you can.

Drawing Energy from Materials That Are Closest

What happens is that the materials of the house not only remember who they are, but they will also feel like you appreciate them because you remind them who they are and they can reconnect with those places. The crystal in the fireplace connects to the mountain again, not just through you, but can do so. The wood connects to trees and the forest and so on. Then someday when you have to do more than you would like and you are tired, you can ask the crystal, not to give you its energy for living, but look around the house or your office and say out loud, "Can you give me extra energy so that I might do this thing, because I do not have enough of my own?" Then see what happens. Maybe you have to touch the stone or the wood when you say so, maybe not. You experiment, you see?

The materials are happy to give you what they have, or reach out to the mountain or the fcrest and ask those beings to pass on any extra energy they have to you. In this case you are not being violent, but you are working in cooperation with other beings. In the long run the purpose is even more. Parents do this with baby, too. If baby wakes up at night with colic or hunger or for whatever reason, mother can touch her stomach or her body with the left hand and feel her own physicality very well, then reach out and touch baby; baby is from more than the mother, but is also from mother. Baby is reminded where she is from. That's the real reason that baby will relax quicker when mother holds it than when father holds it. There is a very little bit of father matter in baby, but lots of mother matter. In this way baby quickly remembers that mother is part of its body, see? And the baby feels secure, remembers where it is from. Ultimately you will be able to ask baby, aside from feeding, to either sleep through the night or sleep with your own hours.

Raising Well-Adjusted Children

In the old-world way, the baby was never separated from mother in its own bed; baby and mother sleep together at least until baby is nine, ten months old. This has gone out of fashion in your time. Perhaps this is because of the influence of the European community, to which many of you trace your roots. But in the old days, including some of the older civilizations still in existence, mother and baby sleep together.

When this happens, mother and baby's rhythm are very much connected; baby wakes only when he or she is hungry, and it is easy for mother to feed. It's not a simple cure, but what the psychiatrist calls separation anxiety is very much rooted in too much separation with mother from baby's life. I know that it is not convenient always to sleep with baby, but if you want to have a happy, well-adjusted child and make for a more pleasant experience when the child is a teenager as well, think about keeping baby sleeping together with mother for the first eight, nine months, okay?

When you have baby in a crib for sleeping reasons only, it is better to be in something like a smaller space and right next to mother's bed, *never* in a separate room. This thing of individuality has gone too far, having baby in a separate room. Baby can tolerate being in the same room with the parents, okay? It's nothing to be ashamed of; as a matter of fact, baby will be more adjusted being in a room with the parents than in a separate room. I recommend it.

Say more about how that affects their teenage years.

When a child grows and becomes an adolescent and then a teenager, things are felt so strongly because you not only experience the leftover desire of having no responsibility and being able to play like the child (speaking generally for most children), but you also have the desire to be an adult and be responsible not only for your own life but maybe even for the lives of others. So you are confused; you have an overlapping experience. If you have the security of knowing that you are not being rushed into independence, such as having the child in separate room and separate bed when they are too young (that's rushing independence, see?), you are likely to feel that you can take more time as an adolescent. You will feel that you can have some privacy when you need it, and you will ask for it. Then it is good for parents, to the best of their ability, to provide privacy if the youngster needs it— which they probably will.

There is more, but I'm using this as an example so that you can appreciate the value of being in one place at one time. That is a lot of the lesson here on physical Earth.

When you are your more whole self and no longer a physical being, you can be outside the body, you can be beyond this realm, you can be many places at once. But when you are here on Earth as a physical individual, it is important to be that individual and to be it in the stages designed into life here.

One of the most important things parents can do for children is to let them take their time, let them be children when they are children and not expect them to live up to the qualities we expect in adults until it is time. And if they want responsibility or crave it, give it to them very slowly in little bits and do not expect them to be responsible like an adult. When they are an adult they will learn responsibility on their own; it is only your job to show it to them in bits and pieces, without expectations or attachments to their suddenly becoming little adults when they are children.

Receiving Energy from Nature

So in all the cases I mentioned, whenever you have to get something done, if you cooperate with the people or ask for energy from your surroundings . . .

Yes. Think about the people who have to live in rugged places. Without your asking, if you are out in nature somewhere, very often the mountains might give you energy. Sometimes people are out on a hike and they go too far and think, "Oh, I'm too tired to go back all the way, but I must, or I will be here all night." The mountain will sometimes reach out with compassion, which is a natural part of Mother Earth's being, and give you energy even if you don't ask for it. But sometimes you will ask in the form of a prayer, if you are in a rush or you are really far away from where you need to be. "Oh, give me strength!" you will say, sometimes in humor, and the mountain will give you strength.

It is easy for mountain to do this because the mountain does not see you as separate from itself. The mountain recognizes that your physical body is not rock like the mountain, but sees your physical body as made up of Earth matter, like a mountain is, so giving you energy is natural. Think about it. Say you are hiking and climbing; it is strenuous and you are exerting yourself. Besides using your energy, when you exert yourself, you throw off extra energy. Where does it go? If you are on a hike, some of it will go right into the mountain, because your extra energy is compatible with the mountain since your body is made up of Earth stuff. So you are, as the hiker, always giving Earth extra energy when you exert yourself, so the idea of the mountain giving extra energy to you is natural, from the mountain's point of view.

I experienced that. In New York State a group said, "Let's go for a nature walk." They didn't tell me that it was straight up the mountain! I got red-faced and couldn't go any farther. Then I felt that I was on an escalator. I swear, an escalator took me up to the top although I couldn't go on.

Please leave that in.

It was a powerful experience, but I didn't ask because I didn't know to ask.

Yes, you did not ask, but it happened. When you discover self-violence, it is then you can pay attention: "When am I just ignoring something I need that I can do?" Once we have learned about self-violence, as tonight, we can go on to other steps—"Or what if? What about this? What about that?" Then we learn more. But first we must discover self-violence; we don't try to do more and more and more without honoring the physical body.

Serve Mother Earth by Serving Yourself

Many people will ask, "What can I do for Mother Earth? How can I serve her?" And I will say, by serving yourself. Mother Earth is you. Your immortal energy occupies Mother Earth's body; however, your immortal energy does not require Mother Earth's body in order to live, to be yourself. But you do require Mother Earth's body to live on Earth. So to serve Mother Earth, first learn how to serve yourself—such as being aware of self-violence, which you don't find Mother Earth doing.

You might say, "Well, Mother Earth has volcanoes and floods and hurricanes and other storms; isn't she being violent with herself?" I would have to say no, she is not, because this is part of her living body. You see, Mother Earth, not unlike you, has internal mechanisms inside her body—underground rivers, underground lakes, underground gases and fissures and oil and minerals and everything. This is part of her internal body just as you have a heart and organs and lungs and blood and tissue.

But Mother Earth also has *external* organs; her blood also runs on the surface in the form of water. This is *not* like you; you can't have blood running on the surface or soon you would be dead. But for Mother Earth, volcanoes and fires and floods are part of her natural process. If you know how you are like Mother Earth and how you are different from Mother Earth, you will experience life here much more benevolently.

I think this is going to be eye-opening for many people. I don't think it's just Swedes from South Dakota who have this work ethic. The need to achieve at any cost is pretty much all over the United States.

Yes, and sometimes all over the world. It is true, one does not need to be Swedish-American to have this quality, although as people might say from the upper Midwest, "But it helps!"

Yes. [Both laugh.]

A little joke, eh? You know, other beings on other planets do not understand how Earth people could be self-violent. We discussed last time that this is a strange thing for them, yet while I talk to you, among those who hear this conversation are many extraterrestrial teachers, who listen and learn and think of ways they can explain it to their people without actually giving them any experience of violence. They usually have to do it in a song or a story so that it is entertaining, understandable and—most important for beings who do not experience self-violence—palatable, meaning they can accept the fact that this is something you do and also that they do not need to do it. The fact that they do not need to do it does not make them better than you, they are told; it is just an experience that is not part of their lives. The teachers see if they can understand it in that way. Then it fits very nicely into their understanding of how they relate to other beings on other planets who are benevolent and who have experiences that don't fit into each other's lives, yet it is all right. If it is presented to them that way, they can hear it. You see, I speak to you as well as to ET teachers in this moment.

If they can understand that many of us have thought for very long that we were mental bodies—that's where the focus has been, that the physical body is just something to carry the brain around. There has been no awareness of the body as having needs.

Learning to Understand the Physical Body:
How Your Body Talks to You

Yes, but now as we gradually learn what the physical body is about and how to understand its language and its feelings and what those feelings mean, then we can take action. And once we start taking action, the physical body breathes a sigh of relief, and says, "Now I don't have to give you such dramatic messages like getting sick or feeling pain."

The body's last-resort message is pain. If you have not listened or been unable to understand the message, the body will say, "Well, let me do this." The body is not being violent with itself, as it sees it; it is just adapting to Mother Earth's natural language. Remember, your body is made from Mother Earth, and her natural language might at any moment be a storm or an earthquake that might change the surface of her body. But that is her way of speaking, her way of demonstrating her passion and feelings. If your body has to produce pain, it is expressing passion and feelings, but it is the message of last resort. It is going to give the message in that way because you have been unable to understand the message any other way. When you feel pain, you are more likely to take action, ask for help, do something. Then perhaps you will wonder, "What does it mean?"

Those of you who occasionally get a headache or other trauma, you take medication or go to a massage therapist or an acupuncturist or whoever helps you—physician, naturopath, whoever's right for you. But also remember, it is all right to take elements of medical science—drugs, precisely measured herbs, teas, all of these therapies available to you today, including what the medical doctor has to offer. If you had wished to avoid these things entirely, you would have chosen to be born in 1600 France, maybe, or 1400 Egypt, maybe—or even 2100 in Iceland, when there will be a colony of people there who are learning how to practice energy medicine for all conditions in order to teach all beings who live in third-, fourth- and even fifth-dimensional Earth how to energetically transform all discomforts. You would have chosen to be born at other times. But when you choose to be born in the twentieth-century Earth (soon to be twenty-first century, eh?), it is because you want to experience in body and soul all that the century has to offer. So don't turn your back on what your times have to offer.

What would you like to talk about now?

The Pleiadian in You

Let me look into it. Let's speak a little bit to the Pleiadian in you all. Very often we—Zoosh and others for other projects with you and others—have discussed the Sirius, the Orion, sometimes the Andromedan, but very little discussion of the Pleiadian. I want to bring that up now, because through your physical experience these days, there is a true correlation between the child and your physical body—the experience of childhood in your physical body, regardless of how old you are. That correlation is simply this: The child knows he or she wants to have fun; it is born with that. The child does not have to learn—the baby or the youngster—that fun is a good thing. It wants to have fun, and it is natural. What does this suggest? Is that just an aspect of childhood, or is it in your very nature?

Do you know that Mother Earth's body is truly a child? She can be millions of years old, yes, but it is in the nature of truly fully realized physical beings to experience themselves more as the purity, innocence and CLARITY of childhood than any other time of life. When you are a child, things are quite clear. As parents know, you can't really fool children, not for very long, because they can tell whether a person is telling them the truth or lying—maybe not right away, but eventually they can understand. So your physical bodies, even though you be adults, have one particular thing very much in common with children: they want to have fun.

I mention this in connection with Pleiadians because they like to have fun; it is in their nature. They like to kid around, joke, laugh, sing, dance and do other fun things. But think about it for a moment: the physical body of you all is born not only with the ability but with the desire to have fun! That means that when you are born you are looking for a good time, if I can say that. This tells you that in your essence, in your purity, in your innocence, in your clarity as a child, fun is natural. As you learn, in your culture, you learn how *not* to have fun. [Laughs.]

Your Body Needs to Have Fun

It's the case for most of you now: Lots of the tension you feel—especially if you are working or studying too hard, or have too many responsibilities—lots of that tension doesn't have to do with the immediate work or study, but with the body's *need* to have fun. This need can be understood in its expression. Yes, love is important—physical love too—all this is important. But the body wants to play.

So here's a suggestion for homework: Some therapists are now doing play therapy with adults. If the therapist has experience and knows what he or she is doing, I strongly recommend this for adults. When done in a nurturing environment, it can remind you of what you're missing. It doesn't work very well, if you think about it, but the physical action . . . remember, so many of you have forgotten physical language. The physical actions you take will have a very profound effect, not only while you are taking them, but perhaps just as important, after you've done them. They will actually cause your body to be relieved and say, "Oh, I've needed to do that!" It's as if your body is saying, "Oh, I've needed to do that for so long. I've been missing that! I've missed rolling around on the floor!" or "I've missed throwing the ball around; I love that!" That's your physical body talking.

Play vs. Work

Learn from the Pleiadians; you do have some things to learn from them, not only to teach them. That is that play is natural and healthy and fun; it is truly the path to fulfillment. Granted, some play is more benevolent; I think you know what kind, so I will not be the strict psychologist here. I will simply say, you know what's benevolent. So play, and don't turn it into what adults do so often—competition. Once you add competition to play, it immediately becomes work. So let play be innocent. If you want to bounce a ball off a wall, fine; but don't try and bounce it more times off the wall every minute, then 50 times the next minute, then 75 times the next minute. Don't make it into work. Those lessons that teach children how to play competitive games, unconsciously given by people with the best of intentions, might make the children good competitors and good business people someday—or good soldiers—but they also teach the child that play is wrong if it doesn't incorporate work. That's how children learn that being themselves, which is their nature—wanting to play, just being themselves—is somehow wrong. Not because an adult comes along, befriends a little child playing and says, "That's wrong," but because the well-meaning adult encourages the child to do play that is competitive or worklike.

I understand why you do this; I understand how it fits into your culture. But I also understand that this is the beginning of the child losing itself and feeling like there's something wrong with her or him. And when those children grow up into adults, it will be harder for them to find themselves, their true natures, their ways of being, their own feelings. They have learned to hide it because it is not safe to show it. They remember as a child, you see—unconsciously. If it is not safe to be shown to others, it's not safe to demonstrate it to yourself, because you might be seen to be doing play that isn't work, you see? As a result, you hide it so well, many of you, that you can't find yourself no matter how hard you try. That's why there are so many necessary therapies that exist today to help people find themselves and know where they are and who they are and what other people are—the child's attempt to get approval from the adult by imitating the adult.

Someday the Pleiadians will demonstrate play to you, not only for pleasure but play as life. The Pleiadians are not foolish people; they do not sit around all day playing silly games, as you might call it. They are not self-indulgent. They know how to do things. They do work, but they make work fun. They might need to work on a ship; maybe there is a Pleiadian mechanic, as you might call him, who has to work on the ship, but it just so happens that mechanics is what this Pleiadian loves to do. It is pleasure, so working on the ship or the craft is pleasure, not work. If the mechanic needs to eat, to relax, to sleep, he or she stops—because all parts in the ship or craft (the flying saucer, as you might call it) are made up of materials that enjoy being what they are. Materials are not ripped out of the Earth to make nuts and bolts without their permission. The materials enjoy being what they are, so the ship hardly ever breaks down. If the mechanic needs to work on it, it's usually to add something, not to fix something. So the ship does not demand that you work hard, and the Pleiadian can take a break and come back and work some more when he feels like it.

I'm not saying that this is like your world, but learn how to make work fun. Some of you know how to do this, and some of you know how to make a demonstration of work as fun to children. And try, if you would, not to get so involved in competition. I know you sometimes think that this is fun, but it is adult fun, and many so-called adult things are really just ways of disapproving of oneself.

Adults disapprove, therefore as children we take that as a judgment and judge ourselves the way we think an adult would?

Yes. If you are an adult, you know, you often feel that you *ought* to be doing this or you *ought* to be doing that. That is a standard way of being for most adults, with the exception of some individuals in a more privileged class. But even the wealthier classes often have responsibilities that the average person might not have. People in a wealthy class who don't have to work would feel, "We ought to be doing something for this group of people" or "We ought to be in service somehow." Many old families have that idea, so their children learn how to be adults in service.

I'm not trying to tell you your cultures are bad; you've accomplished many good things, and you are doing more good things than not. But it's okay to refine things, make them better, so that your goals, the things you want as individuals and as a society, do not keep moving further and further away from you because you haven't adapted your means to achieve those goals to your true nature, but are attempting to achieve your goals by *not being yourselves.* This is a big one.

Separation and Materialism: Lucifer Brings His Tools

When did we lose ourselves? How far back does this go?

It really goes back to the time when that being (with the best of intentions, as your Uncle Zoosh said) left Jehovah's ship, came down and said, "I'm going to give these people tools so they can do it for themselves." This being was absolutely feeling that he was going to give these people independence so that they didn't have to be dependent on something outside of themselves.

That sounds very good in your modern time, but it was also the beginning of separation and materialism in its own right, rather than materialism as an integrated experience. (Integrated materialism is asking materials around you to become what you need, all right? And they simply do that rather than your having to drag them from where they live to become that.) So that's how it started in ancient times. It started by beings who meant well but meddled in a system that was working. [Laughs.]

Was this Atlantis or pre-Atlantis?

In Lemurian times this being presented tools to the Lemurians, who said, "No, thank you; we're happy with our system." Then he went to the Atlantis place. There were many people on Atlantis; they were really people from Lemuria who decided they wanted to start a new colony, but they were going to use the Lemurian methods of creating what was needed, through dance and song and color and, to some extent, ceremony. He went to them—they were just getting started, see, and they were already feeling a little bit the desire to be independent—and said, "Here, I've got something for you so you can be more independent." It was perhaps unintentional, but it was a seduction.

But in the long run it was part of the plan, right?

Oh, certainly. People on this planet and in previous times had experiences like this elsewhere, and the only way to learn it in its more benevolent way is to do it over and achieve benevolence rather than ignore it and try to go on as if it hadn't happened. It's like your people say, "Okay, you fell off the horse, but the horse is not your enemy. Get up and make friends with the horse, touch it, pat it and tell it, 'I'm sorry for falling off and frightening you.'"

It's really true that when people fall off horses, horses get frightened because they are very feeling beings. They get frightened not only for you, but for themselves. So tell the horse, "It's not your fault," or say, "I still like you," then get back on the horse and try to ride. In other words, don't forget it; don't say, "Maybe I will drive a car and forget about the horse." Then the horse is disappointed and feels like you have not forgiven it, and it will always feel uncomfortable around you.

And you will still have the fear.

You will have the fear of the horse and all it represents. When people have experiences before this, such as Orion—or in an individual life, if you have a relationship and it didn't work, you don't usually stop having relationships—you repeat the experience but try to do it in a different way. Eventually you do it in a way that works for you, and that relationship is more successful than the previous one. But you don't stop. If you stop, you get frightened, and not only do you fear relationships, but relationships are uncomfortable with *you*; the experience is uncomfortable with you because you have not forgiven the experience for its discomfort. Then you not only have problems with intimate relationships, but you have problems with friendships and business relationships, even how you relate to tools. Maybe before, when your relationship was not doing too great but was struggling along, you could hammer a nail in straight; but afterward you suddenly seem to bend more nails. [Chuckles.] Everything is connected to everything else; it is not rules and laws I am talking about here, but possibilities.

So with great benevolent feeling, Lucifer brought these tools.

Yes.

Go on with that a little bit.

Lucifer (that was his name then) said, "I've got these wonderful tools for you, and you can build your own houses and cut down these trees." At first when the people heard this, they were horrified: "Cut down trees! The trees are living beings; we would not want to hurt them." But of course, as with any independent colony, there will be someone who will try something. Lucifer himself would go over and say, "Look here, you can cut this tree down," and begin sawing the tree, eh? This is an example. He would not have brought a saw, but it gives you the idea. Mostly the people would shrink back in horror, but there would be one or two who would say, "Let me try that."

I am compressing about a million years of experience into something you can understand, but it is important to see it within that context; otherwise you can't understand the minor thing that Lucifer did. What he actually brought the people was a device. If they stated what they needed into it, the device would materialize it for them. That's what he really brought. He didn't bring hammers and nails.

Lucifer's Device in Atlantis

The people, instead of dancing and doing the ceremonies and interacting with the color and the energy of life as they had in Lemuria to feel comfortable and be in a benevolent state of being all the time and never get too cold or hot, would actually experience the elements, see? If they got cold, then Lucifer said, "Go over to the device and say, 'I am cold; what can you give me to help me be warm?'" Out would pop a snowsuit or something. It was with the best of intentions. Think about how often you would all like to have such a device today.

Sounds like the replicater on Star Trek.

Yes, it sounds just like something from a story. The reason it is such an idealized device is because it was once given to people here, and deep in the memory and in the soil of Earth which makes up your bodies, there is the memory that such tools exist and even now are utilized by many extraterrestrials. But the more advanced spiritual or higher beings or whatever do not use this thing.

They invite the particles, then.

Yes, just as we've discussed before, they invite the particles.

How long did they have this device? We've never read about it or heard about it.

In terms of experiential time, three or four years.

That's all?

That's how long everybody could go up and use it. About that time they started to develop hierarchies. They felt that it might be better if one person asked for things. It was like developing specialties. One person would be in charge of the device, and when someone needed something, he would go to that person and say, "I need this." Then that person would go to the device and say, "So-and-so needs this; would you produce it for her?"

You could see where that would go, not only into the religious and philosophical but into the cultural and nationalistic experiences of today. So the device began to be isolated from the general public. After a while, through other machinations of society, it became available only to certain classes of people. Eventually it was available only to the royalty or to the initiated. When the society was destroyed before the end of its natural cycle, it was taken elsewhere. The device itself could not be destroyed; if you put it in a nuclear explosion, it would not be destroyed because it is a receiver/transmitter extraordinaire. It is not an evil device; it is really a spiritual device, but it is actually like a toy. It is meant to be an aid, this device; it's meant to be an aid to children to learn how to create benevolently for themselves. Initially they have this device so they can see the desired result, you see. Eventually, when they learn how to ask the particles to be what they need them to be, as we've discussed, then the toy is set aside or given to other children who are learning. So this was a *toy*. That's another reason Lucifer felt it was innocent—a child's toy, so why shouldn't it be all right to give it to the people?

What happened to it when Atlantis disintegrated?

It was under the sea for a long time, but eventually it was found. It is now ensconced in a secret place in the Earth. You will find it again— or more likely, it will be reclaimed someday by extraterrestrial civilizations. They will give you some other device that is a little simpler and easier for you to understand, but more important, they will give you the training that goes with the device. When you have regular meetings with the Pleiadians, interaction between all of you (most likely you will someday), you will be happy to have them teach your children how to manifest and create some things with these devices. It will be a good contact in more ways than one.

Losing the Ability to Play

Were we seeking our lost innocence and our lost ability to play? How did that all tie into that tool?

Within the context of my entire discussion tonight?

Yes. I asked when we lost ourselves, our ability to play, and you referred to . . .

I said that in that ancient time in Atlantis there was this toy. People initially went to it and said, "I need this," and the device would create it. But then it came to be less and less available to people. On the positive side, people learned to go to other people and help them. But because the society was shifting into hierarchies, they also learned that the people on the lower end of the hierarchies had to work. And for many at the lowest end of the hierarchy, work was their whole life. Even though they would be created at some point either by cloning or by natural reproduction, they wouldn't be allowed to experience any childhood or fun. Fun would be a *privilege* of work, not a natural state of being. So many of the things you are working out today have to do with that whole hierarchical drama. If you didn't do it right the first time, just like relationships, you'd try another till you got it right. It is about relationships, how you relate.

Anything, anyone—how you relate, then fill in the blank. There are so many confusions these days for you yet there are symbols. You have seen, perhaps, this symbol [draws], not uncommon in your times. This is a square with a circle inside and a triangle inside that. Do you know what that means? Many different things to many different people. Seen from above the symbol looks like this [draws].

Three lines.

Change perspective. We are above the symbol; what does that suggest? That the triangle inside the circle inside the square is not one symbol.

How often do you say, "I want something, but I have a block"? What this means is that there is a big block, like a wall, in front of you—like a square, hm? And beyond that square is the triangle, the three aspects of life—youth, middle age and old age—or the cycles of life, however you put it. And beyond that is the circle—everything you want. But the immediate thing in the moment is

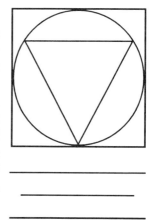

what you want to create for yourself, the object you need, which is part of the triangle— past, present and future, trinity. You have the square in front of you; that is the block. As you learn not only how to do things in new ways, but how to do things in perhaps spiritual ways, you learn how to *step through* the square. You either learn all the steps to get to what you want, or you learn some new spiritual thing and dance through the wall. Or you learn how to walk around the wall instead of just banging against it. Then you get to the triangle, which represents what you want when you want it.

I give you the symbol because the symbol is meant to show you that the square is connected to the circle and the triangle, what you want. In reality the symbol was always intended to be expressed like this, which I think many of you probably know [draws]: a triangle inside a square inside a circle. These symbols are very useful [chuckles].

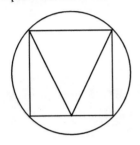

So that means that ever since Atlantis—for who knows how many thousands of years—we've lived this work ethic?

That's when you discovered . . .

. . . that playing is a sin. You've got to feel guilty here.

Yes, that's when a part of you discovered that play is not connected to what you need. If you went to visit Lemuria right now, everybody is playing and dancing and laughing and singing, and you would say to yourself as modern man or woman, "But who prepares the food? Where do they grow the vegetables? What do they eat, and who builds their shelters?" But they do not have to do that; they exist there because everything is one, and they know that. They dance and play because that is their nature, which is also your nature. The food is provided either as substance to eat, maybe for a ceremony, but more likely they never feel hungry because there is no real separation between them and the world they dance in. They breathe, eat, play and interact completely connected. They have their individuality and they also have their One experience.

So we're going to get that back?

Becoming More of Your Natural Selves

Oh, yes; even now you are being given back the parts of yourself, and they have consequences. But those parts are going to have effects on you. Sometimes those effects will feel strange and bizarre, unusual—such as having other people's discomfort or dreams because they don't fit into your life. But it just means you're supposed to mention it to others, and it will get back to them. That is part of being the One. If you walk down a road in a society where everything is known to be the One (meaning it is all connected) and find something that looks like it's part of something else because it doesn't seem to be whole unto itself, then you continue walking down the road and you ask others, "Do you have the rest of this?" or "Is this for you?" Maybe someone takes it and says, "I think I have the rest of that over here; it must have fallen off." [Chuckles.]

Say more about bringing our parts back. Where are those parts?

Zoosh has said that someday you will get back your heart and your ability to know everything, and someday you will know how to instantaneously cure yourself or other people. Someday you will get all the parts back that you left on the other side of the veils when you came to this school to learn what you need to learn to re-create your reality. Those parts are coming back now. Because we can't bring everything back at once, you have to bring something back and work with that for a while. You go through all the experiences you have learned so far here, which have to do with responsibility, consequences, actions and interactions, and bring those parts into the context of your culture here.

It's not only to remember who you are, but you have come here to re-create who you are. So when your natural parts come back to each and every one of you, they will not only bring things that were you before this life, with wisdom and those abilities, but those things will also need to adapt to what you have become here. They will need time to integrate what *you* have learned in this life, just as in this life you will need to integrate *them*. They might feel like long-lost parts, but more likely they will feel like something new that you don't know what to do with. So you will need a time of reacquaintance.

They sound like abilities more than parts.

They are abilities, but I'm calling them parts because they are truly parts of you. When you come here, you leave most of the total you elsewhere so that you don't remember who you are. You can then re-create new abilities for yourself because you don't continue to use your old skills that you sharpened up over many lifetimes. You have had to make new tools for yourself.

So we integrate those old abilities with our . . .

. . .with your now new flexibility. Your new flexibility may not be totally comfortable with what you once were. Even though those parts might have great and powerful wisdom, they will also be previously . . . or otherworldly, other-dimensionally connected to the total you. But they will not have had a personal experience of your life here. So if you have discovered some new way to do something and some part moves through the veils and comes here and reintegrates with you, then you may have new skills and abilities here, new to you from your perspective.

But maybe they won't fit, and they'll have to adapt. Because you didn't have that ability or part of yourself here in this life, you had to create something else. So those two things have to be blended to reach an accommodation with each other: Your old wisdom needs to be updated to the new wisdom, and the new wisdom needs to have time to expand into the old.

Give me some examples.

Getting Your Heart Energy Back

An example: Someday you will get the greater part of your heart energy back. It comes in in bits now, because if you got it all back right now, you'd be like the Pleiadians and you couldn't be here in this world. But when you start to get more of your heart energy back, you will feel things more. Your feelings will be stronger, your passions stronger, your love and your need for love will be stronger. In other words, as a psychiatrist might say, you will be emotionally more powerful and you will need to interact more on the feeling level. There is nothing psychological about this; it is a physical thing. That greater portion of your heart needs to accommodate to what you have done here with the smaller portion of your heart, and the smaller portion needs to have time to adjust to the other portion. In the past (this life, before the parts of your greater portion came in), some things might not have upset you very much; you would have walked by and said, "Oh well, it's too bad, but it's not about me, so I'll just go on." Now when you hear about something—a friend tells you, you hear it on the news or read it in a newspaper or magazine—and you have a huge emotional reaction, it is very surprising to you. You cry or you're enraged or you call your congressman; you have a big reaction. That's because you have more heart energy, more compassion, more identification with your fellow man or woman than you had before. If someone is suffering someplace else, you want to know what to do about it right now. It's no longer just, "Oh, that's too bad, but that's not me. I'm just going to go on with my life." That's an example.

What are the numbers for our present heart energy? The maximum anybody had was 28 percent and the average was 14 percent or so. What are the numbers now?

Now it's gone up to 35 percent.

What's the average?

No more than 35 percent, but these numbers are totally arbitrary for your own mental cognition. At any given moment you might be overwhelmed with feeling, whereas in another moment you might feel very abstract.

What a time to be here!

You all chose to be born during these times, which is why it's okay to take aspirin if you need it.

So we're not only getting more heart energy, but actual knowledge of how to do particular things?

No, no. It can be knowledge of how to do things, but since it won't come back as a body of knowledge, which would change your whole personality, it will come back in little bits. You will feel it, for example, as something being easier to do that you used to struggle with; or it could be that something you used to struggle with, you don't worry about so much anymore, or you can accomplish it much quicker, without having learned anything new.

Or maybe being drawn to something and learning it very quickly.

Yes, or some activity you never were interested in before that you suddenly want to know about. Or even some group of people or some experience, some part of the human experience—you were never interested in that, and suddenly you can't get enough of it. This has somehow to do with some greater portion of you that is incrementally coming in now.

Have we moved beyond 3.48?

[Laughs.] I think that is less important, because remember, you must go slowly to integrate and not be rushed. Do not rush the child to be independent, or the child will revenge itself as an adult. If the child was rushed and did not get to have playtime, when it is an adult it's going to be stubborn and demanding, not because the child or adult is a bad person, but just because it was rushed. Being rushed is not good, so rushing to 4.0 dimension—not good.

All right, we will slowly enjoy the integration. [Laughs.]

If you have a nice cup of coffee or cocoa or hot tea, do you want to take just one sip, then put it down and forget it? You want to enjoy the whole cup.

Perhaps that is enough for tonight.

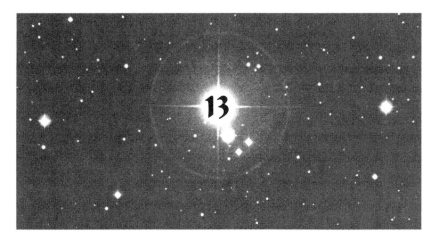

"The Vast You" and Other Realities

December 16, 1997

I sis here: Greetings.

Welcome. We're told that our soul is mostly connected to where we are here now, this physical plane, and that we've got possible and probable realities and other-dimensional selves, but I don't know that we've ever had a really good explanation of that. Are the other-dimensional selves connected to the same soul, or to another part of us?

The Universal Choir Sings Choices for Alternate Realities

Let me start this way. People who have had so-called after-death experiences sometimes describe hearing what seems like the universal choir, a beautiful music. If you can, picture (not just imagine how it might be) the music, if you are a musician, as a form of sheet music where one has lines and dots, where one sees symbols for tones and connections with the right timing to other tones. With the universal choir, one hears something like the fabric of a spiderweb, only the web would be very large and each strand would represent a possibility.

Those sounds are literally sung by beings in the higher dimension, sometimes angels, sometimes beings who have not yet taken on the traditional duties of the angelics. If it were not for that, you would not have as many options in your daily life. You would also not have the opportunity to make dramatic and sudden choices, even simple and subtle choices. That music is the fabric of *choice*, and it allows you to experience potential choices for alternate realities.

For example, what happens to someone who dies suddenly? Everyone dies with his permission, but what happens if someone has plans or intentions for their life, and suddenly they die and are not prepared to go through the veils? They wish to have some version of their intentions play out. Sometimes these people remain on Earth as discarnate spirits, and sometimes these spirits are, over time, gradually rescued and led on through the veils.

But there is also another opportunity. There are alternate realities that are, for the sake of musical comparisons, perhaps a half-tone different (instead of sharp, flat; instead of flat, sharp), for the sake of the musical analogy. Those unfinished goals, expectations, needs, desires and so on might be played out in that alternate reality in all circumstances, which means that all situations associated with the life up to that point will be represented, but in some fashion that would be askew compared to the physical life one had led—meaning not the same, but with striking similarities. In this way an alternate reality is available for such circumstances.

But do these realities exist *only* for those circumstances? No. For such a training and teaching world upon which you are living, there must always be a tremendous number of choices. For example, two individuals in a room or even on a planet will affect the way that planet demonstrates itself to those individuals. Even one individual on a planet will change that effect, and if you have hundreds and thousands and millions and billions, where the planet must be so many things to so many different people, often the planet cannot do it all. Once you have a certain number of souls incarnated on a planet, so many choices could be made that sometimes choices are made within an octave (keeping our musical analogy), which amounts to a mass choice for many individuals who bear a similarity to all the other individuals yet are not quite the same. A simple, mundane example would be the vast movement—suddenly, in terms of the vastness of time—from horseback riding to driving in automobiles. That was a mass event. It took a few years to assimilate, but it happened for many people.

In those circumstances, the planet can easily tolerate such mass events. But in the circumstance where each individual requires a great many alternate choices, one has to have resonances available to take up the slack (that's a nice phrase). So these extra resonances or alternate realities exist to support Mother Earth in her material-mastery capacity so that you as individuals have choices beyond what she personally can provide.

Within the scope of your Creator School, this also offers the choice for dramas. Some people describe moments of an after-death experience where they have initial moments of fear and discomfort and frightening images and feelings, which fade and then become more benevolent. But what is available to provide such fear and discomfort?

Mother Earth cannot do this in her own right, so the individual in such a passage does not go directly through the veils; they go into an alternate reality which can provide that brief moment of after-death experience. This is usually only in the case of an individual who had not processed completely the lessons of discomfort they were learning in an individual life. In this way they can process it without involving Mother Earth directly, but in an alternate way. After they finish that in their not-quite-human/not-quite-spirit state, then they again pass through the veils and continue on with their lives.

The Energy That Fuels These Realities

If Mother Earth doesn't provide the energy for these alternate realities, then who or what does?

As I indicated, it is partly provided by angelics who are not working directly with humans or other beings, since angelics work with beings all over . . .

Oh, the ones singing . . . I didn't understand.

Yes, it is done partly by angelics, but also partly by the rhythm (I'm musical tonight) of all beings on Earth and in your immediate solar system. The immediate solar system would be your Sun and the first five planets, all right? The other planets do not have the closeness; the proximity is not there. Everything on those planets (and for the sake of clarity, everything on Earth) . . . for example, a single blade of grass would have a resonant energy that supports that blade of grass to exist, yet it also has the same choices, even though it does not have the same lessons. The blade of grass itself is not in Creator School. But because it is participating in Creator School for you, it has these choices, though the chances of a blade of grass utilizing choices such as I've indicated for a human being are almost nonexistent. Yet those choices must be there. Therefore all other forms of life have this extra resonance. The more vital and living the planet is with plants and trees and animals and living stone and water and so on, the more extra resonance is available to support the universal choir's resonant sounds, to support variables in life choices.

It is interesting to note that in the 1700s, when life was more lush—

there were more species of plants and animals and fewer human beings—people had their alternative choices because there was more life. Now the more life is represented in more human beings, though fewer animals and plants, fewer pure streams of water and clouds because of atmospheric gases and so on. So how, then, do you still have all these choices? Is it because of the people on the planet? No, it is because you are now at the point where you are beginning to reassimilate portions of yourself that have been previously inaccessible to you. The veils are thinning or lifting, and you are now gradually beginning to become more of your natural selves, through which you have the capacity to experience alternate realities on your own.

The loss of the plants, though sad, is stimulating you to find cures for diseases in a more challenging way. These plants could have provided the cures, but many are now gone, most of which were associated with rain forests and quite a few with desert plants that are no longer accessible. The reacquisition of your natural selves, or your more complete selves, is making it possible for you to access these alternate realities on your own. This is essential. It is as if to say that the people in the 1700s, because there were fewer, utilized the natural world for their pathways to the alternate realities. People nowadays, since there is less of the natural world (certainly in its pure state), must have a means to access these alternate realities, and they do so by your reacquaintanceship with your natural selves.

Experiencing Alternate Realities

Are these alternate realities fully inhabited? If we were conscious there, would it be like Earth, where there are people, relationships, jobs, obligations, possessions?

These realities exist out of the necessities of others. If there were not people on Earth learning lessons in Creator School, these realities would be like empty drawers, to be activated should they be needed. But if you went to those realities, you would experience little or nothing. It would be like a piece of paper ready to be drawn upon or written or painted upon, but it would be a potential. To the extent that it is a reality unto itself, it is strictly reactionary.

Is it like going on the holodeck, where we run a program?

Oh, no. If you went there, it would be absolutely real. It would just be strange; everything would look familiar, but it would be different. We'll pick an example that will amuse you: If you went there, the person you knew as your mother might be your aunt, or the person you knew as your husband might be your coworker. You would probably still know these people, but not in the same capacity.

That would be confusing.

Very confusing for a time, yet the only people who go there are people who are essentially discarnate spirits who feel they must complete something. But it is a very challenging way to do that; it is infinitely easier to simply go through the veils and go on. In a sense, it has to do with attachments.

Now, this is different from the discarnate spirit who might stay behind because he or she dearly loves someone and must see them once again; this is not the same. That would be a circumstance in which that loved one might have a vision of that person, sometimes referred to in the past as a ghost. In reality, the individual who had passed over is allowed to visit the loved one, sometimes more than once, but this is not common.

There have been a few books about, for instance, someone who woke up in his own body but in another reality—a different time frame, where there were railroad trains instead of cars. It would be a strange situation.

Yes. One interesting thing is that it almost always would be present- or past-oriented; it wouldn't be the future. It would be very unusual to wake up in an alternate reality that was futuristic, in which there was no similarity at all. You will almost always, if you read about that in books, find it was present- or past-oriented.

Is there a part of each of us in these realities that functions full-time for years and years?

No, no. You go into those realities only if you need to do it. Even though you might see all the people you know in those realities, the people you are seeing are *not* the people who are in this reality.

So you create them just to have them there like a stage setting?

I wouldn't say that you as an individual create it; it would be more that they are created for you to temporarily interact with until you are ready to go on to pass through the veils. You do understand that I am not talking about other dimensions; I am talking about alternate realities, which is quite different from other dimensions.

Yes, I understand; we're not talking about fourth, fifth, sixth dimensions.

No. You only go there . . .

. . . to finish something up.

Actually, it's not quite that. You go there only if you insist on finishing something up in that way. Even though you are discarnate, it is essentially a willful experience, and you cannot exert will in pure spirit form. As you go through the veils with your guide and so on to continue your life elsewhere, you do not have will. Will is the exertion of an idea by force, whether it is for good or not. This might be a dramatic way to view will, but you can see that if you are all functioning as one in a harmonious world, will has no place there. But it does have a place in Creator School. So if you will yourself to go to an alternate reality, it necessarily binds you to this reality's alternate realities. It would bind you to remain as a discarnate spirit, not going through the veils until you feel you are done or until things become too disorienting. This happens for some who refuse to leave this reality; they will sometimes go into an alternate reality to speed that decision, but if it becomes too confusing, they will eventually be rescued.

I had the idea that these were ongoing existing other parts of ourselves that were functioning all the time. That's not true, then.

Not according to my understanding.

Vertical Integration

When we hear that we are integrating our alternate selves or possible selves or the other parts of ourselves, how would you describe it?

Integrating other parts of yourselves? I would see it the way Uncle Zoosh calls it, more as a vertical experience. I would use that visual, not because alternate realities are horizontal, but so you understand that when you are integrating other parts of yourself, these are parts that exist now but are veiled from you so you can experience the lessons and growth of Creator School. But you do not integrate the kind of alternate experiences I have been discussing, for that is not you, unless we are talking about someone who is actually there.

That's never been explained before. So are these parts other expressions of the soul on the physical plane, or are they on other dimensions?

Which parts are we referring to?

The parts we're integrating now.

Those parts have to do, to some extent, with heart energy, which might be on the physical plane, yes? They are what you would now consider your mystical abilities, your overall being, your overall experience, your accumulated wisdom and so on—that which you identify as the greater or larger or all-encompassing you.

So it's not past selves and lives we've lived that we haven't accepted?

Oh, no; past lives, as you call them—and future lives, for that matter—are on their own strand. When they die they are done, and they go on through the veils just as you do. You are someone's past life now (you could see it that way), and when you're done you'll go on. But you do not accumulate past lives. When you are in an individual life you may be able to access them sometimes, perhaps with the assistance of someone who can do this for you. But generally speaking, each life is on its own thread of living, and as you become more aware of the total you, the total you is conscious of all your lives. That is another way one might become aware of one's past lives or even have leanings or understandings as to what future lives might be.

So they don't totally integrate into our vastness until at some point we're totally beyond Creator School way down the line?

Becoming Aware When Passing through the Veils

They are all together now; when you pass through the veils, you become *aware* of them all being together. I realize that it has been put to you that you're all going to meet at some point in space, but it has been put this way for the sake of a visual example. In reality, here on this school you experience the illusion that you are not united as one being so that you can directly experience the evidence of consequences. Of course, if you knew and had physical evidence that you are one, you would never do certain things that you do here, because the moment you began to do them, you would immediately feel the consequences as others feel it. If you say a harsh word to a person when you know you are all one, the moment that harshness begins to build—even before you actually express it—you would instantaneously feel the impact of that harshness on other individuals and yourself. So you would be disinclined to do that.

But here you are allowed to do that by way of slowing down creation so you can understand its intimate building blocks. All you do when you pass through the veils is simply become aware that you are connected, and for those who are interested, have it explained to you in detail. But once you have the awareness, which is a feeling—not a vague feeling but a very precise and understandable feeling—you usually do not require an explanation. It is an understanding, a knowing. For instance, it is like the difference between thinking about swimming when you don't know how to do it, and thinking about swimming when you know how to do it. You have the *feeling*; it's completely different.

The way people understand and talk about their past lives is: "I was somebody." That somebody is ongoing and existing, you're saying.

This requires an illustration. [Draws.] For the sake of the illustration, the vast you, yes? And veils, yes? We're just drawing a few lives here, but one could make more. Individual lives, yes? Now, this illustration effectively eliminates time, so the individual life goes down here. This [at top] is the vast you, and here are the individual lives, yes? One might, in the vast you, conceivably have had millions of individual

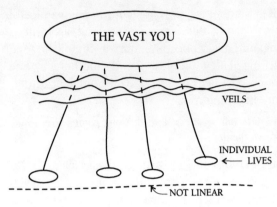

incarnations—but one would only need to access . . . let's say these were all on Earth, hm?

For example, one would need access only to certain others. Let's say there were seven other Earth lives. As one gradually remembers more of one's vastness, one might gradually begin to remember skills obtained in the other seven Earth lives, yes? But it is not a line, not one after the other with these lives. Does that help?

Remembering Past Lives

Let me ask you a question. This represents a human on Earth at this moment in time [points to a circle at the bottom]. As this veil thins here and we access more of this vastness, then we can remember some of these lives shown down here and pull them up into here? Is that what you're saying?

Possibly. More likely you will tend to remember things that have already been completed and reassimilated. It is less likely that you will "remember" lives that may be ongoing within their own time. Speaks of Many Truths will say to you, "I am alive in my own time" because he wishes to focus in that time rather than in his current spirit state when speaking to you so that he can have relevant understanding of physical life.

Remembering a past life is not only a memory. In the case of connecting to the lives that have already been completed in the vast you, one can remember those lives as the veils thin to the extent that one remembers the wisdom accumulated, or perhaps even have a snippet of experience of that life. But if one remembers a life that is ongoing—a life that is still focused in the physical somewhere in its time, not unlike Speaks of Many Truths will say—then you are not just having a memory; you are actually sampling something that is going on for that individual in their living life that could interfere with that individual. It is no interference if you sample something from the vast you that is already completed and reassimilated into your vastness. These things are built-in protections for those lives, because you are protected. You are doing this for yourself, yet the vast everything will acquiesce: "Yes, that is good; let us support that." Protection is meant to keep you on track in a given life rather than be the type that a helmet offers to an athlete.

But you say we could have had millions of Earth lives.

Well, millions of lives, not Earth lives, but as an individual.

All right, hundreds, thousands, whatever. But why are some complete and others not?

Because Earth has not been here very long. In terms of Earth in this place, I don't think anybody on Earth has had more than 101 Earth lives. I am not aware of it. I realize that there are people who feel they have had more Earth lives, but some of these lives are in the future of Earth and some of them are in the past of Earth when Earth was in Sirius—still the planet Earth, but in a different version of itself.

Got it. And there was also an Earth here before this Earth. They could have had lives on that, too?

Not likely.

What about people who do past-life regressions? They go back and remember, for instance, swimming and drowning, then come back and lose traumas and anxieties of this life.

If that is done spiritually, meaning the person does it in a benevolent way, a sacred way, it will not interfere with the past lives. If it is done scientifically without heart and in a harsh fashion, it can very easily interfere with those lives.

So it's all in the way it's done.

Support in This Creation

Everything is in the way it is done, everything. Here is a perfect example: As anybody who lives with animals knows, one can say the most unkind things to a beloved animal living with you, but if you say them in the kindest, most loving way, that being will respond to the feeling. One can say the most wonderful things to that same being but in a harsh way, and again it will respond to the feeling.

All communication is based in feeling *first*—80 percent in feeling, and in precision, three percent. The rest is support from external sources—meaning guidance, inspiration, like that. You are supported all the time. If you were not given that level of support, the disagreements and the misunderstandings would be eternally chaotic. There has to be some support all the time [chuckles].

It takes a high teacher/student ratio to run this Creator School, right?

Yes. The administrators of this school are functioning (since we are musical) in syncopation with all the other administrators. No one administrator can run this school, including your Creator. We know this well by now, simply because of all of Creator's assistants and assistance. And so [laughs] the experience is very vast in terms of the support necessary to run such a dramatic school within an essentially benevolent creation.

You've explained that beautifully. I was really curious about that.

Good. Let's see what else, if anything . . . Once upon a time, yes?

Yes, I love those.

When Children Were the Visionaries

I was working with some individuals on Earth. These individuals were all children; as you would look at them now, these were children. This society (which is no longer on this planet, but was for a time), functioned quite differently than your current societies do, but it has had a lingering effect. In this society it was very well understood by all its members that children were the visionaries and had the capacity to remind adults (bigger people, hm?) what was important, not only because of the needs of the children, but also because of what they said.

In that society, children's questions were pondered by the great thinkers of the time. If a child would say, "But why?" it wasn't dismissed as childish ignorance; it was considered: Why? Every time a child would say, "Why?" (true, this society was not very big), the people would consider why and explain to the child why, up to that point in time. If the child still asked, "Why?" as children still do, it was assumed by the thinkers and philosophers of the time that the child—whether he or she was consciously aware of it or not, you understand—would know at some level that there was some other way, that there was more or that there could be more.

There was always a great deal of respect for children. Children were considered the stimulants of the wisdom keepers, so the wisdom keepers told the stories of the wisdom, but they also were prepared to have the keys to greater wisdom handed to them by children. In this case, children were considered to be children until they were about seven or eight years old. After that they would begin to assimilate the society, manners and culture and would be less likely to ask "Why?" with that resonance that the wisdom keepers could feel—always feeling—that indicated there was more. About the time the child got to be fifteen or sixteen years old, they would never say, "But why?" again in the same way. They might still want to know why, but the knowledge the wisdom keepers could give them would then satisfy their curiosity.

This was one of the societies that existed on Earth before your societies that are generally discussed: Lemuria, Atlantis and so on. It was what I would call a prototype society. It was intended that the beings (who never numbered much more than 1500) have their lives and their experience, which was multilevel in terms of their spiritual integration and not quite as physical as some other societies, but was still integrating the dimensional planes you call three through five, and occasionally seven. They were intended not only to live their lives, but to leave the material mass of their bodies behind to integrate into the soil of Mother Earth so that a child's curiosity would be sustained by the energy of these ancestors.

Where on the planet?

Things look so much different . . . oh, yes, right down here [between the tip of Australia and Tasmania]. You know, there used to be a land bridge between this island and the southern part of this continent. It was the land that existed between the two places. It was right there, and it was a very interesting society.

The land where they buried the bodies then is now in the ocean.

Ancient Burial Methods

They didn't actually bury the bodies. Their burial techniques did not involve digging into the Earth because they had great respect for the Earth as a being, and they felt that digging would injure Mother Earth. So when someone died, they would set the body on the ground, say prayers over it (because they honored the body) and over the spirit they knew had departed. So they returned the body to Earth . . .

. . . by allowing creatures to eat it?

Well, it wasn't the same then; there were not as many carnivorous creatures. As a matter of fact, carnivorous creatures as you know them today did not exist then. There were some that would be considered biological—very small and in the oceans.

They would simply put the bodies out on a platform well away from their encampment. They would lay them down on the ground, completely devoid of anything material, and the bodies would gradually turn to dust. Experiencing the elements, they would turn to dust. But the animals were not carnivorous then.

Then there was the time of the eroding, you would call it geologically, but in terms of its spiritual significance, it is sometimes referred to (and highly misinterpreted in your time) as the sinking of that soil. (Sometimes you read about the sinking of Atlantis, but the sinking of Atlantis for the most part had to do with erosion, not so much with actual sinking. This has become confused in your time.) So when that landmass eroded, it placed these materials in the ocean, which was the best place because of rain and the cycle of rain.

Because it goes all over.

. . . all over quickly.

Isis Works with the Children

That was an interesting society I worked with. I worked especially with the children. When you are very young and must be taken care of, there is the desire and the pleasure at being taken care of, but there is also a need to feel important and a reluctance to have too much responsibility. This is not to say that the child wouldn't welcome *some* responsibility, but for a child to know that its curiosity might alter the world in which it lives is quite a lot.

I worked with the children directly, with a portion of my energy, to support their dreams and, more importantly, their imaginations. The children had a very strong and well-developed imagination, so they could not only access the feeling when they were asking, "But why?" but would also have an imagination. They could mentally (because imagination is partially the mind) have the vision that supported and sustained the feelings that stimulated the question, "But why?"

My working with the children allowed them to feel that they were of service, but not in a way that would change their lives so dramatically that an individual might feel the continuity was disrupted. As you know, continuity is very important for a child or for any being in this Creator School, even if the being is not part of the creator training, such as a cat, a dog, a dolphin. Yes, they might wish to be spontaneous at times, but continuity is quite essential. It is the same for children—and, I might add, for adults, but sometimes adults like to believe they are above such things [laughs].

The continuity is security.

It is a degree of benevolent predictability that supports and nourishes that feeling of sustained security. I worked with them that way so that their questions would not be traumatically life-changing for them.

Were they part of the Explorer Race?

No, but their energy has affected and sustained you very often. Children, as Zoosh has told you, are intentionally born curious here, to the degree that they manage to sustain their curiosity within themselves and externally. You build on curiosity that you have within yourself, wondering about something but not necessarily verbalizing it or inquiring in some way as to the answer. The foundation is the inner curiosity; that is what the energy from that ancient society supports. Your own societies and cultures, to say nothing of family life, do not always support "but why?" from a child these days.

On a soul level, when these beings went back to a benign society, did they retain that curiosity, that feeling? Did it affect their lives when they went back to wherever they came from?

The society was rather benign. As I said, there was no fear of carnivorous creatures. They did not have to eat or drink very much. They had freshwater pools to drink from and they did not have to eat much because the wild food they gathered and could eat was full of life force. Making the transference back to an even more benevolent society was not much of a shift.

Can you say where they came from and where they went back to?

They went back to Sirius. A lot of the early societies on this planet were from Sirius, because it was easiest for Sirian beings to be supported, nurtured and sustained by the soil of a planet that was once in that system. Gradually, as the planet changed to accustom itself to beings from other star systems who gradually became what you now know as Earth beings, the need for only beings or souls from Sirius— beings who have had continuing lives on Sirius or beings who might have come here through a window or portal and set up their society— was decreased over time and adaptation.

Was this something you arranged, that a certain number of souls would come here and live for a certain time?

I'm disinclined to say arranged; I would rather say that I supported and nurtured it. If they wanted to have a future life on Earth, and if Earth happened to be in another star system, well [laughs], you had your future life on Earth, perhaps not exactly what you expected, but with reasonable benevolence, just in a different place. One did not necessarily take the shuttle to a planet in Sirius; one might take the shuttle to Mars [chuckles] (this is a joke, you understand). Things might be unexpected, but you would still be on this planet.

The Destruction of Maldek Created a Great Discordance

Was the planet before this one destroyed because of the explosion of Maldek?

It was not directly the cause, but it was certainly an indirect cause, because the atmosphere of that planet was very delicate. It was very resonant, meaning that if one makes a tone and another tone is discordant to the first, the first tone will be affected. The destruction of Maldek created a very great discordance, and the atmosphere simply could not sustain itself. This gradually created the disruption and ultimate destruction of the planet.

Weren't there civilizations on the moons of some of the larger planets in this system that were also affected, like Titan and Io and Ganymede?

Yes, some of these, but they were not civilizations that started there; they were colonized, so it was easy to evacuate them.

There Are No "Facts": Knowledge Is a Vehicle to Stimulate Growth

I'll tell you a little secret. It won't make you feel good, but stories and all the details in stories are intended to reveal more about yourselves to those to whom the stories are told. That is 99-plus percent of the reason for *all* stories, especially those generated from spirit. Less than a fraction of a percent of the story is at any time absolutely true. This is essential, because every individual—every Pleiadian, every Orion, every Andromedan, every Rigelian, any being—has his own unique memory in the vastness of his personal existence, interacting with all other existence. If there were rigid facts, it would not be possible for a thousand angels to dance on the head of a pin. It would not be possible because there are too many variables in individual memory and wisdom. So all knowledge is intended to produce a result, *not intended to be factual!*

Hmm. I hear you, but something either happens or it doesn't happen.

Oh, you are quite wrong. For example, someone comes up to you and reminds you of a conversation you recently had. You are adamant that the conversation was about this subject, and the other person is adamant that the conversation was about that, and the two things are quite different. Who's right?

All right, but a planet either blows up or it doesn't.

No, you are wrong. Why do I assault you with this? It is because if we become attached to facts, *we never grow at all.* But if we can allow facts to seek their own resonance, then growth is assured. That is why when one starts a joke at the head of a line of people and it passes down, by the time it gets to the end person it doesn't even resemble a joke, much less a conversation. Or why fifteen eyewitnesses to an event all describe the event differently when asked separately: "Oh, it was this," "Oh, it was that." They are adamant, "It was absolutely this." "She wore a red hat," "No, she wore a blue hat."

But if you videotape it, you'd just have one result.

Maybe not!

Maybe not?

An example: Have you ever heard of something being taped on a recording, then later it is not there anymore, or else there is only static or something is there that was not there before—you did not hear it at the time, yet it is there on the recording? I tell you this not only for your personal growth, but ultimately when you are in your vastness—or even just passing through the veils—you become so aware of all things in all times in all ways that this allows you to experience the creator-you. Do you know that for the Creator of this universe, there is *not one fact?* Not one. There are only fluid events, fluid possibilities. I am being very diplomatic here. But I have to be diplomatic, because I am disinclined to uproot the tree of your philosophy and discard it completely. I would rather have you prune it on your own!

Well, go ahead, uproot a little bit. This is for everybody.

Well, up to this point in time it is certainly for everybody, but I am not sure that everybody is ready to hear that maybe Maldek existed and maybe it didn't.

Really? But I was there!

Or maybe not!

Really?

Yes! If you can imagine flexibility to the infinite—this can only be imagined as a feeling, meaning all options available now and indefinitely. This is essential as a creator. This means that "just the facts, ma'am," is only a joke, and that stories are simply a vehicle to pass on *wisdom*, in the case of those who pass on their wisdom with stories. Or that stories are only a vehicle to stimulate growth or, as Zoosh would say, to stimulate questions. This is not inappropriate; it is very appropriate to creators in training. As a matter of fact, it is quite essential.

So I'd better print this.

It is up to you. Be aware that your statement, "It either happened or it didn't" is very much the attitude of many individuals—as a matter of fact, the vast majority. Yet in my perspective, it ain't so.

You see, we (if I might speak for Zoosh and others and myself) are gradually introducing you and reintroducing you to the flexibility of experience. This is also how, when a person has had a terribly traumatic experience in his life, about which they can say absolutely, "This happened," in the vastness of flexibility, in the vastness of your creator selves as you are, those fixed things may or may not have happened. This means that those fixed things do not have to color all your future lives with their traumatic vibration, because when you are the vast you, it was something that *might* have happened. If it did happen, there was much to be learned from it, certainly a great deal of compassion to be understood and applied. But it didn't absolutely happen; if it had, then the rigidity would impact all beings—not only all versions of yourself, not only all incarnations of yourself, not only your vastness, but since we are all one, it impacts all beings. That is why absolutes are only a figment of your intellectual imagination.

And I spent all my life looking for them!

But it is useful to have that belief here, the belief that black is black and white is white and all of this. One can make mistakes and experience consequences (sometimes benevolent consequences—not all mistakes are bad); one can apply things. In short, beliefs based on thoughts, not realities, are sometimes very useful tools to use in a fixed amount of experience, but they do not apply to the vast you.

It is important to give stories respect, because a story might contain wisdom that was intended to be taught, as in many tribes and clans and so on and also the society I referred to a moment ago. Stories allow for flexibility because they need not be told the same way every time, as long as the wisdom is passed on in some way and some form of the wisdom learned still applies (not all wisdom remains permanently applicable). That is useful. But if they are facts, that is rigid and does not last.

That is why you do not have the facts of ancient societies, although their philosophies are often available either in inspirations, imaginations or artistic renderings at some other time or place. You might look at what society has left: the Great Pyramid, Stonehenge and so on, or the artifacts of any society. You might look at it and be greatly inspired. But you did not have the facts of their day, the newspapers—who did what to whom. That's good, because you need inspiration, *not news,* though I do respect your need in the moment for some news, yes.

Speaks of Many Truths wants to do a book about lost societies, lost civilizations. So he would approach it as a teaching, then, to help us understand the philosophies of those people?

All beings such as myself, including Speaks of Many Truths, would always approach it that way. He's not going to tell you about all lost societies that have ever existed, lost only because you don't know about them at the moment; he's going to tell you about the ones that are relevant. This does not mean that the other societies are not interesting, that in some flexible way they might have occurred. It does mean that it will have some relevance to the reader today.

Just as you might have a conversation with your friend a few days ago and she says it was this and you say it was that—who's right? Maybe you're both right. The main thing is, it is less important who's right than what you have gained from it in your overall wisdom that you assimilate and pass on to others.

When You Are in Your Vastness

That's what happens after these lives, and it is why you go through the veils and look back at your life and understand it: "What did it mean?" and "How does it affect me now?" and "Now I understand it; I was never able to understand that before," you might say after passing through the veils and talking to your guides and teachers. Looking at the life you have lived during this cycle, you would say, "I can't imagine that I never saw the value of knowing that; thank heavens I had that experience. Now I understand half the universe better than I did before."

A typical example of that would be ignorance or frustration, then understanding that by having lived even moments of frustration, you are able to understand an entire planetary society's annoyance at not having all their knowledge all the time.

You're giving us sort of a . . .

. . . a provocative overview.

We're close enough to the veil that you're saying we can start to understand . . .

You can begin to think about it; it is like discovering nutmeg for the first time. You might like it. Then there will be someone saying, "Ooo, I'd rather have cloves." Understand that it is a chance to begin savoring the possibility of it. It is also a stepping stone to reassimilate your vastness. It does not have to take experiences away.

When you are in your vastness, you have all levels of experiences, even what could have happened given a certain circumstance or what might have happened. You have that, but you have it in a way that is benevolent to you and everybody else. In this way no one is injured. You still get to learn from it, but you do not have the rigid facts. If you had the rigid facts, everyone would suddenly be sitting at attention, as it were, unable to go forward.

As you go on and assimilate these concepts into your societies in different ways, many of the disagreements you have had from one culture to another will simply evaporate. With this knowledge (if I can call it that), with this feeling, with this experience of such flexibility, one is not likely to experience attachment—certainly an attachment to having somebody else do it your way. This is not to say that you don't put one foot in front of the other, but as you gradually incorporate more of your vastness into your daily lives, it allows you to experience greater levels of that feeling you can use to immediately identify not only your vastness, but your teachers—the feeling of patience. One experiences impatience here because one is confronted with rigidity.

[Laughs.] Including my own.

Well, I am simply providing you with the philosophy that is your own and that of others in the greater you. I am not saying to forget about the day-to-day events, what needs to be done, clarity in communication and so on; I'm not saying forget about that. I am saying that in the larger picture it will not be quite as absolute. It is certainly fine to improve communications here on a daily basis in your life. So much communication is muddled here because people are afraid of what others might think of them or because they are polite—and many things in between. Sometimes it is very useful to say exactly what you are feeling so that the other person will truly understand. It is not always necessary, but sometimes it is.

Reading that should create a lot of interest. It's pretty powerful.

Actually, because you all do understand stories, it's really just another story. Sometimes it is necessary to open up the door a crack even when one is loving the exploration of one's current room. Sometimes one must open up the door a crack to give a glimpse beyond that, if only to know that there is more, not to take away the room that you are in.

And on that note, I'll say good night.

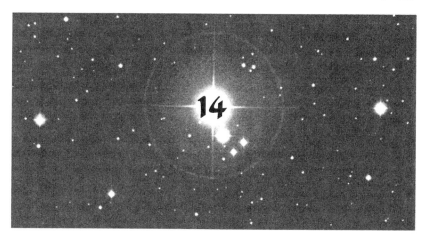

Priestess/feminine Mysteries

January 22, 1998

Isis speaking. This experience is intended to facilitate the reader's journey through the Isis experience (if I might refer to myself in such a broad way), in a way that can best assist them in their journey toward applied spirituality.

Goddess or priestess—of these terms I prefer "priestess," and I will tell you why. When the term "god" or "goddess" is used, it tends to suggest a reflection of an ideal within the spiritual framework as we know it. I prefer the term *priestess* (or *priest*, for that matter) because it is truly recognized as an individual—perhaps initiated on a path, perhaps not—who serves the needs of the people. In this sense it is a very grounded occupation.

Most people have similar needs the world over regardless of their religion, nationality, background, anything. There are certain core issues that go to the heart of being human. If one is a god or goddess, we have someone who is separated from the people. A priest or priestess is someone who, within the religious context, is separated and sometimes elevated from the people, but within the more contemporary (at least to my standards) spiritual practice, who is intended, not for slavish devotion to the people, but to act as a guide, in its best definition.

Is there something you can say about the role of women in the next few years that can give us a focus?

Isis' Vision for Women Today

Yes. I am glad you asked that. The role of women changes radically in the remainder of the '90s and up to perhaps 2003. For the last few thousand years women have been making an effort to please—that really sums things up concisely. And in an effort to please, regardless of what society on Earth we are talking about, a great many false ideals have not only been proposed, but lived up to so much that the actual role of women has been corrupted to the point of being more false than true.

Let me say my vision of the role of women. It is for women to initiate life, meaning to give birth, to nurture, to be nurtured and to provide by example as well as by action ideal basic living circumstances. While this is the role I see, it is, of course, something that will take some time to establish universally. If one has been told that one must be this or that or if one is living up to social demands, one naturally engages a script for oneself to follow.

Many women are conscious of basic realities; although this is not intended to suggest that women are forced into awareness by biological necessity, women are, by biological necessity, forced to be *real*. There are points when women cannot play the role, whatever that might be in your societies—the biological role women have in common that is intended to keep you conscious of the role of the reincarnational life cycle as well as the necessity (to say nothing of the comfort) of love. Women have, in your contemporary society (the last 40 or 50 years) learned in many different ways how to be good men. Although this might be a dubious perfection of skills, it has its advantages, because then one perhaps understands how men can move so far afield from their natural tendencies.

In the coming years women all over the world will become increasingly aware of how much they are alike. Your friend Zoosh has been preaching for some time about how much people are alike and how very little you differ in the larger picture. Women have an innate understanding of this, at least as adults. But in the near future we're going to see more applications of this awareness, and not just in meetings of woman to woman. The simple fact of following the masculine model in the world's body politic has made it quite clear to almost everyone that this does not work. By "masculine model" I mean: *see, change, restructure and format to fit the moment.* That's the basic description. The feminine model would be: *feel, accept, love, nurture, involve.* This is the gesture for *involve,* yes? [See photo.]

So within the context of involve, one has the roots of society. However, within the context of restructuring what you see to fit the thoughts or perceived goals of the moment, as in the male model, one can very easily fall into the "we versus them" experience. With the female model, one is unlikely to fall into that experience unless you are attempting to live up to the masculine model because of the cultural and societal demands on you.

What needs to be done, then, is something that is occurring now as we speak. The inappropriateness of the masculine model of conducting society will become such a conscious and obvious truth to so many people over the next fourteen to fifteen years that true feminine experience, feminine ways—not artificial, glamorized femininity, but real, root femininity—will become an ideal almost to the point of being pursued with a level of religious zealousness. One will have to guard against this, because in the sudden and electrifying awareness that many people will have—that it is much better to be involved than to be in exclusion or to exclude—this feminine model will be idealized. Therefore, I am counting on women to maintain a sense of humor through it all in order to keep femininity at its essence light and enjoyable rather than dogmatic.

As more and more world governments begin to acknowledge and then pursue working with things and people as they are, not as they would like them to be, you will experience an acknowledgment of your true value not only in your day-to-day lives as women, but in the larger sense you will be drafted to become leaders, representatives, government and service employees and otherwise involved in the public forefront to serve what I call in the natural way. The natural way does not use pretense. It also lovingly and gently acknowledges falsehood as it is seen and felt without judging it.

Natural Man vs Unnatural Man

Remember, the natural man is not what most women see or, for that matter, what most men are aware of in themselves. Most men are programmed by your societies to become false ideals stemming from false ideas. When men mature, they will see these things for what they are and begin living a life to the best of their ability based on some model that suits them at the moment, a life of greater value to themselves and others. But it is difficult to recapture the naturalness when the naturalness that they are born with is so heartily disapproved of. Aside from their biological differences, boys and girls are very much the same when they are born, at least until they are two to three years old, and when they are given equal nurturing and love, they have similar curiosities. This is understood by child psychologists. But even with this understanding (which is widely accepted, I might add), the child psychologists have almost no voice in the running of world politics, to say nothing of the local variety. The best voice they have, though even today it is weakly heard, is in scholastic and educational environments.

This tells you something. It says that when learning is involved, especially for young children, even the unnatural male model of society accepts women in the role of nurturing and guiding. This tells you that this is a core function for women. As the nurturer, the guide and, in its higher sense, the wayshower, it will be up to women to gently show men what is natural and what isn't. Of course, the true timing of that will be based upon men saying to women, *How?, When?, Where?* and *When can I?*

So I am putting women on notice here. By the time you get this book or read this in some form, you will have had several experiences that will startle you: Men, and even strong-willed women, let's say, will have come to you to ask how you maintain your happiness and comfort as yourself. When I separate "strong-willed" women from other women, I mean a woman caught up in the business cycle who is acting out a role that might not be that of her core natural personality.

Natural Women: Speak Your Wisdom

For these coming years, you women will have many opportunities then to speak your wisdom. In this case I do not mean telling people what to do, but speaking out or showing people what works for you in whatever your walk of life, nationality or religion might be. It is up to women to speak of wisdom. There are certainly men who speak of wisdom, but more men are lost these days than women. So, women, pay attention to your wisdom, which means what works for you; that's why you do it, compared to what you do that does not work for you but you do it because *you feel you should.*

In coming years the natural woman will come to be aware of the difference between learning how to function in society and embracing society's manners and mores, thereby losing her natural awareness of her true wisdom and personality. In the coming years those who are aware of their true natural personalities (which will vary, of course) will be in a good position to be wayshowers. Remember, don't deny the evidence of your feelings or the physical evidence of what is true, good, loving and continually dependable. And if you share wisdom with others, speak of what works, not what *should* work—not even what *could* work, unless you are striving to achieve that which could work. Women have often in the past confused love and the belief in someone with *what is.* So if you can separate how you see what *could* be from what *is,* then you can speak about wisdom and at the same time about ideals.

Moving Out of Polarized Male/Female

So are we going to swing like a pendulum from total male domination and male values and separation and struggle to almost an unnatural feminine before it comes back to be balanced?

No, that's not what I said. What I said is that men will become aware that the permanent foundations they are attempting to create for systems cannot be permanent. They need shoring up all the time because they are not natural. The natural feminine role *is* the natural masculine role, the only exception being your biological differences, period. So although you see this as a pendulum, I do not see it that way. This is what I see: Right now [draws #1] this is your society, and the natural feminine is forced to take this role in that society (the circle surrounded by the square). In increasingly rapid succession over the years, we will have this kind [draws diagrams 2-8, showing the circle expanding until it surrounds the square, which turns into a triangle, which in turn has a circle within it].

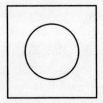

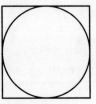

1. Your present society, where the natural feminine is forced into this role inside the unnatural masculine.

2. The expanding feminine (circle).

3. Expanding feminine.

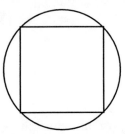

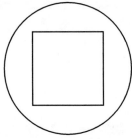

4. Expanding feminine.

5. Expanding feminine.

6. The changing masculine (from square to triangle).

7. Changing masculine.

8. The circle is the true feminine way, the triangle is the true masculine way.

Number eight will happen in about 25 years. The first seven illustrations will develop over the next 10 to 15, perhaps 17 years. The circle in illustration #8 is the feminine way, the triangle the true masculine way. Right now the masculine way is in its artificial self, the square; but in its true self it is the triangle, and here we have the circle within. After 25 years we start getting this [draws #9]. The true masculine symbol is this, which the male society will evolve toward within 50 years.

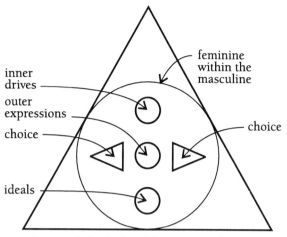

9. The true masculine symbol, which will begin to develop in 25 years and evolve toward in 50 years.

The triangle is the male; the circle is the feminine and the more benevolent within the male, all right? The three circles represent the man's inner drives, outer expressions and ideals. The two inner triangles represent choices—this way or that way. Now, here is the true feminine symbol [draws #10]: circles to the infinite within, meaning the farther you go in, the more circles, even under a microscope—more and more circles. As you go out, it is the same thing—more and more

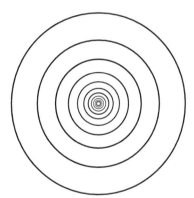

10. The symbol of the true feminine and for ultimate, benevolent, loving perpetual truth. There are circles to the infinite, both outward and inward.

circles to the infinite. That is the true feminine symbol, most of which you had to give up to come here to be women. If you were here all the time, you could never under any circumstances, no matter how obviously necessary, speak anything but the absolute truth in the most loving, benevolent way possible. So this is the symbol for ultimate, benevolent, loving, *perpetual* truth.

Why does the masculine symbol surround the feminine symbol in #9?

The masculine symbol has within it the feminine symbol so that it can *achieve* balance, but the feminine symbol has within it only the feminine

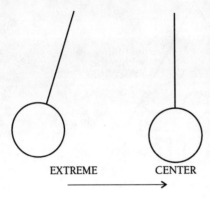

EXTREME   CENTER

11. Pendulum swings to the center.

so that it can *maintain* balance. The society is not going to swing from one extreme to another, but rather (using the model of the pendulum) the pendulum is going to swing [draws #11] to the center.

That's beautiful. We had imaged it all the way over to the side, then back again.

No. As anybody who has knowledge of even rudimentary physics knows, if it were to swing suddenly to the center, it would overshoot and swing farther. If it did that, chances are that it would continue swinging back and forth, which it has been doing.

Because of these back-and-forth cycles (which is not a bad analogy on your part), the latest extreme swing, which you're in now as a society on Earth, needs to be allowed to very slowly and incrementally brought to center *with no more speed than necessary*, so that when it arrives at the center, its natural state of balance, it will be welcome and will want to remain there without any further momentum to take it to the other extreme, thus continuing the cycle.

That means we're coming out of polarity.

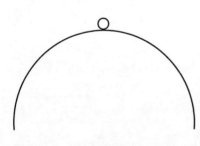

12. Sign for balance, on Earth.

Exactly. The sign for neutral place does not exist, but the sign for balance on your world is this [draws #12]. No offense, but does it remind you of anything? It is obviously a reference to the feminine, because it not only has to do with arcs of circles, but a complete circle, and anytime we're talking about circles, we're talking about the feminine reality.

But beyond the lower dimensions there is no masculine and feminine; there is more of an androgynous . . .

What you now consider androgynous is actually, in its moment-to-moment experience, love, gentleness—in short, qualities now exclusively identified as positive qualities of the feminine . . . or let's use a different word to avoid confusion—*core* qualities of the feminine.

But they are basically core qualities of the masculine too, right?

Yes. When you move out of polarized male/female, ideally the male is intended to give direction, not purpose, when needed. Purpose is the continuity of the feminine cycle of love, and so direction is needed only when the unexpected occurs. This is why the masculine is required for existence.

Using the Ideal Masculine

Let's say we have a trail of ants going from their home to gather seeds for the winter (obviously to feed the young and to survive), and someone places something between the ants and their destination. The ants stop and are confused; eventually they go around that blockage. That is an example of applying the masculine. They don't try to destroy it, but they use the masculine to go around it.

Ants walk from point A to point B on a trail they can smell, which is infinitely more important than what they can see. They are using not only instinct, but the evidence that supports instinct. So if you put a barrier in the path, what they can smell and feel stops suddenly, so they must adapt and go around the barrier.

So they send scouts out.

Yes; that's when they use the ideal masculine, which is based on a necessity because of an unexpected event. The ideal masculine, I might add, is the core from which all the resonance of the true masculine is built. That is why in a world such as this where you have bitter cold in some places and great heat in other places and all extremes in between, without adaptability, which is rooted in the masculine, you would not survive very well except in the most temperate zones. That is why you can't live here on Earth as it is now and as you are now without the masculine. If you did, with all your population, you'd be sleeping five to a bed because you'd all be in one place.

A similar analogy has been used here of the linear mind to the heart. The masculine has been equated to the mind and the feminine to the heart.

But the mind as you experience it now is one way; it has been the linear mind, the progressive mind, the mind that builds on one thing and another, and also builds on experience. But what about at higher dimensions? I am talking about dimensions where the male and female are no longer a factor. In that case one uses the ideal masculine even though the being might be perhaps more predominantly feminine in its expression.

In the polarized world the teaching has been that masculine and mind and brain are similar, and heart is the female, right?

That has been the teaching you've had up to now, yes. But thought based on needs and inspiration, what your friend Zoosh calls vertical thought, is experienced at higher dimensions. However, ideas are not experienced there for their own sake, but rather as an impetus toward actions that will serve benevolently. In more loving dimensions, as a daily experience one does not find thoughts that will prompt or stimulate actions that are in any way destructive or self-destructive. This is not because these thoughts are excluded, but because they are not part of the cycle of life.

The Importance of Continuity

The true cycle of life is based on love, but also on continuity. Continuity is that which continues as a result of itself and as a motivation by itself—and since itself is everything, there is nothing excluded. So you cannot do anything that would cause harm to any part of yourself, even if you are on the other side of the universe. When you feel yourself as one being, you cannot strain or allow one part of your body (the body of *all* beings) to suffer without all parts of the body feeling it.

So what you are evolving toward, truly, is more feeling. When you have more feeling, you are more likely to be presented with undeniable physical evidence of what needs to be done. When you see your fellow man or woman suffering, you might think that you can walk on. Even if you do, perhaps you say, and can justify completely, "I can do nothing," or perhaps you will say a prayer, which is good. And perhaps if you can help, you do, which is good.

But if you have said your prayer and believe you cannot help any further, and you walk on, it does not in any way alter the fact that you personally are in pain because of the pain of another. The more you become involved in the world of feeling, which will happen over the next 10 to 15 years, the more you will be presented in every moment with the physical evidence from your own bodies that other people are suffering on your world and need attention.

The Cure for Cancer

Can I tell you what will give you the cure for cancer? It will happen when everyone has what they need to eat, is loving and is being loved; when everyone is looked after; when no one is left to suffer even though no one can see them suffering, such as prisoners; when all needs are generously and gently taken care of in the most loving ways—then all disease will disappear. And when you are even one-quarter on the path toward that (which will happen in the next 10 to 15 years), cancer will recede to being only an occasional occurrence.

The reason you are all heightened in your feelings these days as you read this is because it is through feeling that you will all find your way home to your natural state of being. So understand that the feelings in your body will inevitably show you what needs to be done, and if you cannot improve your condition and the condition of your neighbors, yet you are still feeling some pain, look toward the condition of those beyond your borders.

Then school will be over.

Yes, school will be over, but not without graduation day.

Say more about that.

Graduation Day for Creator School

Graduation day means that once you have embraced [as in the gesture on page 249] your world and all its people and animals and plants, then, as in any good graduation exercise, you will celebrate the experience and be tested. That testing will be how much you can love beings from *other* worlds. When you learn to love ants [chuckles] and cockroaches (and neighbors you think of in those terms) without its being a drudgery, but instead a genuine pleasure because you have found the way to relate to them and they have found their way to relate to you—when this occurs, then ETs will be here en masse. Obviously, the ETs will know when you can love someone who looks so different from you, like an ant—and loving does not mean you must pick them up and hug them, but simply allow them—and when you can learn from their natural wisdom, discovering what they have to offer you. ETs will then realize that no matter how unusual some of them might look, if you can love the ants and the way they look and act, perhaps you can accept them.

So learn from the animals, from the littlest ones, from the plants. When you speak your inspiration and, more importantly, learn how to welcome and be welcomed with grace, then you will be applying both the feminine principle and the universal principle.

The New Mystery School

How can we bring the new mystery school into existence so that women and men can seek this loving balance within themselves and express it?

Discard the need for mysteries and secrets and embrace simple truths. Women are uniquely qualified, because in order to live, to love and to produce life, that life will be difficult if there are secrets. If all is known, life can be good. In the case of the animals, if there is no grass (perhaps we have horses here), then the herd moves on until it finds grass. In the case of the human being, sometimes people feel that the truth must come to them. But sometimes it is just as well to go to where the truth might be, even if you think it is to find a nice grassy area (in the case of the horses) to munch on.

So talk to each other. If you don't get the answers, travel about a bit even if it's just to the next town. Talk to others, or talk to people who have experiences different from yours. Embrace only that which feels good to you, not only in one moment but in the next. In this way you will practice loving truth.

That which is the mystery school is now to be revealed. The temple that looks within now finds everybody turning 180 degrees and going out. We do not abandon the temple; we take the temple with us and learn by doing. As any physician well knows, it's not what you learn in school that counts so very much; it's what you learn in practice. That's why the best physicians are usually well-experienced. It is the same for priestesses. It is experience that will teach you, and after a few years of experience you will discover the commonalities and glean the wisdom from those you meet as well as from the inspiration you bring through to serve their needs. Sometimes that inspiration will be from spirit, sometimes it will be from a tree or a passing deer. Ask them to help, ask for inspiration. If you have been trained or shown, you will know how to feel and know what they have to offer.

Service, as has been said for many years, is its own reward, not only because you can feel good doing something for the benefit of others, but because you grow and become more in service. Even now on your planet you are all in service to each other. Sometimes this service does not feel so good, other times it feels very good. So understand the rules of school: that you all teach each other all the time. As you begin to pay more attention to good feelings and embrace each other as you are, then in time all wounds will be healed, and even self-destructive epithets, things one says about oneself, will not be heard anymore, to say nothing of hurts and hurtful deeds to oneself or others.

As you said before, self-violence is going to lessen completely.

Yes, that's what I am expanding on a bit tonight.

So there are no more secrets, and we can look forward to graduation as a time when everything is out there and nothing is hidden.

You can look forward to pleasant rather than burning curiosity. Burning curiosity becomes that because of secrets, especially secrets for which solutions are desperately needed. But pleasant curiosity urges, invites and has pleasure in the discovery.

So all women are going to become priestesses, committed to their own discovery and in service to others.

Yes, and ideally they will have some direction, nurturance and support to achieve their true natural state, since ultimately it will be their job to help men to do the same—of course, only when they ask, not because of how they should be or when you want them to be something, but when they are ready. They will let you know when they are ready, because they will ask. Give them only and exactly what they ask for, not your whole life plan. Better to let the hungry eat enough to satiate themselves rather than eat so much that they don't want to go back to that table again.

You said recently that they would become the example and teach by living.

That is why it is essential to live your wisdom so you are enjoying life even when adversity is present. If you live your wisdom, you can weather the adversity in the best way for you. You will find this in cases where people are in adversity, yet are managing to maintain the best humor possible in the circumstance. This is not because they are in denial, but because they have their personal way of experiencing the adversity as simply a passing experience, feeling secure in the recollection of better times and in the certainty that better times will come and that all adversity is fleeting. It is precisely this certainty that causes adversity to be even more fleeting.

My understanding is that each man or woman has both masculine and feminine sides, and that our path is to integrate these two polarities to become whole. It's not really the feminine and masculine in the gender sense, but the intuitive, the feeling, the loving part (in women as well as in men) plus the structure and what we understand as the masculine side.

I do understand that it has been discussed that way before. My perception is if both men and women were raised in the feminine nurturing model of which I speak and which I know is the natural state of being in other places, what you call the natural masculine within is actually not natural, but is culturally deposited within women and to a greater extent in men. I do understand that it is a way to look at things, and it has served well in the past to create equal value for each sex and for the way your societies have been structured in terms of the male or the female approach. But from my perception and from knowing men on other planets, having spoken in my way with them and seeing them, men on other planets are usually quite gentle and nurturing. If they need to be warriors, which is practically never, they do not have to abandon those qualities; they don armor, and when the war is over they take it off and resume their natural personalities.

Since it is my intention to take off the gloves and speak what I know to be so, I would have to say that the internal masculine is true only so far as it has to do with resolution, as in my example with the ants. But all structure comes from cultural infusion.

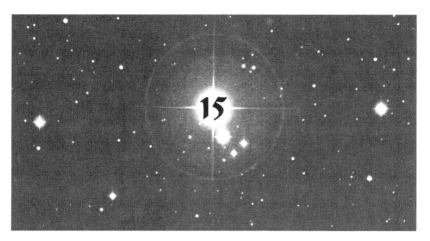

Infinite Transformational Possibilities

February 12, 1998

I sis speaking. What are you interested in?

I have an absorbing interest, and possibly every human does—we're told that we come to this plane and by our actions in one lifetime we can influence the vastness of ourselves, that we can make changes in the larger part of ourselves. Can you talk about how that works?

It is not just this plane, though that is a reasonable assumption—it is this planet at this time. It is a very small envelope of time, space and energy that encompasses this experience of the Explorer Race on this planet. Because this planet is in a pivotal position, as a joint in the arm, it literally has access to the many possibilities and probabilities of both past and future. This is because this place now is a school, and if you graduate, you will have that effect. If you do not graduate, then it will be postponed.

The Milky Way Galaxy Is about Transformation

The school itself is purposely in a position that guarantees it full access. This is another reason it was necessary to move this planet from

Sirius to its current location in this galaxy. We have not discussed this much, but this particular galaxy is about transformation.

The Milky Way galaxy?

Yes. It is about transformation. Anything that is a portion of this galaxy is either working with (or on, perhaps) transformation, being affected by transformation, or affecting transformation in some way. For instance, the Pleiadians are in this galaxy, yes? And as such these beings, as you know, are closely connected to you. As such they are affected by transformation, and because their next generation or two will begin to experience the tiniest degree of polarity, transformation is something they are contemplating as a fast-approaching future event. This is an example of your galaxy's participation in transformation.

As you can see, even if there were no other contingencies involved, it was necessary to move this planet to this exact galaxy. One might ask, "Was it possible for the Explorer Race to go to this planet at this dimension at its previous home in Sirius and have the same effect?" No. On Sirius it would not be polarized, nor could Sirius tolerate it. So, given the polarity it would experience, it had to be someplace that would not support a sustained, extreme polarization.

Look at Sirius. Sirius had that planet that went extreme to the negative, that one planet. That is because the planet itself needed transformation; it needed to have a check system so that it would not go to the extreme. But because it was in Sirius, and the Sirius galaxy supports, sustains and nurtures anything, they couldn't break out of it. It was a cycle that kept becoming more and more extreme, and they couldn't break out of it. Since it was learned that that would not work there, and since that planet is no longer there injuring the galaxy Sirius, then we have the situation where the Explorer Race came to the galaxy you are in now, which would not allow such extremities to take place, at least not permanently.

Theoretically, if this planet went to an extreme of negative energy, the planet itself or the forces and energies (physically speaking) within this galaxy would transform it. This galaxy will tolerate only so much before the energies of transformation are unleashed to the extreme. Even planet Earth has adapted to this galaxy. When the planet was in the galaxy of Sirius, it did not have the transforming capacities that you see it having here. It did not have volcanoes, terrific storms or winds, earth upheavals, none of this. These are all transforming influences that it has adapted to in this galaxy. So you see that the necessity for the Explorer Race to come here was vital.

Past-Altering Attempted by the SSG

Now, within that foundation, in order to have the opportunity to alter your past and your future, you needed to be in a place of transformation, but it would also have to have such a powerful resonance with transformation that anything in your past, even without your permission, would have the capacity to be altered. Now, think of the sinister secret government, how they are attempting to alter your past and your future to maintain their control over you. Within that context, you can see that while some of you might not have traumas in the past or in past lives that need to be changed, others could *put* the traumas there if they felt it was worth the effort and sacrifice.

For example, for a time the sinister secret government had a time machine, or machines that could access time. They still have some small capacities there, although the effort they must make now to move into the past requires extreme sacrifice and great material investment. For instance, it might take a hundred people to perform some function or effort that would be of minute impact, so they have to push very hard to do very little. But they might consider it worth their while to go back into someone's past whom they see as a threat and alter their past even slightly (since they do not have the subtle knowledge of how to do these things), hoping it will have some effect that will benefit them. For all they know, it might have an effect that might hurt them, but they are willing to try, you see.

As a result, there needs to be some safety mechanism in place so that no matter what version of the past the SSG goes to (using them as an example), it will protect all pasts—all versions, all variations for all individuals. Because of the extreme unusualness of your experience here, there is also a potential, however remote, for a collision between pasts or for a warp or tear in the firmness of any past experience. A safety mechanism is needed whereby any discomfort can be at least moderated, and at best cleared entirely, regardless of its cause. It is possible to do this at this time in this place, though it is not true for the third dimension everywhere, only at this time and place. There has been much clamoring of souls to come to this time and place, not because they have so much to clear up in the past, but for the amazing experience of it.

Quantum Expansion: Transforming the Past and the Future

Now, you might ask, "How is the experience different, aside from my obvious day-to-day life?" Think of this for a moment: To have your past transformed one way or the other, then have it cleared by what you do, changes mightily not only who you are, but how much you are, how much you can be, and the quantum capacities of your being. Remember, Mother Earth is working on quantum mastery, so the potential for you to have lessons or experiences on the path of quantum mastery are available to you even though you as beings have not yet evolved enough to qualify to work on quantum mastery. Most of you have not even begun teaching mastery, much less dimensional mastery. This is an opportunity to have potential quantum expansion in your soul being.

What is quantum expansion? Quantum expansion would be an expansion beyond your soul's capacity to expand—you could become more than you could become, if you can understand that. And it could happen very fast. For instance, you might need to have 150 lives or experiences in order to achieve something. One life on this planet at this time in this place might allow you to jump over three-quarters of those experiences. That's how much your soul could expand. Your soul could expand more than it can; it can go past what is possible. It can go beyond the mathematical reference for what is. That is quantum, all right? That is why people want to be here.

Now, a similar situation exists for the future, for the future is a little more sacrosanct or safe. It is easier for things to happen in the past, even though the past is gone from your current perception, than for things to happen to upset the future. This is because what happens in the future is largely based upon the many variables happening in the present. That is why those like the sinister secret government who would attempt to alter your future are really doomed to failure before they even begin. So much is going on in the present that they cannot possibly calculate for it, and so that is why they will sometimes try to alter the past, hoping to slow down your move toward your inevitable spiritual future.

So even with that safety mechanism built in for the future, it is possible to alter the future benevolently, though the necessity for that is going to be greatly reduced compared to the past.

That is inspiring. Define transformational. How do you use the word?

Transformational is that which brings about change, either by what it does or by the effects that encompass one during one's experience.

If the Milky Way galaxy resonates a transformational state, how did it get that way?

The Creator made it that way, with the intention that anything and anyone who came here would have quite a variety of places to go to experience greater or lesser influences of transformation, according to their personal needs.

In my original question, I was thinking more of our own vastness before we came into this creation and that possibly, as a result of our experiences, we had certain attitudes or beliefs or ways of looking at things that would limit us, and by coming to the Earth, there's a chance to change that in the greater part of us by what we do here. But you're talking about our past lives.

I speak to you of your past lives because I do not differentiate between a physical lifetime and an embodiment beyond this universe, or in this or any galaxy or in this universe. To me, a life is a focus of the soul personality within the context of a being, which takes you beyond an organism as a human being or any being that might walk, talk, fly, be in this universe. I used the sinister secret government only as an example of past-altering influences, not to suggest lives on Earth.

Let's take an example of someone who had an attitude that has limited them. Now they're on Earth. How can they, first, find out what they're trying to transform, then how can they do it?

The Transformational Journey of George Washington

Let us take a famous person from your country's history who is no longer in that body, but had an experience. Once upon a time that person was living physically in this country as George Washington, but before he existed as George, he had several lives in this universe, most of which were geared toward the development of statesmanship. One might think that that would have been for his life as the first manager (which is what it really was; although the title was president, it felt more like a manager to him at the time) of the then-fledgling United States. But actually, the president job was also preparatory for him.

Before he came to this universe he was a spirit who understood very well the experience of individuality, which is why he made an excellent president of the United States. He could see people as individuals much better than united groups. On the one hand, it made it difficult for him to manage larger groups, but on the other hand it was very easy for him to appeal to individuals and bring out the best in them. This is how he was able to help people rise to occasions well past their capacities as they knew them.

Now, as a being before this universe who understood individuality well, he needed to learn what effects groups or communities have on the individual, since his main theme has been for a long time (and will be into the foreseeable future) individuals and all that relates to them. That is his theme. He had several lives—one of which was on a very distant star system unrelated to this one—but also in this universe, where he could begin to understand family. Family is the first group that one fully experiences, and he spent a lengthy time understanding, through experience, the family.

When he got to this life, he was experiencing individuality in a context of whatever we call plus and minus charges; he could work with beings with whom he was reasonably comfortable, groups of peers, but it was very difficult for him (in the terms of the minus) to work with beings who were *not* peers. One must remember that in this life Washington was essentially an aristocrat, so he could function well within a group situation that was reasonably aristocratic. But the minute he had to deal with common people, it was a great struggle for him. Because the soldier in the field was the common man, as it were, things did not go well in the beginning of his military campaign.

Also, he could not see clearly how to communicate with people without a shared language and syntax. Therefore, because there was no shared syntax with the slaves who worked for him, he could not communicate with them directly, although people who worked for him would communicate with his slaves. This is why he never fully understood their suffering even though he was treating them better than some. It was a matter of degree, I assure you; they were not very well off.

It was, of course, toward the end of his life that he began to have greater capacities for communication. He freed his slaves at his death, but this was not uncommon for people of his class.

Within the context of such a man's lessons—how his being beyond this universe has changed as a result of lives lived up to that point (he has had two lives since), the greater entity (preceding George Washington as you know him) has now been able to adapt, through the use of color, sound and somewhat friendly ceremonial interactions, and has a greater capacity to relate to beings in the collective, even though they may not be focused toward learning about individuality.

Were his other two lives spiritually important?

Yes. He had a life in the late 1800s as a shoeman, the man who makes shoes. This worked very well for him, because he found himself in a circumstance where he was working with people as individuals. He wasn't making shoes as you make them today in a factory; he made them one shoe at a time, in France. He was able to accommodate greater interactions between people, because he was the sort of person who moved around from place to place making shoes. Even though he could make ordinary shoes for everyday people, he would also make shoes for people of means. This is how he really got along. So he was able to deal with many classes of people, you might say.

There is another life situated not too far from here (I cannot give the name because he is alive at this time) where he is involved in the military. He's a person who trains people in the military when they come in. He's in a female body in this time, but he has kept up that connection to the military and is training military nurses. He (or she) is not giving medical training, but military training for nurses in the military. This allows the formal context of the military, which tends to create a homogenizing effect regardless of people's backgrounds, the only major separations being between ranks. Other than that, the tendency is to create a certain degree of sameness among individuals the military needs, such as professional nurses. The military cannot treat them like ordinary draftees; there has to be a certain degree of benevolence there. Of course nurses come from all walks of life these days, so he's (she's) exposed to that. So the being who was George Washington is alive today, though not in the military of the United States.

Choosing Lives to Become More

People seem to think it has to go A, B, C, D, upward in evolution. It really goes from a high life to a low life to this and that—you pick up little pieces of experience, right?

As I like to say, it moves not forward or backward, but from side to side. That way it takes progression out of it.

How does that work? Let's say someone is a great singer in one life, but maybe in another life is a public person. Would he or she pick a quiet life as a sort of balance?

Let's take an example. Let's say someone is a great singer, but they're a perfectionist; perhaps they're an opera singer. As a performer, he or she has great anxiety about the audience's response. Even performers who have the greatest acceptance and adoration still have this anxiety, because performers are artists, and artists are sensitive people.

Then let's say in the next life, the person lives only a few years, but during that life he is a baby and young child, born to a mother who sings to him. He loves the mother's voice even though it might not be a professional singing voice. The voice is so filled with love, tenderness, appreciation and welcoming that the reincarnated opera singer understands that the degree the audience loves the music has more to do with how they feel about the person than what the person radiates.

So when an audience adores a singer—say, Pavarotti in your time— the audience loves Pavarotti not just for his great voice, but because it loves the *man*. Even if his voice were to crack on stage sometime (it probably won't, but if it did happen), the audience's heart would go out to the man because the people love the man *first*. It was not always this way; when he was young and starting the first day, it was a test. They waited to see if they would love his music, but now they love his music so much it has spread into loving the man. So even if he fell asleep on stage, they would think to themselves, Isn't that amusing? or Isn't that sweet? or He must need to rest; it's fine. Let him go in back and sleep for a while; we will wait. That's real love.

What are some of the qualities, mistaken beliefs or attitudes that the Explorer Race roots had that can be changed here on the Earth by their fragments?

Largely speaking, those who participated came from a great distance, yes?

Oh, yes.

To become what is now the Explorer Race, winding through from one life to another and so on, some here on Earth now and some elsewhere waiting, there are several main things that will change for you all, tracing you back to your points of origin, small in number. You will learn how the whole—large groups working together—can accomplish more than what can be accomplished. That is quantum change.

When you are an individual, no matter how magnificent or grand, who knows everything you can know up to your capacity—as some of the creators who have spoken to you are like—the thought that there is something you don't know would not even occur to you; it wouldn't come up. If someone asked you, you might briefly ponder it, then dismiss it out of hand because you know what you can know up to the limits of what you can know. But since you don't *know* those are limits, then as far as you know, you know everything. You do not perceive your endings, let's say, instead of calling them limits. You do not even perceive that it is theoretically possible.

So you can't become engaged in quantum activities such as remerging as one being, becoming a creator yourself, until you've learned, not necessarily perfected, *teaching mastery*. You will probably have acquired teaching mastery by then because you will have had the opportunity to explore planets and interact with other ETs and so on, and processed that.

You will have to have mastered dimensions, and if you haven't, you will need to have dimensional consultants to support and sustain you who will advise you correctly. Because of who you are and where you are coming from, you will immediately initiate for yourselves the lessons that lead to quantum mastery, though you will just begin. As a result, through this experience you will be assimilating preparatory steps to quantum mastery so that when you become Creator, you will discover that regardless of all the many and varied experiences of all the beings that make you up and remerge as one being, for that moment you will be able to do things beyond any one individual's experience or wisdom. The more you are, the more you are.

When looked at logically, it doesn't make sense. Looking at it through physics, one says that mass can be changed in its appearance or demonstration of itself, but it cannot be made more. It is the same amount, yes? So one can see that in order to fully appreciate one's true experience as being more, one has to first experience being *less*.

Think of the beings you were before you came here, before you joined this experiment. You were that more; you did not think of yourself as missing anything, though you did have a certain degree of joy in discovery or interest in adventure. You didn't think there was something you were missing that you needed, rather that there might be something you didn't know that might be interesting or fun to know; but you didn't need it, you could get along without it.

Now, as you are going to remerge and become a single being, you will discover that you know things you didn't know before, you can do things you couldn't do before, you can be things you couldn't possibly be before and do things for others that are impossible for you to do. These are the foundational, applied lessons of quantum mastery.

Quantum mastery always begins with an experience that leads to a question; you have an experience, usually something benevolent or beneficial, but something that, within the context of your own personality, is impossible (you can't do that, but you did). So it immediately leads to the question, how? The moment you ask or think or engage the question, you are on the path of quantum mastery.

Is there a way for readers to get a feeling for what they are attempting to change in themselves now, to allow expansion?

Yes, yes. Take note of the inspirations or connections that occur between what seemed like separate thoughts, that as a result of reading this, suddenly come together to form a connected unit. After you have thought about your inspiration and what connects to seemingly independent things, go back and examine the connection. The connection itself will show you exactly what area you are working on to expand into the greater you.

Can you give me an example?

Pursuing the Path: the Sea Captain and His Dreams

Let's say that an individual is a functioning member of society, where he is a skipper of a small ship with two or three crew members, nothing fancy. They go out to sea, maybe bringing people out to sea for vacations and fun things to do in the ocean, swimming and so on, and to special, unique places. The skipper, or captain, has to read the charts, know the fun places to do things; he has to be a manager to run the boat well so that the crew can count on their paychecks. He must think about safety and all the other things a captain must do. Within the context of this sea life, however commercial it might be, there is an ongoing need to stay very alert and wake up quickly when it's time for the next watch or action. So he must be quick to become conscious.

Let's say that the person has deep, profound dreams, but he must get up with an alarm regularly even though he has regular waking times. In the charter business one cannot always be certain when one is required, so one has to get up with an alarm. So the captain's dreams are interrupted regularly.

Now let's say that there is a time when the dream is so profound, so deep, so insightful and so all-inclusive (an example might be when you wake up unsure whether the world you're in is your physical world or the dream world; you have all had this experience) that the captain sleeps through the alarm. Even though it rings for five minutes and disturbs other people on the ship, they are busy and cannot come. They assume that the captain forgot to turn the alarm off. So he sleeps perhaps twenty minutes past the alarm.

During that time there is an experience where the dream is so insightful that although the captain knows he's supposed to wake up, he cannot. He hears the alarm in the distance and tries to wake up, but cannot, the dream is so profound. Let's say it is a prophetic dream, which happens sometimes. There is going to be a storm, and if he stays out at sea three more days, the ship will sink and they will all be killed. So although he tries to wake up, at the same time he knows it's important to pay attention. He wakes up eventually and says, "Maybe we ought to change where we are," and takes action on it.

You might ask, "What was the lesson? Was it the dream?" No. The captain learned that to be rigid with the alarm bell is not always the best thing. If the captain applies this method, he would examine that moment of realization after he changed his ship's direction, thereby avoiding the destructive storm, saying, "Well, it's a good thing I did that." He would start thinking, "Maybe these wonderful dreams I'm having are important enough to pay attention to, even if I'm sometimes a little late for my duties." He would examine that decision, understanding that having more flexibility with himself is important, because he might then have visionary skills that will be good for both him and others. The captain, in this case, realizes that in the larger context, he is learning about what he can do for himself and others that benefits all concerned.

Resolving Past Lives

That's beautiful! There are so many people who put duty and alarm clocks and rigidity ahead of their own inner life. This is important. Also, there's been a lot of talk about humans changing their past lives. If a past life that comes up is unpleasant, can you re-create it with imagination? Does that change it? How do you change a past life?

Re-creating it in your imagination or your meditations is a worthy thing, because it will reduce the inflammation. If a past life is a painful experience, the pain of the experience might get worse and worse if you have the capacity in your present life to do something about it. It won't distract you from your present life if you do not have the tools or the means to change it. But once you have the meditative or prayerful skills to change it or do something for it or even soothe or nurture it, then it may begin to become more inflamed in order to catch your attention in some way.

This would compare with having an injury; perhaps you bump your leg, then you put some salve on it. It doesn't heal the injury right away, but it supports that area and makes it feel better. Perhaps it speeds the healing or allows the healing process to work less painfully because you have salve to put on it.

If you have the skills or the abilities to use your imagination or have meditative or shamanic techniques to resolve a past life of your own, by all means go ahead. It might not immediately and totally resolve that past life, but it will support and nurture it, much like putting salve on a wound. It will not flare up so often because you have done what you can with the tools you have. If it flares up again strongly and you feel it, then you either have new tools, new things you can do, or you need to nurture it more than once. Then do what you did before in the most loving, benevolent way in your imagination, your meditations or your shamanic techniques. If you have new things you can do, do that as well.

Is it wisest to allow these things to come up by themselves, or is it okay to search them out with regression therapy or seek them out in other ways?

It is all right to have regression therapies as long as the individuals you go to are skilled and experienced. That is acceptable, or any other means that works for you, as long as the individuals are skilled and are comfortable for you. Sometimes, as you have suggested without saying it, you will have some experience that you do not understand; maybe it has to do with a past life, maybe not. But if it does even in part, then you can go to one of these people to help you. If you do not already know what to do, ask them to give you something you can do for yourself so that it is not only they who are doing it. It is fine for them to do something; however, it is better for you to follow up and continue to follow up, because no one can work with your past life better than you can—though you may need to be instructed.

There's another theory that says you don't have to work with your past lives because if there's something unfinished, it will show up in some large way in this present life, and by looking over the things that stand out in this life, you can get an idea of your past lives or of what has not been resolved in past lives.

The Effect of Self-Love on Your Past

Certainly; I am just commenting on past lives since we are talking about that tonight, but it is certainly not the only way. I feel it is generally better to work with present circumstances. However, one can make an effort to love oneself. When you love yourself in that physical, heartwarming way, you will tend to spread that benevolence throughout your own experience and also throughout all your lives. If any life needs it, it will utilize it, but not in a way that drains you.

As you focus on the heart warmth, it creates an inexhaustible supply. In this way you can help to resolve things you don't know about. If they are not there, then there is no harm; but if they are there and you do not know, or do not know anybody who can help you to know, you can still do the heart warmth and it will work toward soothing that discomfort. Even the discomfort from a time in this life you don't remember that might be affecting your current circumstance, such as something that happened in childhood.

The heart warmth works as a well or spring. Water comes up from a spring down below; it does not come up specifically for this animal or that person or this tree or that bird. It comes up for any and all. When you produce the heart warmth, you bring it up for yourself. To the extent that it helps other parts of you even as you move along, it falls away from you in excess. This will work beneficially in those ways also.

This brings up another question. When we design a life now, in this time on this planet, are we trying to bring in all the old, unresolved things to resolve them all? So many people seem to have so much going on. Have we tried to get as much into these lives in order to resolve as much of the old stuff as possible? Is that how we've set up the lives?

No. You have not tried to do that; it just works out that way.

Let's say you desire to solve certain things, then at a certain point you've resolved them. Then do more old discomforts flow into your life that need release?

Not necessarily. It isn't a cornucopia of discomfort. Rather, to the extent that there are discomforts, then they are there, but they can be resolved to the extent you can resolve them. Let's say you did not do the heart warmth for a few weeks, for example, and there is something in the past that needs to be nurtured more often than that. Then it would come up. You must do the heart warmth again, even though you don't know what it is for. You might resolve something, but you cannot resolve it completely, as one might resolve a stain in a carpet. Those who know the carpet-cleaning business know that sometimes you resolve the stain completely, but after a few weeks of wear, the stain comes back because it was resolved only in the fibers. You do what you can, then if the old wound needs more energy, you do more later.

The Infinite Grocery Store

How is the life designed? Maybe that's what I'm trying to ask. How does one set up the plot for a lifetime? It's a question I'm sure everyone would be interested in. Do we set up a story line with agreements with other people? How do we set it up? How does it change, transform?

Imagine for a moment the infinite grocery store. Not only is it filled with food, but also other items you might need—even ones that do not seem to fit into your life at the moment. Since this is our story, we can say that you have infinite storage capacity. So you go in, and things you need get tagged with your name and a time frame. Those things come to you when you need them, in as much variety as you need—variations of things and different kinds of experiences to the extent you need them.

Let's say we're in the food section and you needed to have a particular experience, which we will call an apple. But one apple doesn't do it. Then you can have as many apples or as many types of the experience that you might need, or even variations. There are many different kinds of apples, you know. So you can have variations, as much as you need and when you need it, but it is not something that you set up beforehand. You basically show up in this place by establishing a life, all right?

Mm-hm. This is you on a soul level.

Yes. You show up, and then you are just there. This place is not a physical place (but it could be, for the sake of our example). You reside there for a moment, and anyone and everything and any circumstance is available in this space. It gets tagged for you and will show up in your life at the time you need it. So it is not something you think about and plan, nor does anybody else sit down and think about it and plan.

But who's doing the tagging, then?

The tagging is done on the basis of what is needed. It is a *response to a need*, so it is a benevolent response. Let's say you go into a glass store and they are selling fine china and beautiful cut crystal, yes? [Laughs.] You begin to whistle a happy tune, then, having perfect pitch, you begin to sing, though not too loudly. Much of the cut crystal will resonate to your voice, responding to you and to your sounds. That will be by way of a tag; it is like that. It responds on a resonant availability. Even if it is not there, it responds.

When you have an intersection in experience . . . to put an amusing touch on it, some time ago, on a highway near a city, two cars filled with two different bands were in a collision with another car, I think a truck. They were upset afterward and were standing around and talking about it with each other. They thought to themselves, "This is pretty funny that two bands should be in a car crash." So they decided to make a song together, like an intersection, right? As they came together and formed this one rock and roll band for this circumstance, this song turned out to be their greatest hit.

They went on after that and didn't stay together. They remained as their own bands. But for this one song they came together, and it turned out to be their greatest hit—very popular. It still gets played now and then.

The main thing is that you might have an intersection where you will meet someone—or many someones—in an unlikely circumstance, and something good might come out of it. Then you go on with your life. It is a variable. Say, for instance, that you have a specific need to meet a specific person on a particular day and time. Let's say that for some perfectly legitimate reason, that meeting can't take place exactly that way. Then there will be variables—you will have as much as you can have. Maybe you will have *almost* an experience like that with someone, not exactly what you need but close; but you will have another experience like that, overlapping perhaps in the future, that covers it.

That's why people sometimes have repetitive experiences, not just because they're slow learners, but because the exact thing they needed was not available then, because it was very precise. They got a piece of it. This does not mean that every repetitive experience would be about this, but for the sake of our example we'll use it that way.

I always thought the soul or self had some specific ideas about what it hoped to gain from a particular lifetime. That's not true?

Yes, it is. Think about it. Our soul goes to the infinite grocery store, yes? And how are things tagged for it?

By one's presence.

But how else?

Desire?

Yes, need. So the soul emanates its native energy, and within that energy is need. Things are tagged according to that need, with variables based on: maybe it can happen, maybe it can't. If not a Gravenstein apple, maybe a Granny Smith. So the resonance is produced by the need of that soul. All others that respond may not just be waiting there; they might be far away from there, but that resonance is felt by them.

This pulls two people into the same town or attracts an accident or something, right?

Or something, yes. You can say that Santa Claus brings you just the right rose.

The Walk-in Experience

[Laughs.] All right, so there's an initial soul going in, and its needs and its resonances set up experiences. There are many people on the planet now who are experiencing various aspects of their souls coming and going—they're called walk-ins, but I don't think they're exactly that. How does that work? The first aspect has completed what it came to do, then another aspect sets up more experiences?

Yes. That is uncommon, but in this rare event of the so-called walk-in, yes. It is the same thing; the vessel of the body is the receiver of different souls in this case, but the function is the same.

The walk-in was different souls. But aren't many humans on the planet pulling in different aspects of their own souls or different parts of themselves?

It is possible.

Do they have agendas?

They might. If nothing steps out, those things will come together to the degree that is mutually compatible. If there is a severe clash in agendas, there will probably be a delay until there is no more clash. If the clash remains through the end of the life, that is a portion of the agenda that will not be worked on.

Story Line of This Creator School

Well, there are over 5 billion humans, but there are not that many stories. Are there themes on this planet?

There are infinite stories. It is just that you utilized, as you say, certain themes to keep you going. Stories of any culture will support and reinforce what that culture is attempting to do, even if it is a homogenized culture such as you have on Earth. Even if it seems that there are not very many stories, that is not so. It is just that there are not that many story lines *here*.

You mean on Earth.

Yes.

How many story lines are there? Can you categorize them?

How high can you count? As many as are needed.

But aren't there themes? Humans come to learn something or to expand or understand something—how would you generalize that?

You must be more specific.

Souls take lives on the Earth, first because they're part of the Explorer Race. They need this and they've agreed to it. They set up their lives. In this duality, first we learn to conquer our enemies and deal with them; then we conquer the parts of ourselves that need it. There doesn't seem to be that many plots. Is there a way to talk about what the themes are, or the archetypal story lines?

Not in this context, no; later maybe we can get into that. You'll need to rephrase that question, because there's no point in my speaking about the obvious story lines when everybody knows them. By the time you are a ten-year-old child, you know what the story lines are, so there is not much point in my adding my two bits there. I will simply say that once you go beyond this school, there are many story lines. But here the story lines that exist are strictly to support what you are doing here.

Tell me again from your perspective what we are doing here.

Growing, changing, expanding, becoming. So stories will all fall within that context. But there are others beyond this Earth, beyond this time, beyond these circumstances, certainly.

Well, we're aware of them, we're printing them, multitudinous ones, all the way up to beyond creators.

Yes. Even so, all the stories you have printed so far follow those general themes because the beings who relate to you must, to a greater or lesser degree, fall into your thematic path. Otherwise they cannot help you, nor can you relate to them.

And they wouldn't interest us, right?

That's right, they wouldn't interest you. There are many beings who have not come through that are present. They are doing something else; they are passing through, observing and so on. But their lives and the context of their lives is meaningless to what you are doing here. And perhaps, to a greater or lesser degree, the other way also. There may not be much advantage for them to know too much about you or for you to know too much about them.

At this time.

At this time, exactly.

I don't want to belabor it. I just thought people would be interested in it.

It is a reasonable question. Stories, as you say, are lessons placed within a theme. Always there is a lesson. Sometimes it seems that the lesson is very hard; other times it seems as if the lesson is so vague that it's hard to put your finger on it. Sometimes you do not really understand your life until it is over, or toward the end. At other times you have the greatest grasp of your life and its full meaning when you are very young, but as you grow up, you begin to lose that as you work into your culture and take your place in society—all points between and more.

Then what's the greatest thing you can do? Just really plunge into life and experience as much as you can, or step back and attempt to get insight?

The greatest thing you can do is to live the best you can in whatever circumstances life offers you.

But "the best you can" means really immersing yourself and experiencing it deeply?

For some. You are looking for the universal, but the universal resolution cannot apply in applied lessons; it can only apply in universal experiences. On this planet you all must breathe, but on this planet there might be thousands of ways to resolve a single dilemma, and each way might be perfect in its own time, in its own place within the context of your life. But if you are looking for a universal morality, we know that that is love. Good night.

Levels of Being

December 18, 1997

Isis Experiences Our Suffering

Isis here. As a fully realized vast being, everywhere on level one, and able to comfortably allow struggle and strife somewhere, Zoosh is on Earth as well as in other places. I'm using Zoosh as an example. He can comfortably allow struggle and strife here, he has compassion for you, he wants to help you and he is doing that. But he does not personally experience your struggle and suffering. For me, as a personal being, I *do* experience your suffering, personally. That is perhaps why I am more inclined to become more directly involved to the extent it is allowed. Please do not think that Zoosh does not care about you and does not love you, but he is a level-one being in his essence.

You have been feeling it for . . .

. . . as long as I have been aware of myself.

I mean, you've been feeling the suffering of this creation for an awfully long time.

But I have been feeling suffering *anywhere* for as long as I have been aware of myself. Even if it were a minor degree of suffering, even if somebody had an itch they couldn't scratch.

On the third level there's suffering like that?

No.

From the third level you feel it on the first level?

Yes, if it is anywhere. Then I tend to be attracted to that place to see if I can help and if it is allowed for me to help. If it is allowed and I can help, then I will do what I can.

That's why you've been pulled here so much!

Yes.

How incredible! You've never suffered before like you have on this Earth, right?

I would have to say that in my experience of my lifetime, I can think of only one other place where suffering was greater.

That's that planet in Sirius.

Yes, that former planet in Sirius that no longer exists within your now sequence of time. It will take quite some experiential time, as Zoosh says (meaning doing things), to heal it. For those beings who come to 3.0-dimensional Earth, it is an ideal place to heal their soul personal experiences, because there is enough discomfort and polarity here that they will feel in a familiar surrounding without going through a typical or normal reincarnational cycle. [This refers to the negative Sirians. Some examples of additional information: *The Explorer Race*, chapters 15 and 22; *ETs and the Explorer Race*, chapter 5; *Shining the Light III*, chapter 30; and *The Explorer Race: Origins and the Next 50 Years*, chapter 20.]

The Vastness of Isis

On the third level are there tens of thousands, billions or trillions—how many beings are there? Is it a rare experience for beings to be from there?

Since all is personal on the third level and on the second level as well, I would have to say that every portion of me is an individual, yet I am united in my entire being. So I would have to count inner and outer. I know this makes no sense to you, but imagine the center of a sphere, counting out and then on the outside of the sphere counting in—that is perhaps easier to understand visually—in order to say how many there are. I am but one personality, so in your now concept of numbers, it would not be comfortable to imagine the vastness of individuals unless one considered united personalities, such as myself, as one. In terms of united personalities there would be at least ten and at most billions. It really depends how far you go.

In my vastness, having become aware of myself on level three, I am able to be everywhere on level three, yes? I am able to be everywhere on levels two and one. But to give you an idea of the vastness, you could take level one; if you moved it to level three, it would be lost there. Level three is necessarily larger because of the personal experience of the beings there. The beings need more space because everything is so intensely personal.

In your totality, then, there are only ten like you?

No, I am saying there are no fewer than ten like me, but to the extent I am aware of, there might be billions, yet the individual parts that make me up would be higher than your numerical system goes.

But you have a sense of the coherence of all those parts that make you up.

Yes, not only a sense, I have a personal experience, so it is like a cell of my body, as in a cell of your body. It is a part of my personal self.

Let's just assume ten. Do they feel the pain on Earth? Or have any of them ever been involved in this Explorer Race experience?

That's another book.

[Laughs.] I'll take it! Well, that's mind-blowing enough for tonight, I guess.

Yes, perhaps that's enough. If we come up with another book idea every week, we will have books and books and books.

That's okay!

Good.

You're wonderful.

Thank you. Good night.

December 23, 1997
A Turning Point in the Explorer Race Experience: The Shift Away from Cynicism

Can you give us details about what happened when this Explorer Race experiment suddenly became guaranteed? It was not guaranteed the last time we talked to Zoosh. What was the turning point?

The turning point really had to do with the increased consciousness that is seeping into places that are not known for consciousness and heart. They might be known for courage and perhaps less wonderful things, but in recent years many peoples on the Earth have gone through a long embracing of cynicism. This cynicism has been used as a shield to protect oneself from disappointment, but one cannot reside in cynicism for too long, because there is a point at which it no longer protects, but nullifies your experience. Good things that might happen will be nullified because you do not wish to give them any credence or validity whatsoever.

In recent years, places where one would expect cynicism to be entrenched have started to move as a body consciousness—not all individuals at the same time, but a gradual movement toward an acceptance of possibilities that things might change for the better individually. This has happened in three particular places of note: in war zones, with soldiers and civilians in war zones, and in prisons.

The reason Zoosh talks at length about prisons and prisoners and speaks to people ensconced in such places is because Zoosh recognizes the vital importance of people in such places to act as a turning point to help to propel society beyond its conventional wisdoms. If people in the most dire of conditions can see a possibility for some future benevolence for themselves and even their friends, in the face of the worst possible experiences, then this belief is to be nurtured as well as acknowledged.

What has occurred is this change. People in these places I mentioned, in the face of all evidence to the contrary, are beginning to have signs that they believe show it's going to change, and there is now evidence they can bring forth in the moment that this will be so. It is not only faith, though it is surely that; it is more than that. It is a feeling, as if someone in the future were pulling a string to which you were attached, and although the string is not turning you into a slave, it is a reminder like a string around a finger. People in such places have been feeling this reminder. So it's more like a feeling without any evidence to support it.

That's wonderful. And that will spread.

I believe it will because of the nature of the military, of war zones, of civilians in war zones and of prisons. These circumstances tend to spread around a bit. And people come and go from prisons as well as the military, and certainly civilians come and go from war zones. So the spreading of this feeling is guaranteed.

Is it a part of our future, then, where somebody is gently reminding us?

Yes, and it is a part that involves faith to the extent that there is no evidence that says, "See, look; this must be so" or "Try it yourself; you can prove it"—not that. It is a feeling only. This is another reason

Speaks of Many Truths and Zoosh have been helping you and working with people to access the full meaning of their feelings and to apply feelings in ways that are benevolent to them and others. When your feelings are sharpened and you have some idea of what they are or at least what is a good thing and what isn't, you can respond to something that feels good even if there is no explanation whatsoever.

No logic . . .

Yes, as to what it is or even what it might be. In that sense it is faith coupled with physical evidence on the feeling level.

Part Two

Isis wanted to do a book where she would work directly with a priestess group, answering their questions based on going into a deeper level of their work with themselves and with those they were assisting—and working energetically and through their dreams with the group.

This project didn't come together. We are publishing the material here that would have been the beginning of the second Isis book and asking any or all Isis groups or practitioners to submit any questions that have come up in your training or your work that you would like to ask Isis—also submit something about your group or practice. We will put any additional channeling generated by your questions in the next printing of this book.

Publisher

Introduction to Part Two

On Initiation

Many years ago when the initiation process was invented, it had to be done differently than you know it today. Today one is initiated by being given something—wisdom or even a material object, to say nothing of trust. When initiation was invented, it had to work the other way: Since everyone at that time knew everything, initiation was promised to be the path of wisdom unattainable. Think about it. If everyone knows everything, then what can be offered? Only the impossible. If you know everything, the concept of the impossible is within your grasp, even though it may not be something you can apply in a practical sense. So the first initiation was granted to those who were prepared to take a perilous journey that no one before their time had ever taken. That journey would start out, and the very first step would be the path of ignorance.

It was hard to convince anyone in the beginning to take that step. After all, if you know everything—all there is to know—why would you want to give that up for the unknown, given that you would not know when, where, how, who, why or any of the things that you took for granted in your normal existence? Yet initiation was a success.

Now you experience initiation as the *return* of your wisdom. Sometimes it comes in the form of faith, trust or responsibility, but other times it comes in the form of challenge. When initiation comes in the form of challenge it is often difficult; sometimes the path is even treacherous. Yet ultimately what is achieved is a balance greater than the sum of its parts. Consider those who began the initiation process so long ago: Why begin something such as that with beings who knew everything? What could be the outcome? At the beginning it seemed to be, not unreasonably, a waste of time, as you might say today, a bit of foolishness, somebody's crackpot idea. Yet there are, as always, the brave ones who say, "I will give up knowing everything strictly as an act of—what? Faith! An act of faith that something is to be gained or the process wouldn't be given to us in this moment."

When those original beings took that step, they really took a step for all of you as well, because there is nothing like the experience of regaining wisdom, even if it seems to be something you did not know before. Yet how many of you can say that you have never had the experience of the wondrous, felt reality of some great truth? Perhaps it was like being thunderstruck, perhaps it was great inspiration. You have all had this at one time or another. When you have that exultant feeling, that is not the result of mind, because feeling is the forte of the physical self. Therefore, the physical self recognizes wisdom once lost and now not only regained, but regained in a broader, more practical way.

One considers, how do you reach for the stars and still maintain a life that can be lived daily? It is done by application, by living, by doing, by consequences, by responsibility, by life. Yet when these things are done in this way, one constantly reinvents oneself. The reinventing process in its own right is perhaps the most valuable gift of the first initiates. How could they know—those beings who knew everything? And I do not just mean in a context of a given culture or society, not just in the context of planetary wisdom, but universal, multiuniversal, multilevel wisdom. How could they know that what they were giving up was not a permanent loss? They could not! But because they were open to taking that first step, which required that they forget all their wisdom, they took a step for you.

Even now the threads of those beings are amongst you. You are all where I am as well as on this planet—everywhere—connected, corded, if you would, to those original initiates. You could not exist here in these times and this place as the Explorer Race if ignorance had not been discovered to be a great opportunity, though masked. When your body celebrates with that exultant feeling of a great truth known—as you say, "eureka! I understand!"—that feeling is directly associated with those original threads.

Remember, ignorance is a gift of the physical plane. Built into ignorance is the guarantee of growth. I am not saying to pursue ignorance; what I am saying is, ignorance was granted as the means of personal expansion. So do not judge those who are ignorant even if it is a painful ignorance. Only that ignorance will guarantee growth. As you read this book and experience it, do not judge yourself, others or even these words; they are intended to spark and stimulate exultant feelings within you, in your physical body, which is made up of a profound wisdom-keeper, Mother Earth. It is your physical body that will tell you, and it will be stimulated by some things here when you are regaining the wisdom you once had, with a little extra thrown in because of your experience, because of your courage and because of your commitment. Never forget that the path of wisdom, albeit emerging from and weaving through ignorance, is guaranteed to expand your consciousness in a practical, physical, spiritual, day-to-day realistic way.

Isis

January 15, 1998

Who Is Isis?

January 15, 1998

(A Session for a Priestess Group who had not heard or read
any of the previous material in this book)

Isis speaking.

Welcome. Can you talk about whether you were here in physical form, where you were and who you embodied in Egypt?

A People in a Time before Egypt's Golden Age

I myself never have been a physical being. Once upon a time there was a young woman I worked with. Why? Because she asked. (What often holds the individual back is not asking. Remember that asking is all right.) This young woman lived in a society that certainly predated what you've come to know as, at least artistically, the golden age of Egypt. In this society she had been blessed with, some would say— others would say drafted into—a position of leadership, not a form of leadership with command or authority, but the kind of leadership where one is an example and can help individuals move from an essentially agrarian lifestyle to one that will become highly symbolic. It was in the same land, but predated the golden age of Egypt. It was understood that something needed to change. The people were happy, there was no great suffering. Yet certain elders knew that something needed to change—not for the sake of the people, but rather for the sake of future generations.

You know, even today you will find parents sacrificing, saving and trying to create the opportunity for their children to have better lives. Whether the children choose to do that or not is up to them, but the parent naturally wishes that the child would be better off than its mother or father. Yet in these times, these people who had lived on the land for generation after generation, living to preserve and nurture the land as well as to be preserved and nurtured by the land, had the foresight and wisdom to respond to what was truly an inner feeling in all of them. Future generations, perhaps not even in their society, required them to change so that some unknown destiny could be fulfilled. It was quite a circumstance.

The Young Girl They Chose

They took almost a generation (people didn't live as long then, about twenty-three years) to pick the best candidate to show them the way. They finally decided, after much consultation, on a young girl of the time. She was chosen absolutely—no maybe, maybe not. This youngster was picked for her intuitive skills, of course, since no one knew what they would be doing, but they had to change, yes?

She was a youngster by your standards, but nine years old in those days was the threshold of womanhood, and it was considered necessary that she make sacrifices. One of the sacrifices she would be required to make was to have no children of her own, considered at this time a terrible sacrifice. Just imagine these days the feeling of giving up all you have known, all you have loved, all you would wish to love by giving up having children of your own. She was also required to give up having a love mate.

This was the beginning of what you now know as the temple priestess, though it was not called that at the time. It was understood that in order to proceed in some way, the person who would guide them (not lead them) would have to make this sacrifice, because if she lived the same cycle as the rest of the people, how could she have time to feel into what must be done? How could she even be considered able to make some major change? It would not be possible if you were living the same life as the rest of your people. This was the beginning in modern times of setting apart the spiritual being, at least in that part of the world.

So this youngster was granted a great deal of love and nurturance from many because she would have to sacrifice her personal happiness. It was understood that if her own mother or grandmother were not present to guide her, love her, nurture her, be her friend, help her along in her difficult journey, that anyone from the culture was expected to fill in. As you can see, this was the nucleus of the head priestess with her entourage, as it were. She was given this nurturance for several years, but she did not have a vision. How could she? She was, as you say, a product of her environment even though she was intuitive.

When the Girl Asked the Birds for a Vision

So one day she went out on the land and spoke to the beings that she felt could offer her the best likelihood of assisting her with this burden of responsibility. She spoke to the birds, because it was well understood in those times that birds could see beyond. Because they could fly so high, they could see things that mortals could not. Even though the people understood that birds were mortal, they had a special feeling for birds, who were considered the representatives of immortals

Candice McGinnis demonstrating Isis' appearance to students.

not only because they could fly, but because when you looked them in the eye, they seemed to know all that needed to be known. And when people dreamt or asked for dreams, they would ask the birds to fly them to what they could see.

You have to remember that in those times flight was considered magic. No one even considered the possibility that human beings could fly in any way, at any time.

So she went to speak to the birds. She walked off a ways, and when she spoke to the birds, she did what in present days your shamans or mystical people do: She would kneel on one knee, spreading her arms wide.

That is the way she would speak to the birds because it was a way she could offer her greeting and call them. She knew she was speaking to the bird spirits, but because she had this special ability, which the people knew about, when she assumed that position birds would always come. They would fly over her or land on a branch of a distant tree.

The land was different then, not a desert as you know it there today, but soil, lands, grasses, trees, and the birds would be nearby. Then she would ask the birds to fly to the immortals, who could grant her a vision. Of course, she was expecting to have this vision in her sleep, because in those days people did not think of dreams as you do today; there was a wakeful state, then there was a sleeping state when you had visions. Dreams were never considered anything but visions.

How Isis Responded

So she asked, and because I had some knowledge of what the people needed to do, I sent a portion of myself, initially in the form of a bird, partly because I wanted her to pass on greater visioning capabilities to those she worked with. Since the people cherished the bird spirits, it seemed a reasonable way to show up. So I flew as the bird out of the Sun; from her perspective she would have to look up and see. She had a feeling (the mystical person responds to feelings), then looked up (squinted, of course) and saw flying out of the Sun a magnificent bird. Instead of flying over her as birds usually did or landing nearby in a tree, this bird, this portion of myself, flew right up to her, alighted about two or three feet in front of her, put its wings out to match her position, and then slowly folded its wings.

She remained in her position. This bird portion of myself repeated this gesture several times until she realized she did not have to hold her arms out anymore. It was a way to show her she could relax. Then the bird sat down, the way birds nest, so she sat down. Then for a long time the bird spoke to her in words, pictures and symbols, some of which she could not understand. It showed her future things that in some ways the Egyptians created in the golden age: artworks, some of the pyramids, some of the great beauties that Egypt is known for today. She was also shown the path that people would be on today, with reverence toward the intellectual and the detached, with an abhorrence of feeling, passion—if not abhorrence, in some places distrust—the enjoyment of it, but distrust of it.

She could not imagine how any society could live like that, so she was informed that they could not; they must be shown how to find their way back to their wisdom. So she was given symbols, pictures and even, to some extent, ceremony. Not much has survived today, but some has. It was suggested that she share this with those who helped her and those she could help with this wisdom. This formed the nucleus for the great things that Egypt is known for today.

You can see how the picture came about that you identify as Isis, but who was actually my student. Some of that is apparent from what I have said, but some was encoded into the feeling of the material from which the artworks were created. She was informed that the artworks had to be as big as possible, much bigger than was necessary or practical, and that the people did not need to know why. [Chuckles.] But in fact, these massive sculptures were so big and of such a material that was not so durable because they were expected to dissolve over time, and the sands that had once been the stone would drift and be carried all over the Earth, waiting in its encoded way for those who would claim parts of this soil to someday form the bodies of what is now the Explorer Race.

This story, in a form, was told to her and she told it to others. In time those people came to be known as the great Egyptian people whom you honor these days. The beginning of it was very sacred. In time many of the accouterments of the ceremonies were gathered and applied to the regal class of beings in ancient Egypt during its golden age. But all of this was taken from the original priestess group, at least in that part of the world.

Your Endearing Quality: Sacrificing What Is Dear for Future Generations

This is a brief version of the story, but I wanted you to understand how it is that I am considered to be this wonderful student who made such sacrifices of her happiness, not only for her people but, perhaps more profoundly, for the people of today. An entire culture was prepared to give up their way of life, even though they were perfectly happy with it, for some unknown generation of beings—perhaps their own people, perhaps much further in the future. Think about that, if you would, because it is that very quality which endears Earth people to people from other planets—the complete willingness to abandon all that is held dear if somehow, in some way, someone in the future that one might never meet would benefit from it.

I must tell you that though people make sacrifices for the betterment of their own kind, their families and their cultures on other planets, to make a sacrifice like this is essentially unknown, at least in this universe. That is why so many beings come from other planets, more in the past than today, but they still come. To them, that is your most endearing quality. Some of them have even used it as a tenet of their philosophies, not for the sake of sacrifice for its own sake, but rather as a leap of faith [chuckles].

This quality is well-known here on this planet, even taken for granted—after all, when you are youngsters in school, even preschool, you often make a leap of faith: "I don't know whether she or he will like me, but I'll take a chance." That's a leap of faith; it may be an ordinary leap of faith, but it is a leap of faith nevertheless. You would be surprised how uncommon that is! Yet here on this planet it is so common as to be almost mundane.

So sometimes things get started and you do them; you know not why, but you have a good feeling for them, so you go ahead. That is where these now-considered-commonplace experiences began. After all, things that are commonplace in any time began somewhere.

Today's Priestess

Could you comment on the task for the priestess today?

Thank you, yes. The priestess today takes a vow, regardless of her initiation rite. The vow might be different, depending on the rite, but the inner vow is the same today as it was in ancient times: *to make things better.* The nice thing about that vow is that it is translatable from society to society. When I say better, I mean benevolently better. After all, one could have an extreme point of view, perhaps a violent point of view, and making something better might not be so benevolent for everyone. So let your vow be to make things better in a benevolent way.

You might say something like this: *I vow to make things better in the best way I can, in the most benevolent way for me and all those I come in contact with as well as all those I will never meet.* This ought not replace vows you take for your voyage on your path, whatever priestess vows they might be, but it is a nice vow because it really sums up your initial motivation for wanting to be involved in the process in the first place. Remember, everyone here these days—and you are living descendants of this practice—really wants to make things better. This is translatable only to a degree, so we add the term "benevolent" because that is understood by all to be a worthy goal.

Given the many and widely varied practices of any priestess or priest today, if you follow that guideline as a foundation yet do not discard your own, then anything that falls well outside those boundaries can be left for others. Priestesses and priests today do not have the responsibility to be everything, to do everything, to apply everything, so your responsibility lies in the path of betterment—for yourself and for others, some of whom you will never meet. You must be able to allow others to do what they must, even if you cannot think about it because it is painful in thought, to say nothing of deed.

I want to give you general guidelines. I am using a wide brush, painting broad strokes. But for right now I'd say that if the priest or priestess can openly join with that vow, you will honor in these times and in times immemorial the purpose and function of the priestess and priest class. By "class" do I mean above, below, to the side? No. It means you must learn even as you teach, as in school, because it is the very nature of being a priest or priestess.

Osiris and She Who Would Be Understood by Thee

Isis, what can you say of Osiris, please?

In terms of the ideal?

No, the quality of the energy or your relationship with him or it.

In the larger sense, Osiris represents the mind and the practical application of the mind's perception. My experience is more perhaps of the heart and the connectiveness to all who express this. My relationship to my definition of Osiris has more to do with defining my point of view in ways that Osiris can understand and also helping others to understand. What we are doing now, communicating in words (also known as symbols), is a function of the Osiris energy. What will be read by others, regardless of language, will be symbols necessitated and then propagated by the Osirian energy. So my relationship to Osiris is the relationship of She Who Would Be Understood by Thee. To your society now, it is specifically Osiris' job to structure the symbolic, apply it in its most practical way and await further input.

Understand this: I do not make light (or perhaps I ought to say, trite) of the Osirian energy, but rather remind you how you could not find your way out of the Tower of Babel, in which you are, at least in the illusory context, fumbling about to some extent now—different languages, different cultures—without Osirian energy. It is Osiris' job to weave the thread of common ground in a practical way that *secures* the seam and is not just the . . . well, for those of you out there who make your own clothes, it functions as basting. We don't want to pin the seam; we want to secure it so that connections between all beings are not only understood, but appreciated. Again, the broad brush stroke.

Resurgence of Interest in Isis and the Mysterious

What do you see as being behind humanity's renewed interest in your essence, your nature?

Good question. Always when you hear or feel that urgent change for the better is needed, yet there is no clear-cut answer, all over the world will be found people turning to what they have known or, more often, what they have known but not understood. At times of great uncertainty, certain things always become popular. One is art, because art by its very nature, even though it is graphic, contains within it the mysterious, which means that whatever side of whatever scene the artist chose to show you, there must be a side you cannot see. If it is sculpture, you can walk around the back and see the other side, but you cannot see the inside. If it is a painting, what is off the frame? What might have been seen from a different point of view? If it is a photograph, what else was there? What was the photographer thinking when she or he took the picture?

In other words, what is popular in these times is the partly understood but necessarily mysterious. It is at times like this that people will lunge with renewed vigor toward that which is not understood, but which holds within it or seems to imbue an essence that says, "If you figure me out, I will reward you." This is why to this day, of course, your famous painting, the Mona Lisa, is revered almost religiously by your society: What's she smiling about? Or is it a smile at all? I perhaps am not unlike the enigmatic Mona Lisa in the sense that there are symbols, are there not? "Look—what are those wings about? And what on Earth are those horns and that light on top? It must mean *something.*"

You have been given symbols of the mysterious not only to remind you of the common mysteries that draw you inexorably back as a greater individual to the wisdom you have known once, but also you are encouraged in many ways to discover *why.*

I would have to say that many individuals might be drawn to the symbolic representation of my student (I understand that it is considered to be me, and perhaps a little bit so) because (can you not agree?) the picture, the sculpture, the representation, ask the questions, *Why? How? What? Who?* and perhaps most importantly, *How can I?*

Your Journey Has Brought About Your Wisdom

Not unlike other enigmatic symbols from culture to culture, many individuals are asking these days, *How can I?* If you stop to remember that story, how those people long ago gave up their culture, though it was working very well for them, to propagate symbols that would be enticing in some vague future they did not know, you will appreciate that those seeds placed carefully in the past now inspire your fertile minds and hearts to bring forth the flowers of wisdom that these symbols only symbolize. The flowers of wisdom are within you, and as you know, it is the journey that brings about wisdom, not the arrival.

So understand that the interest in me now will bear the same fruit as the interest in many others, because the journey, while not exactly the same for all individuals, will bring about the same result.

I think we will say that is enough for tonight. It is a beginning, is it not? Now you have some idea of who I am, or at least who I claim to be, and perhaps I have done my duty—maybe stimulated a few questions. That is, after all, my ultimate purpose with you. Good night.

Prelude to the Next Isis Book

Now that you have read this opening book in the series of books that I will do through this channel and with this publisher, know that it is my intention to open up a dialogue with you. If you have any questions that pertain to how you feel about me or what you might have heard about me, I ask that you send it to the publisher so that such questions can be addressed in a future volume—or article, more likely, associated with the book, perhaps in an appendix. [Mail to: Light Technology Publishing, P.O. Box 3540, Flagstaff, AZ, 86003]

I also ask that you consider that the Isis speaking to you now through this channel is the larger being. I do not dispute how I might have been defined in other ways and times; I feel that different definitions for different times are perhaps appropriate. You need to see the big picture—at least the big picture insofar as it is relevant to you and what you are doing here. Within that context, I want you to understand that this book is only the beginning. There will be many more. Be thinking about what you'd like explored. If you do not have questions, then perhaps you could send in topics you'd like explored, and we will or will not get to them; it depends. But I'd like you to know that I consider this book participatory; several things I discussed in this book were in response to questions that beings who have had contact with me would have asked if they had been here.

On that note, I will say good day and good life.

APPENDIX

Transformational Techniques

An Exercise to Feel and Increase Your Feminine Energy

Isis through Robert Shapiro

There are so many people now who are out of touch with their feminine energy. Also, many men who are unable to be close to women—close enough to have that feminine energy nurture them. And there are women who, because of your modern times, are coming more into their masculine energy out of necessity. What will be most benevolent for this planet has to do with the feminine energy.

So I want to give you all something you can do that is both for the planet and for you. It will help you to actually feel the feminine energy even if you are living on a mountaintop by yourself, even if you are living in conditions where feminine energies are not present, even if you are living in the hustle and bustle of the business cycle. This exercise will help you feel the feminine energy within you. It requires a diagram and pictures.

Here's the gesture. Use your left hand. Move it like this [to begin, hold left arm outward to the side, palm facing forward; raise arm, moving palm to face leftward; then lower arm, rotating palm to face toward right] and repeat the gesture. Now I will draw the full pattern of movement to the right [see figure, next page].

When you are done moving your left hand from left to right, bring your hand back so that the palm is facing your chest. Move it to the left again and repeat the cycle. It was intended that this help integrate the feminine energy for you as a person.

When you are on the downstroke, move a little slower. The key for this to work is to move very slowly, especially at the very bottom of the stroke.

Both the gesture and the speed at which you make it are equally important. After a while you will experiment with it. If you make it too quickly at first, when you slow down, you will begin to feel the energy better. Those who have good instincts will be able to know on the basis of how you feel exactly what speed to use.

What is it doing?

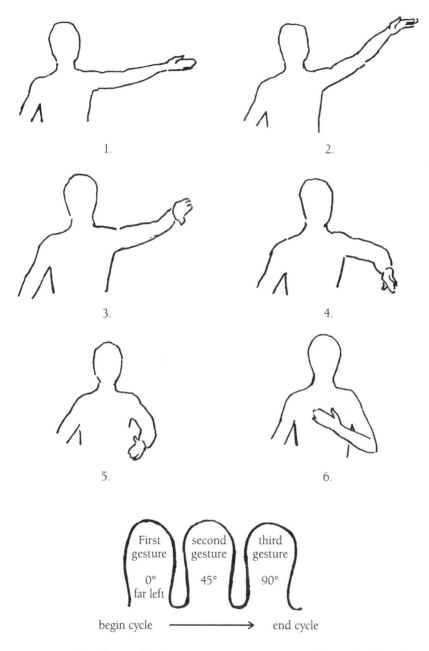

It actually allows the feminine energy in your physical self to be more present. It attracts benevolent feminine energy to you, not just any feminine energy. It attracts and integrates all in one motion. If your life is a strain or there is much rushing or you are living in difficult circumstances, you might need do it more than once a day.

For those living in more benevolent circumstances, it might be necessary to do it once a week or less. The main thing is that it have a felt energy. Those who feel the energy, stay with it as an exercise. Those who just experience it as an exercise, see if it helps.

If you feel it right away, do it as long as it feels good. If you don't feel it very much, then try to do it for at least a few minutes each time. If you have done it on ten different occasions (not all in the same day) and you still don't feel anything, then let it go. It works for people at different times. You might try it again at a later time in your life when your life is either more benevolent or when you feel you have too little energy.

It works in concert with the Earth in many ways. Because you are parts of Earth's body and are made up of her body, Earth needs to give you energy every day. When you do this, you make it easier for Earth to give you that energy. It will spare her the struggle and at the same time create a more benevolent experience of the feminine energy for you. For those who want a more scientific model, it's not unlike a moving antenna.

Later, I will give later information on what this gesture does and can do for you and many others in the future. But begin now. I want you all to have time to try it. To those for whom it works and who feel that warmth and that benevolent energy, I will give you more that you can do with it in the future.

For more gestures that can help the Earth and yourself, see the first Shamanic Secrets book: *Shamanic Secrets for Material Mastery*.

The Heart-Heat Exercise

Speaks of Many Truths through Robert Shapiro

P ractice feeling love as heat in the chest. Use your hands over your chest to help focus energy not touching body.

When you can hold this warmth, add the feeling (not visualization) of gold light.

Keep practicing back and forth until you can feel both at the same time, then hold it for at least 10 or 15 minutes.

After you learn to do this, while you are feeling this heat or love or both, say out loud:

"I give all beings permission to be loved, to be fed, clothed, healed and comforted."

You can add other appropriate things, but keep it simple. The heart heat will naturally radiate even when the gold light is absent.

Because one of the most important levels of creator training is to be able to feel what others feel, you might have nightmares and wake up with horrible feelings or have other experiences that result in such feelings. As soon as you can, ask:

"Let benevolent love bless and transform all I am feeling."

Then feel gold light. This is alchemical training to transform the pain of others through being aware of their feelings.

When you come together as a group to feel heart heat and gold light:

Talk about what's bothering you so you have some feelings to transform. Focus on the physical warmth in your chest or solar plexus, which is the physical evidence of love.

Strike a chime or make some signal, then imagine gold light there while you feel the heat with total focus so that the alchemical transformation can take place.

In a group these feelings are amplified. This exercise can transform any discomfort that arises and you will feel ecstatic; it is the closest feeling to the Creator energy that you are. The larger the group, the wider the area it will transform to cheerful, loving feelings. Eventually it can become first nature to you and you will feel it all the time. It will lead to unifying all beings, everywhere.

The Disentanglement Basic Process

SSJOooo through Robert Shapiro

Lie on a flat surface on your back, hands by your side, palms down and slightly away from your body—preferably three hours after eating and before you go to sleep, but it works anywhere, anytime. Remove any metal buckles and take coins or metal keys out of your pockets. Do not cross your legs or feet. This position allows you to get used to being open in your most receptive areas.

Say out loud (if possible), *"I am asking gold lightbeings, Earth gold lightbeings, lightbeings who can work through gold lightbeings, and lightbeings who can radiate or emanate to gold lightbeings, to disentangle me from all my discomforts and pains."*

Squeeze your eyelids shut and then focus on the light patterns—don't think. If you catch yourself thinking, gently bring your attention back to the light patterns and continue.

Do this for twenty or thirty minutes or for as long as you feel you need to do it or until you fall asleep. This can be done once or twice a day.

After a few weeks, make a list of every person and event in your life that makes you feel uncomfortable. Say the above statement and add, "I am asking to be disentangled from the discomfort and pain of _____ _____," reading one or two names or events from the list. Do each name for two-three days or until you feel clear with the person.

Speaks of Many Truths adds:

"You may notice that if you say those specific words or names during the course of your day, after you've done disentanglement on them three to five times, that you no longer feel physically as uncomfortable about them as you once did."

"This means the disentanglement is working. The objective is to feel physically calm. Keep saying those specific words or names in your disentanglement process until you feel physically calm. When you do, move on to other words or names, never more than one or two at a time."

THE EXPLORER RACE SERIES

ZOOSH AND OTHERS THROUGH ROBERT SHAPIRO

Superchannel Robert Shapiro can communicate with any personality anywhere and anywhen. He has been a professional channel for over twenty-five years and channels with an exceptionally clear and profound connection.

The Origin...
The Purpose...The Future...of Humanity

If you have ever wondered about who you really are, why you are here as part of humanity on this miraculous planet and what it all means, these books in the Explorer Race series can begin to supply the answers—the answers to these and other questions about the mystery and enigma of physical life on Earth.

These answers come from beings who speak through superchannel Robert Shapiro, beings who range from particle personalities to the Mother of all Beings and the thirteen Ssjooo, from advisors to the Creator of our universe to the generators of precreation energies. The scope, the immensity, the mind-boggling infinitude of these chronicles by beings who live in realms beyond our imagination, will hold you enthralled. Nothing even close to the magnitude of the depth and power of this all-encompassing, expanded picture of reality has ever been published.

This amazing story of the greatest adventure of all time and creation is the story of the Explorer Race, of which humans are a small but important percentage. The Explorer Race is a group of souls whose journeys resulted in incarnations in this loop of time on planet Earth, where, bereft of any memory of our immortal selves and most of our heart energy. We came to learn compassion, to learn to take responsibility for the consequences of our actions and to solve creation's previously unsolvable dilemma of negativity. We humans have found a use for negativity—we use it for lust for life and adventure, curiosity and creativity, for doing the undoable. And in a few years we will go out to the stars with our insatiable drive and ability to respond to change and begin to inspire the benign but stagnant civilizations out there to expand and change and grow, which will eventually result in the change and expansion of all creation.

Once you understand the saga of the Explorer Race and what the success of the Explorer Race Experiment means to the totality of creation, you will be proud to be human and to know that you are a vital component of the greatest story ever told—a continuing drama whose adventure continues far into the future.

Light Technology Published Books

the
EXPLORER

RACE

Zoosh. End-Time Historian
through Robert Shapiro

Book 1...
the EXPLORER RACE

You individuals reading this are truly a result of the genetic experiment on Earth. You are beings who uphold the principles of the Explorer Race. The information in this book is designed to show you who you are and give you an evolutionary understanding of your past that will help you now. The key to empowerment in these days is to not know everything about your past, but to know that which will help you now.

Your souls have been here for a while on Earth and have been trained in Earthlike conditions. This education has been designed so that you would have the ability to explore all levels of responsibility—results, effects and consequences—and take on more responsibilities.

Your number one function right now is your status of Creator apprentice, which you have achieved through years and lifetimes of sweat. You are constantly being given responsibilities by the Creator that would normally be things that Creator would do. The responsibility and the destiny of the Explorer Race is not only to explore, but to create. SOFTCOVER 574P.

$25⁰⁰ ISBN 0-929385-38-1

Chapter Titles:

THE HISTORY OF THE EXPLORER RACE
• The Genetic Experiment on Earth
• Influences of the Zodiac
• The Heritage from Early Civilizations
• Explorer Race Time Line, Part 1
• Explorer Race Time Line, Part 2
• The Experiment That Failed
GATHERING THE PARTS
• The ET in You: Physical Body
• The ET in You: Emotion and Thought
• The ET in You: Spirit
THE JOY, THE GLORY AND THE CHALLENGE OF SEX
• Emotion Lost: Sexual Addiction in Zeta History
• Sex, Love and Relationships
• Sexual Violence on Earth
• The Third Sex: The Neutral Binding Energy
• The Goddess Energy: The Soul of Creation
ET PERSPECTIVES
• Origin of the Species: A Sirian Perception
• An Andromedan Perspective on the Earth
  Experiment
• The Perspective of Orion Past on Their Role
• Conversation with a Zeta

BEHIND THE SCENES
• The Order: Its Origin and Resolution
• The White Brotherhood, the Illuminati, the New
  Dawn and the Shadow Government
• Fulfilling the Creator's Destiny
• The Sirian Inheritors of Third-Dimensional Earth
TODAY AND TOMORROW
• The Explorer Race Is Ready
• Coming of Age in the Fourth Dimension
• The True Purpose of Negative Energy
• The Challenge of Risking Intimacy
• Etheric Gene-Splicing and the Neutral Particle
• Material Mastery and the New Safety
• The Sterilization of Planet Earth
THE LOST PLANETS
• The Tenth Planet: The Gift of Temptation
• The Eleventh Planet: The Undoer, Key to
  Transformation
• The Twelfth Planet: Return of the Heart Energy
THE HEART OF HUMANKIND
• Moving Beyond the Mind
• Retrieving Heart Energy
• The Creator's Mission and the Function of the
  Human Race

Book 2...
ETs and the EXPLORER RACE

In this book, Robert channels Joopah, a Zeta Reticulan now in the ninth dimension, who continues the story of the great experiment—the Explorer Race—from the perspective of his civilization. The Zetas would have been humanity's future selves had not humanity re-created the past and changed the future.

$14⁹⁵   SOFTCOVER 237P.
ISBN 0-929385-79-9

Joopah, Zoosh and others through Robert Shapiro

Chapter Titles:

- The Great Experiment: Earth Humanity
- ETs Talk to Contactees
- Becoming One with Your Future Self
- ET Interaction with Humanity
- UFOs and Abductions
- The True Nature of the Grays
- Answering Questions in Las Vegas
- UFO Encounters in Sedona
- Joopah, in Transit, Gives an Overview and Helpful Tools
- We Must Embrace the Zetas
- Roswell, ETs and the Shadow Government
- ETs: Friend or Foe?
- ET Presence within Earth and Human Genetics
- Creating a Benevolent Future
- Bringing the Babies Home

Book 3...ORIGINS and the NEXT 50 YEARS

This volume has so much information about who we are and where we came from—the source of male and female beings, the war of the sexes, the beginning of the linear mind, feelings, the origin of souls—it is a treasure trove. Then in addition there is a section that relates to our near future—how the rise of global corporations and politics affects our future, how to use benevolent magic as a force of creation and then how we will go out to the stars and affect other civilizations. Astounding information.

$14⁹⁵   SOFTCOVER 339P.
ISBN 0-929385-95-0

ORIGINS and the NEXT 50 YEARS

Zoosh, End-Time Historian through Robert Shapiro

Chapter Titles:

THE ORIGINS OF EARTH RACES
- Our Creator and Its Creation
- The White Race and the Andromedan Linear Mind
- The Asian Race, the Keepers of Zeta Vertical Thought
- The African Race and Its Sirius/Orion Heritage
- The Fairy Race and the Native Peoples of the North
- The Australian Aborigines, Advisors of the Sirius System
- The Return of the Lost Tribe of Israel
- The Body of the Child, a Pleiadian Heritage
- Creating Sexual Balance for Growth
- The Origin of Souls
THE NEXT 50 YEARS
- The New Corporate Model
- The Practice of Feeling

- Benevolent Magic
- Future Politics
- A Visit to the Creator of All Creators
- Approaching the One
APPENDIX
- The Body of Man/The Body of Woman
ORIGINS OF THE CREATOR
- Beginning This Creation
- Creating with Core Resonances
- Jesus, the Master Teacher
- Recent Events in Explorer Race History
- The Origin of Creator
- On Zoosh, Creator and the Explorer Race
- Fundamentals of Applied 3D Creationism

Light Technology Publishing Books

EXPLORER RACE

CREATORS AND FRIENDS
THE MECHANICS OF CREATION

*Creators and Zoosh
through Robert Shapiro*

Book 4...
CREATORS and FRIENDS
The Mechanics of Creation

Now that you have a greater understanding of who you are in the larger sense, it is necessary to remind you of where you came from, the true magnificence of your being, to have some of your true peers talk to you. You must understand that you are creators in training, and yet you were once a portion of Creator. One could certainly say, without being magnanimous, that you are still a portion of Creator, yet you are training for the individual responsibility of being a creator, to give your Creator a coffee break.

This book will give you peer consultation. It will allow you to understand the vaster qualities and help you remember the nature of the desires that drive any creator, the responsibilities to which that creator must answer, the reaction any creator must have to consequences and the ultimate reward of any creator. This book will help you appreciate all of the above and more. I hope you will enjoy it and understand that maybe more will follow. SOFTCOVER 435P.

$**19**^{95}$ ISBN 0-891824-01-5

Chapter Titles:

- Andastinn, Prototype of Insect Beings
- Kazant, a Timekeeper
- Founders of Sirius, Creators of Humanoid Forms
- A Teacher of Buddha and Time Master's Assistant
- Designers of Human Physiology
- Avatar of Sea Creatures; and Quatsika, Messenger for the Dimension Makers
- The Empath Creator of Seventeen Planets
- Shapemaker of Portals
- Creator of the Inverse Universe, Our Creator's Creator
- Creator of the Void, Preamble to Individuality
- The Tornado-Shaped Creator of Creators
- The Center of Creation
- The Heart Council
- Creators of Gold Light and White Light

- Creator Talks About Itself and the Explorer Race
- Creator Talks About Friends
- Creator Speaks of the Stuff of Creation
- Creator Discusses Successes and the Outworking of Negativity
- Synchronizer of Physical Reality and Dimensions
- Master of Maybe
- Master of Frequencies and Octaves
- Spirit of Youthful Exuberance
- Master of Imagination
- Zoosh, the End-Time Historian
- Master of Feeling
- Master of Plasmic Energy
- Master of Discomfort Speaks of Himself and the Explorer Race
- Master of Discomfort Discusses Light Transference

Appendix: The Lucifer Gene

Book 5...
PARTICLE PERSONALITIES

All around you are the most magical and mystical beings. They are too small for you to see as single individuals, but in groups you know them as the physical matter of your daily life. These particles remember where they have been and what they have done in their long lives. We hear from some of them in this extraordinary book. SOFTCOVER 237P.

$14⁹⁵ ISBN 0-929385-97-7

Chapter Titles:

- A Particle of Gold
- The Model Maker: The Clerk
- The Clerk; a Mountain Lion Particle; a Particle of Liquid Light; and an Ice Particle
- A Particle of Rose Quartz from a Floating Crystal City
- A Particle of Uranium, Earth's Mind
- A Particle of the Great Pyramid's Capstone
- A Particle of the Dimensional Boundary between Orbs

- A Particle of Healing Energy
- A Particle of Courage Circulating through Earth
- A Particle of the Sun
- A Particle of Ninth-Dimensional Fire
- A Particle of Union
- A Particle of the Gold Lightbeing beyond the Orbs
- A Particle of the Tenfold Wizard
- A Particle of This Creator

Book 6...
EXPLORER RACE and BEYOND

With a better idea of how creation works, we go back to the Creator's advisors and receive deeper and more profound explanations of the roots of the Explorer Race. The liquid domain and the Double Diamond portal share lessons given to the roots on their way to meet the Creator of this universe and finally the roots speak of their origins and their incomprehensibly long journey here. SOFTCOVER 360P.

$14⁹⁵ ISBN 1-891824-06-6

Chapter Titles:

- Creator of Pure Feelings and Thoughts, One Circle of Creation
- The Liquid Domain
- The Double-Diamond Portal
- About the Other 93% of the Explorer Race
- Synchronizer of Physical Reality and Dimensions
- The Master of Maybe
- Master of Frequencies and Octaves
- Spirit of Youthful Enthusiasm (Junior) and Master of Imagination
- Zoosh

- The Master of Feeling
- The Master of Plasmic Energy
- The Master of Discomfort
- The Story-Gathering Root Being from the Library of Light/Knowledge
- The Root Who Fragmented from a Living Temple
- The First Root Returns
- Root Three, Companion of the Second Root
- The Temple of Knowledge & the Giver of Inspiration
- The Voice Historian, Who Provided the First Root
- Creator of All That Is

Light Technology Publishes Books

Book 7...EXPLORER RACE: the COUNCIL of CREATORS

The thirteenth core members of the Council of Creators discuss their adventures in coming to awareness of themselves and their journeys on the way to the Council on this level. They discuss the advice and oversight they offer to all creators, including the creator of this local universe. These beings are wise, witty and joyous, and their stories of Love's Creation creates an expansion of our concepts as we realize that we live in an expanded, multiple-level reality.

SOFTCOVER 237P.

$14⁹⁵ ISBN 1-891824-13-9
(to be published Fall 2001)

Chapter Titles:

- Specialist in Colors, Sounds and Consequences of Actions
- Specialist in Membranes that Separate and Auditory Mechanics
- Specialist in Sound Duration
- Explanation from Unknown Member of Council
- Specialist in Spatial Reference
- Specialist in Gaps and Spaces
- Specialist in Divine Intervention
- Specialist in Synchronicity and Timing

- Specialist in Hope
- Specialist in Honor
- Specialist in Variety
- Specialist in Mystical Connection between Animals and Humans
- Specialist in Change
- Specialist in the Present Moment
- Council Spokesperson and Specialist in Auxiliary Life Forms

Book 8...EXPLORER RACE and ISIS

This is an amazing book. It has priestess training, Shamanic training, Isis adventures with Explorer Race beings—before Earth and on Earth—and an incredibly expanded explanation of the dynamics of the Explorer Race. Isis is the prototypal loving, nurturing, guiding feminine being, the focus of feminine energy. She has the ability to expand limited thinking without making people with limited beliefs feel uncomfortable. She is a fantastic storyteller and all of her stories are teaching stories. If you care about who you are, why you are here, where you are going and what life is all about—pick up this book. You won't lay it down until you are through, and then you will want more. SOFTCOVER 317P.

$14⁹⁵ ISBN 1-891824-11-2

Chapter Titles:

- The Biography of Isis
- The Adventurer
- Soul Colors and Shapes
- Creation Mechanics
- Creation Mechanics and Personal Anecdotes

- The Insects' Form and Fairies
- Orion and Application to Earth
- Goddess Section
- Who Is Isis?
- Priestess/Feminine Mysteries

Book 9...EXPLORER RACE and JESUS

The immortal personality who lived the life we know as Jesus, along with his students and friends, describes with clarity and love his life and teaching on Earth 2000 years ago. These beings lovingly offer their experiences of the events that happened then and of Jesus' time-traveling adventures, especially to other planets and to the nineteenth and twentieth centuries, which he called the time of the machines—the time of the troubles. So heartwarming and interesting, you won't want to put it down.

14^{95} ISBN 1-891824-14-7

Chapter Titles:

- Jesus' Core Being, His People and the Interest in Earth of Four of Them
- Jesus' Life on Earth
- Jesus' Home World, Their Love Creations and the Four Who Visited Earth
- The "Facts" of Jesus' Life Here, His Future Return
- The Teachings and Travels
- A Student's Time with Jesus and His Tales of Jesus' Time Travels
- The Shamanic Use of the Senses

- The Child Student Who Became a Traveling Singer-Healer
- Other Journeys and the Many Disguises
- Jesus' Autonomous Parts, His Bloodline and His Plans
- Learning to Invite Matter to Transform Itself
- Inviting Water, Singing Colors
- Learning to Teach Usable Skills
- Learning about Different Cultures and People
- The Role of Mary Magdalene, a Romany
- Traveling and Teaching People How to Find Things

Book 10...EXPLORER RACE: EARTH HISTORY and LOST CIVILIZATIONS EXPLAINED

Zoosh reveals that our planet Earth did not originate in this solar system, but the water planet we live on was brought here from Sirius 65 million years ago. Anomalous archaeological finds and the various ET cultures who founded what we now call lost civilizations are explained with such storytelling skill by Speaks of Many Truths that you feel you were there!

14^{95} ISBN 1-891824-20-1
(to be published late 2001)

Chapter Titles:

- Lost Civilizations of Planet Earth in Sirius
- Ancient Artifacts Explained
- Ancient Visitors and Immortal Personalities
- Before and after Earth Was Moved to This Solar System from Sirius
- The Long Journey of Jehovah's Ship, from Orion to Sirius to Earth
- Jehovah Creates Human Beings
- Beings from the Future Academy
- Sumer
- Nazca Lines
- Easter Island
- Laetoli Footprints

- Egypt and Cats
- Three More Civilizations
- Medicine Wheels
- Stonehenge
- Carnac in Brittany
- Egypt
- China
- Tibet and Japan
- Siberia
- Natural Foods/Sacrament of Foods
- SSG's Time-Traveling Interference in Israel Imperils Middle East: How to Resolve It

Light Technology Publishing Books

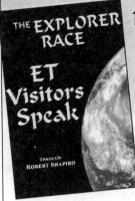

Book 11...EXPLORER RACE: ET VISITORS to EARTH SPEAK

Even as you are searching the sky for extraterrestrials and their space ships, ETs are here on planet Earth—they are stranded, visiting, exploring, studying the culture, healing the Earth of trauma brought on by irresponsible mining or researching the history of Christianity over the last 2000 years. Some are in human guise, some in spirit form, some look like what we call animals as they come from the species' home planet and interact with those of their fellow beings that we have labeled cats or cows or elephants. Some are brilliant cosmic mathematicians with a sense of humor presently living here as penguins; some are fledgling diplomats training for future postings on Earth when we have ET embassies here. In this book, these fascinating beings share their thoughts, origins and purposes for being here.

14^{95} ISBN 1-891824-28-7

Chapter Titles:

- Stranded Sirian Lightbeing Observes Earth for 800 Years
- An Orion Being Talks about Life on Earth as a Human
- Sensient Redwood
- Quah Earth Religion Researcher
- Visitor to Earth Talks about Pope Pius XII
- Observer Helps Cats Accomplish Their Purpose: Initiating
- A Warrior of Light, the Ultimate Ally
- Penguins: Humorous Mathematicians
- Xri from the Ninth Dimension
- Nurturing the Birth Cord
- Sixth Dimensional Cha-Cha Dances with Humans
- Starlight for Regeneration of Earth's Crystal Veins
- Starlight for Regeneration of Earth's Crystal Veins
- ET Resource Specialists Map and Heal Planetary Bodies
- The Creation and Preparation of the Resource Specialists' Ships Part 3
- Future Zeta Diplomat Learns to Communicate with Humans
- Warrior of Light
- Sirius Water-Being—A Bridge between ETs and Humans
- The Rock-Being Here to Experience Movement
- We Need Benevolent Alien Implants to Go to the Stars
- Ketchin-sa—ET in Dog Form
- Balanced Beings Attempt to Remove Earth Beings' Discomfort

Book 12...EXPLORER RACE:
The HEART is the DOOR to the FUTURE

The opportunity to change the way you live is not only close at hand, it is with you right now. Some of you have felt a change in the air, as you say, the winds of change. And other times it is ephemeral, hard to grasp. It is the ephemeral quality that can help you to know that the good thing that is out of your reach has to do with the future time line. The future time line is also an experience line. It is a sensation line. It is associated with the way your physical body communicates to you and others. It is a way of increasing your sensitivity to your own needs and the needs of others in a completely safe and protected way so that you can respond more quickly and accurately to those needs and appreciate the quality of life around you, much of which you miss because the old time line discourages you from observing. It encourages you to study and understand, but it discourages you from feeling. And it is feeling that is the ultimate answer to your discomforts as well as the pathway to true benevolent insight and fulfillment.

Chapter Titles:

14^{95} ISBN 1-891824-26-0
(to be published late 2001)

* Zero Four
* Time Traveler
* Fluid of Time
* Ordinator of Souls
* Energy Three
* Mother of All Beings

Book 13...EXPLORER RACE:
THE ULTIMATE UFO BOOK

This is a UFO book with a twist. The beings who channeled through Robert are the ET beings who were on the ships with humans in the famous case files—Betty and Barney Hill, Betty Andreasson, Travis Walton and many, many others. Here is a completely different perspective on the reality of off-planet/Earth-human interactions. As the various beings describe who they are, your understanding of our neighbors in space will expand.

Chapter Titles:

14^{95} ISBN 1-891824-19-8
(to be published late 2001)

* ET Contacts
* Daughter of Isis
* Zeta Coordinator
* People of Zeta
* Roswell
* The True Purpose of the Zetas
* Andromedan Diplomatic Liaison to the Zetas and the Parent Race
* Parent Race of Zeta ET Contacts
* Faces of the Visitors
* Visitors' Book & Sirian Mapper
* Bears, Meditation Beings
* Criminals, the Vega Star System and Microbes
* Botucatu, Brazil: Joao and the Andromedans
* Pascagoula, Mississippi: Hickson and Parker
* Guardians at Pascagoula
* The Andromedans: A Tale of a Minister
* Andromedans in Mexico and Professor Hernandez

Light Technology Publishing Books

SPEAKS OF MANY TRUTHS AND ZOOSH THROUGH ROBERT SHAPIRO

SHAMANIC SECRETS for MATERIAL MASTERY

Learn to communicate with the planet

This book explores the heart and soul connection between humans and Mother Earth. Through that intimacy, miracles of healing and expanded awareness can flourish.

To heal the planet and be healed as well, we can lovingly extend our energy selves out to the mountains and rivers and intimately bond with the Earth. Gestures and vision can activate our hearts to return us to a healthy, caring relationship with the land we live on.

The character and essence of some of Earth's most powerful features is explored and understood, with exercises given to connect us with those places. As we project our love and healing energy there, we help the Earth to heal from man's destruction of the planet and its atmosphere. Dozens of photographs, maps and drawings assist the process in 25 chapters, which cover the Earth's more critical locations.

19^{95} SOFTCOVER 498P.
ISBN 1-891824-12-0

Chapter Titles:

- Approaching Material Mastery through Your Physicality
- Three Rivers: The Rhine, the Amazon and the Rio Grande
- Three Lakes: Pyramid Lake, Lake Titicaca and Lake Baikal
- Mountains: Earth's Antennas, Related to the Human Bone Structure
  - Three Mountains: The Cydonia Pyramid, Mount Rushmore and Mount Aspen
  - Mountains in Turkey, Japan and California
  - Eurasia and Man's Skeletal Structure
  - Greenland, the Land of Mystery
  - Africa and North America
  - South and Central America and Australia

- Shamanic Interaction with Natural Life
- Africa and the Caspian and Black Seas
- Mauna Loa, Mount McKinley and Shiprock
- The Gobi Desert
- Old Faithful, Cayman Islands, Blue Mountains and Grandfather Mountain
- Meteor Crater, Angel Falls and Other Unique Locations on the Planet

PART II, THE FOUNDATION OF ONENESS
- The Explorer Race as a Part of Mother Earth's Body
- Spiritual Beings in a Physical World
- Earth Now Releasing Human Resistance to Physical Life
- Healing Prisoners, Teaching Students
- The Shaman's Key: Feeling and the Five Senses
- How to Walk, How To Eat
- Breathing: Something Natural We Overlook
- How to Ask and Let Go, and How to Sleep
- Singing Our Songs
- Some Final Thoughts

Light Technology Published Books

SHAMANIC SECRETS for PHYSICAL MASTERY

The purpose of this book is to allow you to understand the sacred nature of your own physical body and some of the magnificent gifts it offers you. When you work with your physical body in these new ways, you will discover not only its sacredness, but how it is compatible with Mother Earth, the animals, the plants, even the nearby planets, all of which you now recognize as being sacred in nature. It is important to feel the value of oneself physically before one can have any lasting physical impact on the world. The less you think of yourself physically, the less likely your physical impact on the world will be sustained by Mother Earth. If a physical energy does not feel good about itself, it will usually be resolved; other physical or spiritual energies will dissolve it because it is unnatural. The better you feel about your physical self when you do the work in the previous book as well as this one and the one to follow, the greater and more lasting will be the benevolent effect on your life, on the lives of those around you and ultimately on your planet and universe. SOFTCOVER 600P.

$19⁹⁵ ISBN 1-891824-29-5
(to be published late 2001)

Chapter Titles:

- Cellular Clearing of Traumas, Unresolved Events
- Cellular Memory
- Identifying Your Body's Fear Message
- The Heart Heat Exercise
- Learn Hand Gestures
  —Remove Self-Doubt
  —Release Pain or Hate
  —Clear the Adrenals or Kidneys
  —Resolve Sexual Dysfunction
- Learning the Card Technique for Clarifying Body Message
- Seeing Life as a Gift
- Relationship of the Soul to Personality
- The New Generation of Children
- The Creator and Religions
- Food, Love & Addictions

- Communication of the Heart
- Dreams & Their Significance
- The Living Prayer/Good Life
- Life Force and Life Purpose
- Physical Mastery
- His Life/Mandate for His Ancestors/ Importance of Animals/Emissaries
- Physical Mastery
- Talking to Rain/Bear Claw Story
- Disentanglement
- Grief Culture
- Closing Comments

SHINING THE LIGHT SERIES

The Truth about ETs, Alien Bases
and the Sinister Secret Government

ZOOSH AND OTHERS THROUGH ROBERT SHAPIRO

Robert Shapiro grew up with the experience of ET contact. Throughout
his life there have been communications with beings from several star systems
and dimensions. He has been a professional channel for over 25 years, most
often channeling Zoosh, who describes himself as an End-Time Historian.

YHWH THROUGH ARTHUR FANNING
(Shining the Light I-IV)

LIGHT TECHNOLOGY
BRINGS YOU THE TRUTH!!
About the Secret Government and their ET Allies/Enemies

For many years you have all wondered, what is that thing that seems to
keep things slow? What stops wonderful goals from being accomplished,
even if everyone is in favor of them? Is it strictly the things within yourself?
Sometimes. Or is it also that there is an invisible network behind many
things? These books will attempt to explain the invisible network and give
you tangible things you can do to improve the quality of life for yourself and
others and to gently, perhaps, but firmly dissolve the stranglehold on your
societies by this sinister invisible network that we choose to call in these
books the sinister secret government.

—Zoosh through Robert Shapiro

The Shining the Light series exposes the malevolent, controlling and
manipulating actions of the sinister secret government (SSG) as it
attempts to keep humans from accessing soul and spiritual functions and
from ascending into the fourth dimension and beyond. In future books,
mentors of humanity will continue to expose the SSG's nefarious deal-
ings, but they will give us step-by-step instructions in the ancient lost
arts of benevolent magic—spiritual wizardry—enabling us as creators in
training to blend our hearts, minds and souls to become creators of our
own destiny and thwart the SSG's goals.

SHINING THE LIGHT I
THE BATTLE BEGINS!

Despite official denial and tactics of derision, active minds are demanding the truth. This truth is stranger than all the fictions about ETs, alien bases and the sinister secret government. The revelations are shocking and enlightening. A crashed UFO leads to information on:

✦ The sinister secret government's time-travel spacecraft
✦ Renegade ETs mining on the moon
✦ The U.S. peace-avatar president
✦ The prime directive—now
✦ Underground alien bases and populations
✦ Ancient Pleiadian warships
✦ Many more startling facts!
SOFTCOVER 193P.

$12⁹⁵ ISBN 0-929385-66-7

Chapter Titles:

- UFO Crash in Sedona?
- Global Shadow Government
- Father to Call Back His Light/Life Force
- The Shadow Government and Its Alien Allies
- Underground Bases and the Secret Government
- UFO Researcher Witnesses Battle in the Sky

- Battle in the Sky—What Really Happened
- Another Sedona Sighting
- UFOs, ETs and More
- Last Chance for Redemption
- The Battle Begins

SHINING THE LIGHT II
THE BATTLE CONTINUES

Current status of the sinister secret government and those who want to usurp its power. Actual cosmic photographs of hidden crafts, beings and events. Photon Belt "Doctor" comes to save Mother Earth. The truth becomes even stranger as the story of alien involvement in Earth history continues. SOFTCOVER 418P.

$**14**^{95} ISBN 0-929385-70-5

Chapter Titles:

- Update on Humanity
- The Light Is Returning Home
- The Sinister Secret Government Is Back in Sedona
- Zoosh Explains the Sightings
- Nineteen Time-Space Anomalies
- Time-Space Anomalies Explained
- Contactee Children
- Bringing the Babies Home
- Evolution of Earth and Humanity
- Sinister Secret Government Moves Entrance to Underground Base
- Awakening to the Master within Your Physical Form
- Xpotaz-Sinister Secret Government Shootout over Grand Canyon
- The Face of God: Robert Meyer's Photos Explained
- Interdimensional Entities Become More Visible

- You're Getting Shifted to the Center
- The Creator and His Friends
- Cosmic Holograms (photos)
- The New Vortex
- Interlude with the Planet—Your Lady
- More on the Sinister Secret Guerrilla War
- The Awakening of Humankind's Dreams (photos)
- You Can Now Integrate the Fourth Dimension
- Earth: A Planet of Peace
- The Photon Belt: A Planetary Troubleshooter
- The Earth's New Dance Partner
- The Photon Belt "Doctor" Is In
- Return of the Ancient Lemurians (photos)
- Nefarious Computer Chip Activated
- The Ancient Gods in You Are Starting to Move

Epilogue: Book III
Shadow Government Attempts to Mine on Hopi Reservation

SHINING THE LIGHT III
HUMANITY GETS A SECOND CHANCE

The focus is on humanity as we began to learn to render the sinister secret government powerless by being the light that we are. Earth becomes a member of the Council of Planets and the universe time-shifts to preserve the Explorer Race.

✦ Ninth-dimensional Mars   ✦ The null zone
✦ ET helicopter pilots   ✦ Sonic mapping
✦ Material masters   ✦ Time collapses
✦ Exploding planets   ✦ Cosmic photographs
✦ The Photon Belt   ✦ And more

SOFTCOVER 460P.

$14⁹⁵ ISBN 0-929385-71-3

Chapter Titles:

SHINING THE LIGHT IV
HUMANITY'S GREATEST CHALLENGE

Includes information on Hale-Bopp, SSG, all updates since Volume III and material on the uncreating of Hitler in 1993.

✦ Negative Sirians coming to the third dimension
✦ The express bus to creatorship
✦ The Poison HAARP project
✦ Luciferian traits and critical mass
✦ ETs in Brazil
✦ Comet brings lightbeing-filled vehicle bigger than Earth
✦ Sinister secret government (SSG) under control of beings from the alternate negative future

$14⁹⁵   SOFTCOVER 557P.
ISBN 0-929385-93-4

Chapter Titles:

- I Love God
- Feedback in the Ripples of Time
- Masculine and Feminine Balance
- Negative Sirians Coming to the 3rd Dimension
- Freedom, Power and Light Moving
- The Null-Charged-Particle Effect
- The Sifting Time
- Anchoring Your Higher Self
- Resistance Being Removed from the Soul!
- The Express Bus to Creatorship
- Divinity: Freedom, Life Forever, Light Forever
- The Poison HAARP
- HAARP: High-Frequency Vandalism in the Sky
- How to Create Solutions for Positive Change
- Project HAARP, Expansion of the Montauk Project
- The Untethered Satellite
- Humanity Decides "Let's Be Free Again"
- Behind Current Events
- Contemplate, Listen, Apply: Become a Master
- Luciferian Traits and Critical Mass
- ETs in Brazil
- How Your Thought Affects Every Living Thing
- Pull Down the Lightbody and Raise Your Frequency
- Crop Circles: Symbols of Soul-Group Origins
- Prepare for the Outrageous Journey to Rescue the Planet

- The Silver Lining behind Tampering with Genetics
- FEMA and fema
- The New Brain
- Gloom & Doom? No!
- Angel Warns of Quake
- Humanity Passes Test: Quake Dispersed
- The Hate Gun
- Hate Gun Shorted Out!
- Alien Invasions and the Sinister Secret Government
- On-Off Circuitry: Shutting Off the Old, Opening the New
- An Alert
- The Lucifer Gene
- Look Up and See Ships in the Sky
- Ancient Records to Be Revealed in the '90s
- Comments on the Montauk Project
- More Comments on the Montauk Project
- Hitler Uncreated
- The Sinister Secret Government's Satanic Origin
- World War II Is Still Happening Now
- More Sinister Secret Government
- The Dark and the Light Sides of the Explorer Race
- Hale-Bopp Comet Brings Lightbeing-Filled Vehicle
- The Ship: The New Collective Teacher
- SSG's Worldwide Agenda

SHINING THE LIGHT V
HUMANITY IS GOING TO MAKE IT!

Zoosh and others blast the cover off past events and hidden forces at work on this planet and reveal opportunities for immense growth and power. This is a pivotal time as the secrets and mysteries that have so long bewildered humanity are illuminated at last by the light of truth.

✦ Revelations about Area 51 by a rocket scientist ✦ A 75-year-long Zeta restructuring of the past ✦ Cloning: the new ethics forum ✦ Recent UFO activity in the skies ✦ The first humans and the original dark side, our shadow ✦ Angels: guides in training (30% of humans are angels) ✦ Using manifestation powers to avert man-made disasters ✦ The angel of Roswell ✦ Symbiotic spacecraft engines and faster-than-light travel ✦ The true purpose of the Mayans ✦ The SSG downs military planes ✦ The SSG realizes they need customers, not slaves ✦ Grid lines rising above the planet ✦ Homework for changing your past

14^{95} SOFTCOVER 330P.
ISBN 1-891824-00-7

Chapter Titles:

Light Technology Publishing Books

Light Technology Published Books